Feasibility Analysis for Sustainable Technologies

Feasibility Analysis for Sustainable Technologies

An Engineering-Economic Perspective

Scott R. Herriott

BEP BUSINESS EXPERT PRESS

Feasibility Analysis for Sustainable Technologies: An Engineering-Economic Perspective

First published in 2015 by
Business Expert Press, LLC
222 East 46th Street, New York, NY 10017
www.businessexpertpress.com

ISBN-13: 978-1-63157-027-8 (paperback)
ISBN-13: 978-1-63157-028-5 (e-book)

Business Expert Press Environmental and Social Sustainability for Business Advantage Collection

Collection ISSN: 2327-333X (print)
Collection ISSN: 2327-3348 (electronic)

Cover and interior design by Exeter Premedia Services Private Ltd., Chennai, India

First edition: 2015

10 9 8 7 6 5 4 3 2 1

Printed in the United States of America.

for Vicki

Abstract

This book leads the reader into a professional feasibility analysis for a renewable energy or energy efficiency project. The analysis begins with an understanding of the basic engineering description of technology in terms of capacity, efficiency, constraints, and dependability. It continues in modeling the cash flow of a project, which is affected by the installed cost, the revenues or expenses avoided by using the technology, the operating expenses of the technology, available tax credits and rebates, and laws regarding depreciation and income tax. The feasibility study is completed by discounted cash flow analysis, using an appropriate discount rate and a proper accounting for inflation, to evaluate the financial viability of the project. The elements of this analysis are illustrated using numerous examples of solar, wind, and hydroelectric power, biogas digestion, energy storage, biofuels, and energy-efficient appliances and buildings.

Keywords

biofuels, biogas digestion, energy efficiency, energy storage, feasibility analysis, feasibility study, hydroelectric power, renewable energy, renewable power systems, solar photovoltaics, solar thermal electric power, sustainable technologies, wind power

Contents

Acknowledgments

I thank my MBA students for their valuable research assistance: Yi Dong, Yali Jiang, and Sisi Zhang on home energy efficiency; Joseph Collett and Fei Zhao on municipal waste gasification; Lulu Jia, Longhai Ji, and Fan Yang on geothermal heat pumps; Zengyu Yu, Renfang Zhao, Sheer-el Cohen, and Maartan Schoots on solar photovoltaics; Gyan Kesler on hydroelectric power; Ray Baptiste and Tony Lai on wastewater treatment; Annette Wrighton on insulation; Haiyan Song on wind power; Alvaro Montaserio on solar water heating; Guanting (Agnes) Cui and Haiqui (Eric) Mao on lighting; and Hassaan Iqbal on hydrogen fuel cells.

I would like to express a special thanks to Dr. Sharon George, Director of the M.Sc. program in Environmental Sustainability and Green Technology at Keele University in the UK, for her insightful comments on an early draft of this book and her encouragement of this project.

Introduction

The push toward sustainability is a defining theme of the present decade. Governments around the world have come to recognize the significance of global warming and have responded with international collaborations such as the European Union Emissions Trading System to limit the production of greenhouse gases, forcing companies to find low-carbon methods of production. Within their own domains, governments have created financial incentives, such as income tax credits and production tax credits, to support the development and implementation of sustainable technologies. However, the intelligent use of these technologies requires a careful assessment of the financial and environmental context in which they are to be used. Solar and wind power, for example, in their current forms are financially viable only in certain locations. *Feasibility analysis* is the task of determining whether or not a technology is financially viable in a particular context and use. This task requires managers to understand the basic engineering and economics of technology and the public policies that apply to technology. Those are the focus of this book.

Chapter 1 is a synopsis of the main ideas in the book. It gives the reader a taste of the concepts and analytic techniques that will be developed in later chapters. The goal of the book is to demonstrate the elements of feasibility analysis that would be used by a consultant or technology specialist to make a real decision about whether or not to fund a particular application of a technology. Through the first eight chapters, the presentation in this book works its way up to the complexity necessary for a realistic feasibility analysis, reaching that level in Chapters 9 and 10.

Feasibility analysis is an interdisciplinary task in which both engineers and financial analysts have their roles. Each has to understand the needs and the capabilities of the other. This book is written for the business student who is interested in becoming a financial analyst, or the professional who is already working in that capacity, who must work with engineers to complete a feasibility study. As such, this book presents the basic ideas of the engineer's toolkit—drawing on concepts such as capacity, efficiency, constraints, and durability in Chapters 2 to 5—so the analyst can be sure that the right questions are being asked and answered. However, this book is also written with a respect for engineers who want to play more of a role in the financial analysis, so Chapters 6 to 8 take the reader through the elements of financial analysis that are familiar to a business student—concepts such as cost structure, break-even analysis, net present value, and rate of return on investment. Chapters 9 and 10 bring together the basic ideas of engineering and economics, presenting the elements of a realistic feasibility analysis.

This book focuses on practical applications, not theory. Interesting examples illustrate every major concept and analytic technique. Special *Tech Focus* sections give the reader a deeper look into the engineering and economic features of specific technologies.

An important companion to this book is the *Study Guide* that is available by download from the Business Expert Press website for this book. The *Study Guide* includes a problem set for each chapter to illustrate the application of the concepts. The exercises and cases in these problem sets apply the engineering–economic perspective to a much wider range of technologies than those that appear in the book's examples, and the *Study Guide* is updated annually with interesting, current applications.

S.R.H.

July 2014

Fairfield, Iowa

CHAPTER 1

Sustainable Technologies

Overview

Feasibility analysis, as applied to the use of sustainable technology, is an interdisciplinary task. This book presents an engineering–economic perspective on technology that yields insights into the circumstances that make a technology economically viable. This chapter presents the main ideas of the book, giving the reader a taste of the engineering–economic perspective but without the depth that the later chapters provide. This chapter addresses the following questions:

- In the context of technology, what does *sustainability* mean?
- How do engineers use the concepts of input, process, and output to describe technologies?
- What concepts enable a technology analyst to describe devices of different sizes, and on what basis can technologies be compared with each other?
- How does an economist's perspective on technology differ from that of an engineer?
- How does a financial analyst compare the costs of two devices that have different lifetimes and different costs to operate?
- How can one establish an objective value for a device, such as a solar panel or a wind turbine, as a point of reference in comparison with the price that a vendor is charging for it?
- What role does public policy have in promoting sustainable technologies, and how does government implement its policies?

What Makes a Technology Sustainable?

Table 1.1 presents a brief list of what people would generally consider to be sustainable or nonsustainable technologies across a variety of domains. Read through the list and see if you can identify the characteristics of a technology that distinguish it as sustainable.

Generalizing from this table, there seem to be three features that distinguish the sustainable from the nonsustainable technologies. One feature of energy technologies is *renewability*—energy from renewable sources such as the sun and wind is sustainable; energy from nonrenewable sources such as deposits of oil and natural gas is not sustainable. Another feature is *efficiency* and is seen most obviously in technologies that use energy. Our drive toward sustainability requires efficiency in the use of our limited resources. The third feature, which occurs in waste management, building technologies, and agriculture, is *nontoxicity*. Sustainable technologies do not create toxic effects for human life or the natural environment.

Table 1.1 Sustainable and nonsustainable technologies

Category	Nonsustainable	Sustainable
Electric power generation	Coal-fired power plants Oil and gas-fired power Nuclear power (?)	Solar power Wind power Biogas power Hydrogen fuel cell
Energy storage (including fuels)	Lead-acid batteries Gasoline Ethanol (?)	Pumped hydro (dams) Biodiesel
Energy usage (lighting, heating/cooling, transportation)	Incandescent lights Old home furnace Gas-fired water heater Internal combustion car	LED lights Energy Star™ furnace Solar water heater Battery-electric vehicle
Waste management	Disposal in a landfill	Recycling Biogas capture or digestion
Building technologies	Interior lighting Gas furnace High-VOC paints Common thermostat	Day lighting Geothermal heat pump Non-VOC paints Programmable thermostat
Agricultural technologies	Chemical-based agriculture	Organic agriculture

VOC, *volatile organic compound.*

The business press tends to equate sustainability with renewability, but efficiency is also very important to the future of human society. It is therefore not surprising that the U.S. Department of Energy established the *Office of Energy Efficiency and Renewable Energy* (EERE; www.eere. energy.gov) to promote each of these aspects of sustainability.

As a field of study, *sustainable business* goes beyond renewability, efficiency, and nontoxicity. It considers the social impacts of business, looking for ways to make businesses more resilient in the face of change and to help them nourish the lives of their stakeholders and flourish as organizations.[1] Our study of sustainable technologies in this short book is developed around feasibility analysis, focusing on the attributes of technology seen through the eyes of the engineer and economist. The social impact of technology has its origin in how technology is used, not in the technology itself. The theme of sustainability raises important questions about *appropriate technology*—how the choice of technology depends on local knowledge and culture,[2] but those are beyond the scope of this book.

What Is Technology?

Technology transforms one configuration of energy and matter into another configuration. For example, an automobile's engine transforms the chemical energy in gasoline into the mechanical energy (motion) of the vehicle. Technology changes the state of matter–energy, so technology is best understood as a *transformation process*. From a scientific perspective, we may say that technology is the application of *the laws of nature* that govern the transformation process. From a business perspective, it is useful to think of technology as the *intelligence* by which one configuration of matter–energy becomes another. In that perspective, the progressive development of a technology is the refinement of the intelligence that is expressed in the transformation process.

Technology and Its Devices

When we define technology in this way, as a process, we focus our attention on the laws of nature by which the inputs become outputs. This perspective sees technology fundamentally as *knowledge*. So, what is a car or a computer? It is the device that embodies the knowledge. But even in such a context, the word *technology* can have different meaning at several levels of generality. The automotive engine can be called a technology. Within that class, a gasoline engine and a diesel engine might each be called a "technology." Within the class of gasoline engines, the one that can also burn a fuel consisting 85 percent of ethanol (E85) might also be called a technology. Even more finely, we may still use the word technology to describe different sizes of E85-burning engine, such as 150 horsepower (HP), 250 HP, or 350 HP motors.

We may use any of the several words for these realizations of a technology. We might call a car or a computer a *device*, because it is a small and self-contained form of technology. We might call a solar photovoltaic (SPV) system an *installation*, because it is an assembly of components. We would call a large factory a *plant*, as in "electric power plant."

In common parlance, people do not distinguish precisely between a technology and the devices, installations, or plants that realize the technology. In this book, we hold to the perspective that the technology is the process by which inputs become outputs, but we may at times refer to all devices that use a particular technology as the "technology," abusing our own terminology for the sake of readability. In Chapter 3, for example, we speak about the economies of scale of a technology. Properly, we should refer to the economies of scale evident in the collection of all devices that realize the technology, but that seems to burden our language excessively for a small gain in precision. We will be content, for example, to speak about the economies of scale in the SPV technology.

To many people, sustainable technology means renewable energy, and the familiar examples are solar and wind power. Energy-saving technologies are not often featured in the business press, but they are very important for a sustainable economy, and so too are the techniques for analyzing energy efficiency. The use of energy in buildings is an excellent example of energy efficiency. In buildings, energy is used for heating, lighting, and running equipment—these are among the principal technologies that appear as examples later in this book. To illustrate this, we take a quick look at the concept of a *net-zero energy building* in the following Tech Focus feature.

Tech Focus: The Net Zero Energy Building

In the United States, approximately 40 percent of the nation's energy consumption takes place in residential or commercial buildings.[3] The U.S. government itself has taken a leadership role in promoting energy efficient buildings. In 2009, President Obama signed Executive Order 13514, which required all new federal buildings that enter the planning process after 2019 to be designed to achieve zero net energy by 2030. The executive order also required that at least 15 percent of each agency's existing facilities and building leases that have 5,000 or more gross square feet should meet the "Guiding Principles for Federal Leadership in High Performance and Sustainable Buildings"[4] by 2015, and it requires annual progress toward 100 percent conformance.[5]

Definitions of zero net energy buildings vary slightly according to the scope of the energy used (site or source) and whether the focus is on energy, cost, or emissions.[6] In net zero site energy, the building produces on site, over one year, at least as much energy as it consumes.

To understand the array of technologies that would be involved in reaching net-zero energy for a building, we have to look at the types of energy used in a building and the uses of that energy. EERE has published data on the energy use of typical or *reference* commercial buildings in the United States for various locations around the country. Table 1.2 gives the EERE data for a typical medium-sized office building constructed after 1980, which has a gross area of 4,982 square meters (53,625 sq. ft.) over three floors, uses a gas furnace with electric reheat for space heating, and a gas water heater that has 78 percent thermal efficiency. The energy use

Table 1.2 Energy use in a medium-sized office building

Energy use (kWh)	Chicago		Phoenix		San Francisco	
Heating and cooling	389,317	37%	368,355	36%	152,891	19%
Water heating	10,270	1%	6,942	1%	9,389	1%
Electric lighting	342,056	33%	342,139	34%	342,089	43%
Electric equipment and appliances	296,256	29%	296,255	29%	296,255	37%
Total	1,037,899	100%	1,013,691	100%	800,624	100%

of the reference building differs by location only in terms of heating and cooling and water heating. It is interesting to see that Chicago and Phoenix have similar total needs, although Chicago would be heavy on heating and Phoenix heavy on cooling. The uses for lighting and equipment are identical or nearly so in the reference building.

The point of interest in Table 1.2 is the amount of energy used for heating and cooling, water heating, lighting, and equipment (plug-in loads) as a percentage of the total in each city. In Chicago and Phoenix, where the buildings have similar total energy needs, there is an equal split (33 percent each) among heating and cooling, lighting, and equipment. In San Francisco, which has a lower need for heating and cooling, lighting and equipment are both approximately 40 percent of the total. Water heating is almost negligible in this commercial building.

These data show that the energy intensity of a typical medium-sized (5,000 sq. m.) office building in Chicago or Phoenix is approximately 200 kWh per square meter per year. The table also shows where efforts should be put to reduce energy consumption through efficiency. Lighting and appliance technologies are at least as important as heating and cooling technologies in the drive toward energy efficiency in commercial buildings. Examples that analyze energy-efficient lighting and appliances appear throughout this book.

The achievement of net-zero energy requires the reduction of typical energy use through efficiency and the generation of energy on site from renewable sources. How much of a typical building's energy can be reduced through efficiency, and how much will need to be supplied on site? The International Energy Agency reports that the proper design of a building's *envelope* (roof, ceiling, floors, walls, doors, and windows) can reduce energy needs by 40 percent.[7] Even further reductions can be achieved by using an energy-efficient furnace and a computerized energy management system, which monitors the sun's impact on a building to adjust heating and cooling in specific zones. The need for electric lighting can be reduced by designing a building to use natural light as much as possible (daylighting), and the replacement of incandescent lights and old fluorescent lights by LEDs and more efficient fluorescents can reduce the consumption of electric energy by as much as 75 percent. The potential reductions in energy use by energy-efficient appliances and other plug-in loads will vary by type of appliance, but the Environmental Protection Agency reports that reductions of up to 60 percent are possible in energy-efficient photocopiers.[8] So it is not unreasonable that Taisei Corporation in Japan, in its plan for zero net energy use in a medium-sized office building, is seeking a 75 percent reduction in overall energy use compared with a traditional building, with the remainder of the energy to be supplied by solar panels on the building.[9]

Renewable energy production is essential in the net zero energy building. SPV and solar water heating (SWH) technologies are most suited to use on buildings. They are featured prominently in the examples that appear in later chapters. Electric power from solar thermal systems, wind energy, biogas digestion, and biomass combustion all count in the *net-zero source* definition although not in the *net-zero site* definition of a zero energy building (ZEB). These technologies are also analyzed throughout the book.

This example of the net zero-energy building shows only the engineer's perspective, which focuses on energy use, energy efficiency, and energy production. A complete feasibility analysis of the technologies used in a ZEB will examine their costs as well as their effects. Here in Chapter 1, we survey the basic elements of each perspective, engineering, and economics. A more complete treatment of each perspective is taken up in the rest of the book.

The Engineering Perspective on Technology

Technology transforms one configuration of matter and energy into another. Technology is a transformation process. The engineering perspective on technology describes that transformational process.

Inputs, Outputs, and Process

A transformation process converts inputs into outputs (including byproducts), so the engineering perspective on a technology starts with a description of the inputs, the outputs, and a name for the transformation process (Figure 1.1).

A few examples illustrate these ideas in Table 1.3.

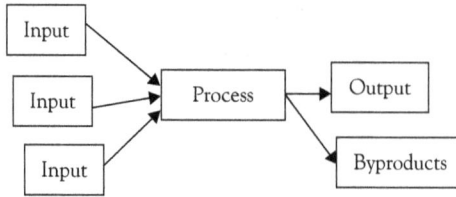

Figure 1.1 Input–output diagram

Table 1.3 Examples of the engineering perspective on technology

Technology	Inputs	Process	Output
Solar thermal	Solar radiation	Absorption of radiation	Heated water
Gasoline engine	Gasoline	Combustion	Motion (mechanical energy)
Hydroelectric generation	Potential energy (water at height) → mechanical energy (spinning turbine)	Electromotive process	Electrical energy
Healthcare	Sick person, medicine, rest	Healing	Well person

Capacity

Any particular example (instance or realization) of a technology—think of a machine or plant—has some limit to the amount of output it can produce in a given unit of time. That limit to its production is the *capacity* of the machine. The *capacity* measures the maximum output rate of the particular machine or plant. Some examples are shown in Table 1.4.

Notice the example of wastewater treatment. It is different from the others. The capacity of a wastewater treatment facility is described not as an output measure (clean water gallons per day) but as an *input* measure (dirty water treated per day). In Chapter 2, we see a few other exceptional cases where capacity is not measured as an output rate.

Efficiency

The efficiency of a technology is a measure of its output *per unit of input*. This calculation can also be derived as the rate of output production

Table 1.4 Measures of capacity

Technology	Output	Capacity example
Solar thermal	Heated water	Gallons of water at 120°F per day
Gasoline engine	Motion (mechanical energy)	200 horsepower (energy/time)
Hydroelectric generation	Electrical energy	1000 kW (electric energy/time)
Wastewater treatment	Clean water	10,000 gallons/day of waste-water treated

Table 1.5 Measures of efficiency

Technology	Inputs	Output	Efficiency
Solar thermal	Solar radiation	Heated water	*Percentage* of solar energy absorbed as heat (versus reflected)
Gasoline engine	Gasoline	Motion	Miles per gallon
Hydroelectric generation	Potential energy (water at height)	Electrical energy	*Percentage* of potential energy converted to electrical energy
Healthcare	Sick person	Healthy person	*Percentage* of people cured (cure rate)

divided by the rate of input usage. Efficiency can therefore be measured only in relation to one input. When a technology has several inputs, each input will have its own efficiency measure. Table 1.5 illustrates the concept of efficiency for a variety of technologies.

Notice that when the input and output are measured in the same units (energy in an engine or furnace, or water in a treatment plant, or patients in a hospital), the efficiency can be expressed as a *percentage*, which is a dimensionless quantity because the units cancel in the calculation of output–input.

Example 1   Efficiency of a Home Furnace

Your old furnace has an efficiency of 80 percent in converting the heat energy of natural gas fuel into warm air for your home. Your recent monthly heating bill showed a natural gas usage of 100 therms. [One therm is equal to 100,000, British Thermal Units (BTUs), a quantity of heat energy.]

(1) How much heat energy (in therms) did your house *receive* during the month?

Solution

The 100 therms in the statement of Example 1 is the amount of natural gas heat energy that you *bought* during the month. That was the input to the furnace. We find the amount of output using the definition of efficiency as output–input. We can write that definition in the form of the general efficiency equation,

Output rate = Input rate × Efficiency   (*Efficiency Equation*)
Output rate = 100 therms/month × 80%
Output rate = 80 therms/month.

So the house needed 80 therms in the month, and you had to buy 100 therms of natural gas to get it.

The Economic Perspective on Technology

Recall our diagram for the engineering perspective on technology, which shows the inputs, process, and outputs (Figure 1.2).

When we look at technology through the economic lens, we focus on the cost to create or operate the technology. In the economic perspective, we add information about the prices of each input, from which we can

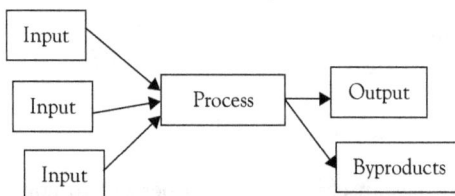

Figure 1.2 Input–output diagram

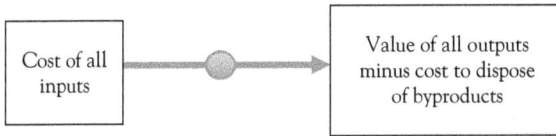

Figure 1.3 The economic perspective on technology

calculate the total cost of all inputs together, and we *suppress the details about the process* of transforming inputs into outputs. The economic perspective is therefore shown in Figure 1.3.

Cost to Create—Cost and Economies of Capacity

Whether the technology is built or purchased, the cost to acquire it is its *capacity cost*. Commonly, capacity cost is expressed in dollars *per unit* of capacity and in that case would properly be called the *unit capacity cost* of the technology. Of particular interest to economists is how the (unit) capacity cost changes when you build or buy larger devices that embody the technology. When larger devices are cheaper (per unit of capacity), the technology exhibits *economies of scale*, or more precisely, economies of capacity.

Example 2   Wind Turbines

Consider the following two facts:

- A large wind turbine has a capacity of approximately 1.5 megawatts (million watts, MW) and has an installed cost (turbine plus siting and installation costs) of approximately $4.5 million, meaning it has a capacity cost of $4.5/1.5 = 3.00$ dollars per watt.
- A medium-sized wind turbine has a capacity of approximately 85,000 W (85 kW) and has an installed cost of approximately $350,000, meaning its capacity cost is approximately $350,000/85,000 = 4.10$ dollars per watt.

Does wind turbine technology exhibit economies of scale or diseconomies of scale, in this range of the technology?

Solution

It exhibits economies of scale, because the larger wind turbine was *cheaper* per unit of capacity.

Example 2 describes the cost to manufacture or purchase a device. In that context, the description of the technology is its cost *per unit of capacity*, which shows whether one device is *relatively* more expensive than another. A different question is to ask about the profitability of operating a device. A simple question about profitability is the break-even problem, which asks how many units the device must produce in a period of time, such as a year, so that the benefits from using the technology exactly equal its cost of operation. Operated above the break-even level, the device is profitable; below the break-even level, it results in an economic loss. The next examples take up the elements of the break-even problem.

Cost of Possession—Fixed Cost per Year

The cost of owning or leasing a device is called *fixed*, because it must be paid whether or not the device produces output. In economic analysis, the fixed cost is expressed per unit of time, typically per year, so devices that have different lifetimes may be compared. The purchase price or manufactured cost of the device is the starting point for that analysis. That price must be *levelized* over the useful life of the device to yield an annual cost that is equivalent, in financial terms, to the purchase price over the useful life of the device. The levelized cost of a device is like the price that would be paid per year to lease the device. In finance, an interest rate or discount rate establishes the general equivalence between cash now (the purchase price) and cash in the future (a series of annual lease payments). Therefore, a discount rate figures into the calculation of the levelized purchase price of a device over its useful life. Fortunately, spreadsheet programs such as Excel or Open Office have built-in functions to perform that calculation, as Example 3 shows.

Example 3   Levelized Cost of a Toyota Prius

Toyota's gas–electric hybrid car model, the Prius, has a purchase price of $25,000. If the car will have a useful life of 20 years, what annual cost over those 20 years would be equivalent to that purchase price, assuming financial investment decisions are made using a discount rate of 8 percent per year?

Solution

The levelized cost of the car will be that annual payment which, paid over 20 years, would have a present value equal to the $25,000 present cost car. In Microsoft Excel, the *payment* function PMT calculates this quantity, based on the discount rate (*rate*), the number of time periods (*nper*, here measured in years) in the useful life of the device, and the present value (*pv*) of the device, here interpreted as its installed cost. The syntax of Excel's PMT function is

$$=PMT(rate, nper, pv)$$

Using 8 percent as the rate, 20 as the *nper*, and 25,000 as the present value, the answer would appear in an Excel spreadsheet by typing

$$=PMT(8\%, 20, 25000)$$

Notice that the *pv* number must be typed in the function without an embedded comma. This is because Excel has optional parameters in the PMT function that may follow the three numbers shown here, and the comma delimits all parameters in the function. Open Office uses the same syntax as Excel, but Open Office uses the semicolon as a delimiter, so it permits a comma in large numbers.

Typed into a cell of a spreadsheet program, this function would give the answer

$$(\$2,546.31).$$

In that form, the answer appears as a negative number, which reflects Excel's convention for the sign of numbers in a cash flow. If you were to receive (cash inflow, positive) a car worth $25,000 today, your lease payment (cash outflow, negative) would be $2,546.31 per year for 20 years.

Cost of Operation—Variable Cost per Unit of Output

To describe the operating costs of a device, we must distinguish between the *variable inputs* of a technology and the *fixed* inputs. The variable inputs are those that must be increased to produce more output. Examples of variable inputs are energy, materials, and personnel time, which get *consumed* in the process of creating the output. The fixed input is the device itself, so the fixed cost of the device is the expense of leasing it per unit of time, such as a year, as discussed in Example 3.

The total cost of all variable inputs used to produce one unit of output from a device is the *variable cost* (per unit) of operating the device. One way to think about an automobile is that the number of miles driven is the quantity of its output, and the number of miles driven per year is its rate of output. The cost of the gasoline necessary to go one mile is the variable operating cost of the car, the cost per unit of output. The variable operating cost plus the expense of leasing the device for the time it takes to produce one unit is called the *average total operating cost* of the device (per unit of output).

Example 4   Automobile

The output of an automobile is the number of miles driven. The input to the car is gasoline. Suppose that gasoline costs $4 per gallon, and the car has an efficiency of 20 miles per gallon. Suppose also that the car leases for $350 per month and the user drives it an average of 1,000 miles per month. What are the variable operating cost, fixed operating cost, and average total operating cost of the car (per mile)?

Solution

The variable operating cost of the car will be the cost of the gasoline consumed in driving one mile. The efficiency datum tells us output per unit of input (miles/gallon). However, to determine the cost of gasoline per mile driven, we need to know how many *gallons per mile* the car uses when it is operated. We get that information by inverting the efficiency measure:

$$20 \, \frac{miles}{gallon} = \frac{1}{20} \, \frac{gallons}{mile}$$

The total cost of gasoline used, per mile is therefore

$$4 \, \frac{dollars}{gallon} \times \frac{1}{20} \, \frac{gallons}{mile} = \frac{4}{20} \, \frac{dollars}{mile} = \$0.20 \, per \, mile.$$

The complete variable operating cost of a car should also include the cost of other consumable inputs, such as oil and the labor cost of periodic maintenance and repairs, and the deterioration (*depreciation*) of a car's value due to usage even when it is properly maintained and repaired, but those are ignored here to simplify the example.

The fixed operating cost of the car, at a usage of 1,000 miles per month with a lease expense of $350 per month, is $350/1000 = $0.35 per mile driven.

The total operating expense of the car is therefore $0.20 + $0.35 = $0.55 per mile.

This example (Example 4) was constructed to explain why the U.S. government permits businesses to expense $0.565 per mile for the use of automobiles when the cost of the gasoline is only $0.20 per mile. The reason is that the full operating cost of a car includes both the variable operating expenses (gasoline, oil, and so on) and the fixed expense of leasing the car or equivalently of owning it and making monthly loan payments. However, unlike the variable operating expense per mile, the fixed expense per mile depends on an assumption about the rate at which the vehicle is being used, meaning the number of miles driven in a month. The complete consideration of fixed costs per unit of output requires a consideration of the time value of money, and we will take up the details of that calculation in Chapter 3. Here, we may simply understand that the extra $0.365 per mile that the government allows as an operating expense, above the variable cost of $0.20 per mile, reflects the cost of financing the purchase of a vehicle that is used at some "average" mileage per year.

Another example of operating cost, or usage cost, for a technology is found in lighting.

Example 5   Light Bulbs

The output of a light bulb is the amount of light created at a one-foot distance from the bulb, but the usage is the amount of light given off over time, say one hour. The rate of output may be 445 lumens, but the amount of light used in one hour is 445 lumen-hours. The input to the light bulb is electric energy. If the 445-lumen bulb draws 40 W of electric energy, then *over one hour*, it will draw 40 watt-hours of electric energy. If that energy costs $0.12 per kilowatt-hour, then the variable operating cost of the bulb is 40 Wh × 0.12 $/kWh = 4.8 $/k = 4.8/1,000 dollars = $0.0048, or just under one-half of a cent *per hour*.

The Valuation of a Device

The goal of our economic analysis of technology will often be to answer a question about investment, *Does the device cost more than it is worth?* The concept of value is central to economics. In common life, we may say, *Beauty (or value) is in the eye of the beholder*, but when a device costs money to buy, costs money to operate, and produces a flow of revenue or savings and other benefits that have a monetary value, the field of financial economics offers concepts and techniques to narrow the valuation to a fairly precise estimate.

The central concept of financial economics is the *present value* of a flow of cash in the future, and the key to finding the present value of a cash flow is to know how to discount money in the future to an equivalent amount of money in the present. The discount rate used for financial decision making establishes that equivalence. For example, if the discount rate is 8 percent per year, it means that $100 today is worth $108 next year, so a legal contract that would pay $108 one year from now is worth only $100 today. As Example 5 shows, the use of a discount rate involves a very simple calculation when a single payment in the future is brought back to its present value equivalent. More complicated cash flows require more complicated mathematics, but fortunately for us, spreadsheet programs such as Microsoft Excel, Open Office, and Apple Numbers have built-in functions to perform those calculations, as Example 6 shows.

Example 6   Residential Solar Photovoltaic Array

A 3 kW system of solar panels, with associated wiring, batteries, and DC–AC inverter, costs $14,400 to purchase and install. The owner can get a 30 percent income tax credit from the U.S. government for this investment. For an owner in Los Angeles, the solar panels will produce enough electric energy to save $1,050 per year that would otherwise be paid to the local electric utility company. The solar array should last 25 years. If the owner decides not to invest in the solar array, he or she could use the money to pay down his or her home mortgage, which will save him or her paying interest on the mortgage loan, which has an interest rate of 6 percent per year. Should he or she invest in the solar array?

Solution

The first step in solving such a problem is to be clear about the cash flow. The initial cost of the system is the $14,400 sticker price minus the income tax credit of 30% × 14,400 = $4,320, for a net price of $10,080, which has to be paid today. The cash flow from the investment would be the $1,050 in saved energy expense per year for 25 years. To a spreadsheet program, the constant $1,050 per year is called the *payment* (think of the $1,050 as a payment back to the homeowner as a result of the investment) and the 25 years is the *nper* of the cash flow. The discount rate that shows how money now is related to money in the future is the 6 percent rate of return that she would get if she *invested* the $10,080 to pay down her mortgage. To a spreadsheet program, that is called the *rate*. The present value of this 25-year cash flow of $1,050 per year can be calculated using the spreadsheet function PV using the following syntax,

$$=PV(rate, nper, pmt)$$

Typing =PV(6%,25,1050) into a cell of the spreadsheet program—and notice that the payment was given to the spreadsheet as 1050 with no comma—gives the answer.

$$-\$13,422.52.$$

To reiterate, spreadsheet programs return the answer as a negative number, because spreadsheets keep track of cash inflows (positive) and cash outflows (negative). The interpretation of this problem is that you would be willing to pay out $13,422.52 (cash outflow, negative) today to buy the solar array in order to get the stream of future benefits described as the payment $1,050 per year (cash inflow, positive).

We interpret the answer to mean that the benefits from the solar array are worth $13,422.52 today. With the 30 percent tax credit, the system would cost only $10,080. Our analysis has shown that the system is worth $13,422.52. Therefore, the system's value is greater than its cost, so the SPV system should be purchased.

It is interesting to note in Example 6 that, without the 30 percent tax credit, the homeowner would have to pay the full sticker price of $14,400, and in that case the system would not be worth the price. That question, asking **what if** *there were no tax credit?* is an example of the kind of *sensitivity analysis* that a financial analyst would perform when conducting a feasibility study on the implementation of this technology.

Technology and Public Policy

Technology is a matter of public interest, requiring some form of support or regulation from government, because the private market decisions of buyers and suppliers, of investors and firms, are not sufficient to bring about the socially optimal development and application of technology.

Public policy related to sustainable technologies takes many forms that must be accounted for in a feasibility analysis. The most obvious are federal and state income tax credits. Federal tax credits are available through 2016 as high as 30 percent of the cost of a renewable energy project, meaning effectively that the U.S. government pays for 30 percent of the project's cost. State tax credits vary widely, from none to 25 percent. Even energy-efficient improvements to buildings have recently qualified for a 10 percent tax credit, although the law providing that incentive expired in 2013. In addition, there are federal, state, and local programs that provide low-interest loans for some applications of sustainable technologies.

Governments also put pressure on public power companies to promote energy efficiency and renewable energy, and one way that the utilities have responded is to offer rebates to individuals and companies that make investments in these technologies. Rebates differ from tax credits, because rebates are treated for federal and state purposes as taxable income, but they figure into the economics of these investments.

Less visible to the general public are laws that attempt to regulate greenhouse gas emissions. Formally, these apply to public power companies and large industrial plants, and in the United States these laws are created at the state level. The establishment of emissions trading systems and renewables portfolio standards has created, respectively, the markets for carbon emission credits and for renewable energy certificates, each of which can be generated by a renewable energy project and sold for their economic value. These marketable *environmental attributes* of renewable energy projects are the subject of Chapter 10.

Take-aways

This chapter surveyed some of the key ideas in the engineering–economic perspective on technology. The rest of the book will explore these ideas in depth and bring out even more subtle points that help us understand how technologies differ and how they can be evaluated financially as a basis for decision making. The *big ideas*, which you should take away from this chapter, are as follows:

- Technology is fundamentally the *knowledge* of the laws of nature by which inputs are transformed into outputs. The refinement of technology over time is driven by the advancement of knowledge about those laws of nature.
- Sustainable technologies are either renewable or nontoxic, or both. They should also be efficient, not wasting resources, and they should have a low lifecycle impact on the environment.
- In the engineering perspective on technology, we look inside the *black box* that performs the transformation of inputs to outputs, quantifying the inputs and outputs of the process,

defining capacity as a measure of the *size* of a device and examining efficiency through the ratio of output to input.

- The economic perspective on technology is more abstract, omitting the details of the transformation process and looking mainly at the costs of purchasing the inputs that are necessary to produce a specific level of output.

- When a device creates output that can be sold, or provides output that enables the owner to save money that would otherwise be spent, the device has an objective, economic value that is independent of the price that a vendor is charging for it. The net present value of the cash flows from a device is the point of reference that enables the analyst to determine whether the device is worth the price that is being charged for it.

- The two perspectives—engineering and economic—come together in the task of doing a feasibility analysis for the implementation of a technology.

CHAPTER 2

Capacity

Overview

Engineering is the application of science—the knowledge of laws of nature—to the betterment of mankind. Through the engineering perspective on technology, we come to understand how technology transforms matter and energy into forms that are more readily usable, such as solar radiation into electric energy. We can describe any transformation process in terms of its inputs and its outputs.

The word *technology* refers to the process of transformation or, more deeply, the knowledge of the laws of nature that underlie the transformation process. We may also use the word *technology* to refer to a class of devices that use the same transformation process. Devices that employ the same technology differ most noticeably in their size. The *capacity* of a device is a measure of its size, and usually—but not always—we measure capacity by the output rate of the device. For example, power technologies produce energy, so their capacity is measured in energy output per unit of time, such as British thermal units (BTUs)/hour for a furnace or watts (W) for electric power.

In this chapter, we look at a variety of transformation processes to see the range of the concept of technology. We see how to describe the capacity of devices for various technologies, and we also take a close look at power technologies and their associated measures of energy. This chapter addresses several fundamental questions:

- How do engineers describe the *size* of different devices?
- The output of a power technology can variously be measured in BTUs per hour, in kilowatts (kW), or in horsepower (HP). How do those units compare with each other, and in what contexts are they used?

- Which units of measurement are used to describe energy, in which contexts, and how do they compare with each other?
- What does the capacity factor of a device tell about the operation of the device?

Technology Is a Transformation Process

Technology transforms inputs into outputs (and byproducts) under specific environmental conditions. Figure 2.1 reminds us of the basic relationships between inputs, process and outputs in the transformation process.

Examples of technologies described in this manner are shown in Table 2.1.

In the following sections, we consider many examples of sustainable technologies, looking specifically at how to measure the inputs and outputs based on the science underlying the transformation process. We give

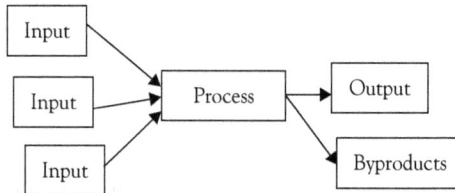

Figure 2.1 Input–output diagram

Table 2.1 Inputs, process, and outputs

Technology	Inputs	Process	Outputs
Solar thermal	Solar radiation	Absorption of radiation	Heated water
Automobile engine	Gasoline	Combustion	Motion (mechanical energy)
Hydroelectric generation	Potential energy (water at height) → Mechanical energy (spinning turbine)	Induction	Electrical energy
Agriculture	Seeds, sun, water, labor, land, fertilizer, equipment	Cultivation, growth	Fruits and vegetables

special attention to power technologies in this chapter, so we begin with a look at these technologies from the engineering perspective.

Processes (Inputs to Outputs) for Power Technologies

Table 2.2 shows how various power technologies differ in their inputs, process, and outputs.

Notice in the table that some technologies involve several stages of transformation of energy. Each transformation is a technology in itself. For example, a coal-fired electric power plant uses *combustion technology* to transform fuel energy into heat energy, then *steam engine technology* to transform heat energy into the rotational (kinetic) energy of a turbine, and then *electromotor technology* to transform rotational energy into electric energy.

What is the steam engine? It had been invented in the early 1700s, but it was James Watt's refinements to the steam engine in 1769 and 1781 that created the power behind the Industrial Revolution. The steam engine

Table 2.2 Inputs, process, and outputs for power technologies

Power technology	Inputs	Process	Output
Solar photovoltaic	Solar radiation	Photovoltaic effect	Electrical energy
Solar thermal heating	Solar radiation	Absorption of radiation	Heat
Solar thermal electric	Solar radiation → heat	Steam engine	Electrical energy
Car engine	Fuel (chemical energy)	Combustion and piston engine	Motion (kinetic energy)
Home furnace	Fuel (chemical energy)	Combustion	Heat
Hydroelectric power	Potential energy (water at height) → mechanical energy (spinning turbine)	Electromotive	Electrical energy
Coal- or oil-fired electric power plant	Fuel (chemical energy) Heat → mechanical energy	Combustion and Electromotive	Electrical energy

uses steam to drive a piston that does mechanical work. Watt figured out how to make it more efficient and how it could produce rotary motion suitable for driving industrial machinery.

What is the electromotor? The discovery of the electromotor effect began with Pixii's experiment in 1832 that had a wire coil in a rotating magnetic field to create an electric current. In the 1860s, the electric generator (dynamo) was further refined. A generator uses kinetic energy as an input and produces electric energy as the output. Working the other way, the generator becomes an electric motor, using an electric current as an input to create rotational motion of an electric coil in the presence of a magnetic field.

Capacity as a Measure of Size

Any specific *device* that expresses or realizes a technology has some limit to the amount of output it can produce in a given unit of time. That limit to its production is the *capacity* of the device.

The capacity measures the maximum output rate of the particular machine or plant. Some examples are shown in Table 2.3. For power technologies, the output is energy, and the capacity is measured in units

Table 2.3 Examples of capacity

Technology	Output	Capacity example
Solar thermal	Heated water	Heat energy absorbed by water (BTU) per day
Home furnace	Heat energy	60,000 BTU per hour
Automobile engine	Motion (mechanical energy)	200 HP (energy/time)
Hydroelectric generation	Electrical energy	1000 kW (electric energy/time)
Wastewater treatment	Usable water, fertilizer	100,000 gallons per day
Farm (agriculture)	Fruits and vegetables	160 acres
Hospital (healthcare)	*Treated person* (as a process measure, not an output measure)	100 beds (treated persons per day)
Light bulb	Light	445 lumens 40 W (electric energy/time)

of energy per unit of time. The table shows that there are various units to measure power depending on the context. Electric power is measured in kilowatts. Heating power is measured in BTUs per hour. Automotive power is measured in horsepower (HP). Later in this section, we will see the definitions of those terms. For now, just become familiar with their use.

Notice the examples of the farm (agriculture), hospital (healthcare), and the light bulb. They are different from the others, because they are not described by an output measure. A farm's *size* of 160 acres is a measure of one input to the production process, land. A hospital's *capacity* of 100 beds measures the number of people treated per day, which is a throughput measure, whereas the number of people cured per day would be a strict output measure. In the example of the light bulb, the common way to describe a bulb is by the amount of electric power it draws, measured in watts, which is an input measure, not an output measure. The correct capacity measure for a light bulb, *lumens*, is a measure of light output. However, the lumen is not a measure of light *per time* but of light intensity (candlepower) falling on one square-foot of area, one foot away from the light source. This example shows that capacity, even as an output measure, is sometimes calculated in relation to a variable other than time.

Capacity Measures for Power Technologies

A power technology transforms energy from one form into another. The capacity of a power technology is therefore expressed in units of energy per unit of time. However, different systems of measuring energy have evolved in different contexts, and the student of sustainable technologies needs to learn their definitions and uses.

Water Heating Technologies (BTU)

A furnace burns fuel to create heat. In scientific terms, it is a technology that transforms the chemical energy in a fuel into heat energy through the process of combustion. Heat energy is traditionally measured in BTUs. One BTU is defined as the amount of energy needed to heat 1 pound of water by 1°F. So the amount of heat energy (E, in BTUs) needed to raise a mass of water (M, in lb.) from a temperature of T_{low} to T_{high} (°F) is

$$E = M \times (T_{high} - T_{low})$$

Example 1   Heat Energy

How much heat energy is needed to raise the temperature of a 50-gal hot water tank from 45°F (the temperature of water coming into a house from an underground line) to 120°F (a standard for the hot water tap in a home)?

Solution

To solve this problem, we need to know the weight of a gallon of water. Sources on the Internet give 8.34 pounds per gallon as the density of water. The 50-gal hot water tank will therefore hold $50 \times 8.34 = 417$ lb. of water. To raise this amount of water by $120 - 45 = 75$ degrees would require

$$H = M \times (T_{high} - T_{low})$$
$$H = 417 \times (120 - 45)$$
$$H = 417 \times 75$$
$$H = 31{,}275 \qquad \text{BTUs of heat energy.}$$

How long would it take a water heater to raise 50 gallons of water from 45°F to 120°F? That depends on the *power* of the heater, meaning its rate of heat production, which is measured in BTU *per hour*.

The technical descriptions of water heaters, as found on retail websites such as Home Depot and Menards, list several features that describe the ability of a water heater to heat water. Three features are prominent in these descriptions:

1. **BTU rating**. This is listed in the product descriptions as BTU, but it really means BTU/hr. It is used for water heaters that are fueled by natural gas or propane, whose energy contents as fuels are measured

in BTUs. Thus, the BTU rating of a water heater represents the maximum fuel usage rate of the device. Home water heaters tend to have BTU ratings in the range of 32,000 to 40,000 BTU/hr.

2. **Recovery rate**. The recovery rate of a water heater indicates how many gallons of water the device can raise by a specific temperature difference (usually 90°F) in one hour. For example, a Richmond 38-gal gas-fired water heater has a recovery rate of 48.5 gal/hr for a temperature increase of 90°F.

3. **Tank size**. The tank size is the number of gallons of water that the water heater can hold. Typical residential tank sizes are 30 to 50 gallons, depending on the number of people in the household.

Example 2   Capacity of a Water Heater

Which of the three descriptors of a water heater is a measure of the capacity of the device?

Solution

In the engineering perspective, capacity reflects the *size* of a device, but its specific meaning is the device's rate of output per unit of time. The output of a water heater is heated water. Therefore, only the recovery rate (gallons heated by 90°F per hour) is a measure of capacity in the engineering sense.

The BTU rating of the water heater is a measure of the maximum fuel use of the device, so that measures the rate of input use, not the rate of output.

Tank size captures the common English meaning of the *size* of the device, and people often refer to tank size as the *capacity* of the water heater, but that is not the meaning of capacity in the engineering sense.

The Metric Version of BTU Is Kilocalorie

In the metric system, heat energy is measured in kilocalories (kCal), also called *food calories* or *large calories*. Analogous to the definition of BTU as the heat energy required to raise 1 pound of water by 1°F, the kilocalorie is the amount of heat energy needed to raise 1 kg of water by 1°C. A kilogram is 2.20462 pounds, and a 1°C change is exactly a 1.8°F change, so one would expect that

$$1 \text{ kCal} = 2.20462 \text{ (lb.)} \times 1.8 \text{ (°F)} = 3.9683 \text{ BTU}$$

However, due to a minor difference in the definitions in the International Table of calorie and a thermochemical calorie, the official conversion coefficient is

$$1 \text{ kCal} = 3.9657 \text{ BTU}$$

Home Heating and Insulation Technologies (BTU/hr again)

Home heating systems typically use natural gas or electric energy to heat air. Their ability to deliver heated air is measured, like that of a water heater, in units of BTU/hr. A small home or a home in a moderately warm climate can get by with a furnace having a capacity of 40,000 BTU/hr. A furnace for a three-bedroom house in a moderately cold climate might need to have a capacity of 60,000 BTU/hr.

How do heating, ventilating, and air conditioning engineers decide on the capacity of a furnace for a particular house and location? The principle is simple—the furnace must be able to *generate heat at the same rate that heat is being lost* from the house due to cooling when the environment is at its coldest. For this reason, the design of a heating system is intimately related to the design of the insulation system in a building.

This section of the chapter is about power technologies. It might therefore seem odd to include an analysis of windows, doors, and walls. However, a window is analogous to a power-generating technology in the sense that it transmits heat energy from inside the house to outside, when the outside is colder. The study of the *flow* of heat energy through any surface is essentially a study of power, so, not surprisingly, that flow is measured in BTU/hr.

The *rate of heat energy loss* through a device such as a window, door, or wall depends on three factors, shown here with their units of measurement.

1. The surface area of the device (A, square feet)
2. The difference in temperature from one side of the device to the other (D, °F).
3. The *thermal conductivity* of the device (written as U, see below for its units).

Building materials such as drywall and plywood, which vary in thickness, are known by their thermal conductivity expressed in BTU/hr per square foot (of area) per inch (of thickness). The thermal conductivity of devices such as windows and doors, which come as ready-made assemblies, is described in BTU/hr per square foot (of area). The thermal conductivity expressed in this way is called the **U-value** of the device or the material.

The formula for the rate of energy loss through a device that has a given U-value, an area of A square feet, and that separates a temperature difference of D degrees Fahrenheit is

$$\text{Energy loss} = A \times D \times U \qquad \text{(BTU/hr)}$$

As energy loss is measured in BTU/hr, the unit of measurement for the thermal conductivity U is BTU/hr per square foot per degree Fahrenheit.

The inverse of the U-value describes the thermal *resistance* of the device or material and is called the **R-value**. Thus, $U = 1/R$. Insulating materials are known by their R-value, because a higher R-value means a higher resistance to the flow of heat, a higher insulating value. The formula for the rate of energy loss through a device is therefore more commonly written as

$$\text{Energy loss} = \frac{A \times D}{R} \qquad \text{(BTU/hr)}$$

Example 3   Heat Loss Through Windows

(a) You have a window that is 2.5 ft wide and 4 ft tall. It is now winter and the temperature outside is 20°F. You keep your home warmed to 70°F. The current window is a common single-pane window having an R-value of 1. What is the rate of heat loss through that window? (b) If you were to replace the window with a thermally efficient window that has an R-value of 3, what would the new rate of heat loss be?

Solution

(a) The area of the window is $2.5 \times 4 = 10$ sq. ft. The temperature difference between inside and outside is $70 - 20 = 50°F$. The R-value of the window is 1, so the rate of heat loss through the window is $\dfrac{10 \times 50}{1} = 500$ BTU/hr.

(b) If the window had an R-value of 3 rather than 1, the rate of heat loss would be $\dfrac{10 \times 50}{3} = \dfrac{500}{3} = 167$ BTU/hr, rounded to three significant digits.

The replacement window would have the effect of saving lost energy relative to the old window. That savings is a benefit to the owner of the window, as if the new window were *generating* heat energy for the house. This is why insulation technology and home heating technologies have a similar purpose.

The R-values of some common building materials are shown in Table 2.4.

The R-values of some common building assemblies are shown in Table 2.5.

The Annual Loss of Heat from a Building

The amount of heat lost through a window depends on the difference in temperature between the inside and outside. For this reason, building engineers describe the climate of a region by its number of *degree-days*.

Table 2.4 R-values for insulating materials

Material	R-value per inch
Cellulose blown (attic)	3
Cotton batts (blue-jean insulation)	3.7
Fiberglass batt	4
Polyurethane (foamed-in-place)	6
Soft wood	1.25
Brick	0.2
Plywood	1.2
Gypsum drywall ½ inch	0.9

Table 2.5 R-values for assemblies

Device	R-value
Single-pane window	0.9
Single-pane with storm window	2.0
Double insulating glass, ¼ in. air space	1.7
Double insulating with film and low-E	4.0
Solid core door 1 ¾ in.	3.0

One degree-day is one day in which the environmental temperature was 1°F less than the reference point of 65°F. The number of degree-days in a year is the sum of the temperature differences from 65°F across the days of the year. For days below 65°F, the sum is called the number of *heating degree-days* (HDDs), which measures the need for heating. For days above 65°F, the sum is called the number of *cooling degree-days* (CDDs), which measures the need for air conditioning (somewhat; most people would not turn on the air conditioning unless the outside temperature was above 78°F.)

For example, data from the National Climate Data Center website show that central Iowa had 7,363 HDDs in 2007. We can form a realistic estimate of the CDDs by using 80°F as a reference point for air conditioning. If the 92 days of June, July, and August were to average a temperature of 83.3°F, that would yield an estimate of close to 300 cooling degree-days.

The amount of energy lost through a window *over a year* depends on the number of HDDs of the climate for the region of the country where the window is located. We have seen that the amount of energy lost in one hour is calculated as $A \times D/R$, where A is the area of the window, D is the temperature difference, and R is the R-value (thermal resistance) of the window.

Over a year, the energy loss has the same equation, but we must multiply by 24 hours in a day and add up all the temperature differences across the year. To get the energy loss over a year, which must be compensated for by heating, we add the number of HDDs of the climate, which is the sum of the temperature differences from a standard 65°F across all days that the temperature is less than 65°F. To find the energy gained during the year, which must be compensated for by air conditioning, we add the number of CDDs, which is the sum of the temperature differences from a standard 65°F across all days that the temperature is greater than 65°F. The resulting equation, for the total heat loss per year, is

$$\text{Energy loss} = \frac{A \times 24 \times (HDD + CDD)}{R} \qquad \text{(BTU per year)}.$$

The energy saved by installing an energy-efficient window is the difference between the energy lost by the old window and the energy lost by the new window.

Example 4   Annual Loss of Heat Through a Window

Suppose that an old window has an R-value 0.9, and a new energy-efficient window has an R-value 3.0, the window area is $A = 10$ sq. ft., and the window is located in Iowa, which has 7,363 heating degree days and an estimated 300 cooling degree days. How much of a savings in energy would result from replacing the old window with a new, energy-efficient window?

Solution

The old window would lose the following amount of energy.

$$E = 10 \times 24 \times (7663 + 300)/0.9$$
$$E = 2,123,466 \qquad \text{BTU per year, lost.}$$

The new window replacement would lose

$$E = 10 \times 24 \times (7663 + 300)/3.0$$
$$E = 637,040 \qquad \text{BTU per year, lost.}$$

The replacement window would therefore result in a savings of $2,123,466 - 637,040 = 1,486,426$ BTU per year.

In Chapter 7, on the economic analysis of technologies, we will return to this example to see how these engineering calculations, when taken together with data about the price of energy, enable a financial analyst to determine whether the window replacement is worth the expense.

Refrigeration Technologies (BTU/hr)

Air conditioning and refrigeration technologies are designed to remove heat from a building, but their capacity is measured in the same way as heating technologies, namely, in BTU/hr.

- A window air conditioner for a small room withdraws 6,000 BTU/hr of heat from the room.
- A commercial central air conditioner has the capacity to withdraw 60,000 BTU/hr of heat from a building.

A seemingly odd convention in the air conditioning business is to measure the chilling capacity (power) of an air conditioning unit in *tons of refrigeration* or just *tons*. One *ton* is defined to be a power output of 12,000 BTU/hr. Thus, the 60,000 BTU/hr commercial air conditioner mentioned above would also be called a five-ton air conditioner.

It does not weigh five tons. Why is it called a five-ton unit? The answer is that one *ton of air conditioning power* is defined as the rate of heat withdrawal needed to turn 1 ton (2,000 lb.) of 32°F water from liquid to ice in 24 hr.

Electric Power Technologies (Watts, Kilowatts, and Megawatts)

Technologies that produce electric power have their capacities measured in watts. The watt is the unit of power used in the International System of Units (SI units). Its larger multiples are expressed as kilowatts (1,000 W = 1 kW) and megawatts (1,000,000 W = 1 MW). A few examples of devices that require electric power give a sense of the magnitude of the watt as a unit of power.

The large wind turbines that people see in wind farms near highways have capacities that range from 1,000,000 W (1 MW) to 3,000,000 W (3 MW). A 2.5 MW windmill can power approximately 1,000 homes. A 1,000 MW electric power plant can serve approximately 400,000 homes.

Table 2.6 Power outputs of various devices

Device	Watts (W)	Kilowatts (kW)	Megawatts (MW)
Bright light bulb	100	0.1	
Solar photovoltaic power module	125	0.125	
Hair dryer, max setting	1,000	1.0	
Typical household	2,500	2.5	
2014 Nissan Leaf electric car engine	37,022	37 (107 HP)	
Wind turbine for a farm or small business	10,000	10	
Wind turbine for a small community	85,000	85	
Commercial wind turbine	1,500,000	1,500	1.5
Industrial gas-fired or diesel power plant	20,000,000	20,000	20
Large-scale solar thermal electric power plant (in Abu Dhabi)	100,000,000	100,000	100
Large-scale oil, coal, or nuclear electric power plant	1,000,000,000	1,000,000	1,000

Measures of Power

The watt and the BTU/hr are both measures of power. They measure the rate of energy flow per unit of time. To four significant digits, the conversion factor is

$$1 \text{ W} = 3.412 \text{ BTU/hr}$$

Example 5   *Electric Water Heater (BTU and kW)*

An electric water heater has a heating element that is immersed in the water and thereby transfers essentially all of its electric power into heat. If the capacity of a water heater is expressed as a recovery factor of 40 gallons per hour (at a 90°F temperature difference), how much electric power will the water heater require?

Solution

Using the methods of Example 1, we can calculate the power output of the water heater in BTU/hr. We use the fact that one gallon of water weighs 8.34 pounds. In one hour, the 40 gallons raised 90°F gains heat energy amounting to

$$40 \text{ (gal)} \times 8.34 \text{ (lb./gal)} \times 90 \text{ (°F)} = 30{,}024 \text{ BTU}$$

Therefore, the water heater's output rate in that hour was 30,024 BTU/hr. Convert this to watts by dividing it by 3.412 BTU/hr/W:

$$\frac{30{,}024 \text{ BTU / hr}}{3.412 \text{ BTU / hr / W}} = 8{,}799.5 \text{ W.}$$

Thus, when the electric water heater is heating cold water, it will draw power at a rate of almost 9 kW. That is like running nine hair dryers at the same time.

The Human Body as a Heat Generator

The common unit for heat energy in Britain and America is the BTU, but we noted in the previous section (after Example 2) that the metric version of the BTU is the kilocalorie or food calorie, and the conversion rate is 1 kCal = 3.9657 BTU. Anyone who has tried to diet knows about food calories. What does the *burning* of calories in the human body tell us about ourselves as generators of heat? As a point of reference, here are two facts:

- A human at rest burns 70 food calories per hour.
- A human walking briskly burns 350 calories per hour.

Example 6   The Human Furnace

A light bulb typically uses 60, 75, or 100 W of power, and all of that energy ends up heating its environment. How does a person at rest compare to a light bulb? In other words, how many watts is 70 kCal/hr?

Solution

From the conversion factor stated previously, we see that 1 kCal/hr = 3.9657 BTU/hr, and from the table of power conversion factors on page 37, 1 BTU/hr = 0.000293 kW or 0.293 W, so 70 kCal/hr = 70 × 3.9657 × 0.293 = 81.3 W. So a person at rest generates about as much heat as a light bulb.

Automotive Technologies (Horsepower)

It is a quaint nod to history that in the Anglo-American system we continue to use the horsepower as a measure of the power output of automobile engines. The horsepower (HP) was originally defined in terms of the ability of horses to raise water from a well or coal from a mine, there are now several varying definitions of the horsepower depending on the context of the application. The mechanical and hydraulic horsepower, although differing slightly, are each close to 345.7 W. The electrical horsepower is defined to be 346 W exactly. The metric horsepower is 735.5 W, and to really confuse matters, the boiler horsepower is 9,809.5 W.[1]

Common automobile engines are typically powered in the range of 100 to 400 HP. The 2014 Toyota Prius has a system power, including both the gasoline engine and the battery, of 134 HP. A 2014 Infiniti QX80 sports-utility vehicle has 400 HP.

Unit Conversion Table for Power Measures

In the examples of this chapter, we have seen the use of the BTU/hr, the watt (or kilowatt) and the horsepower as units of power. The factors that convert one unit to another are shown in Table 2.7.

The numbers in the table correspond to the column measure divided by the row measure. For example, the table shows that the ratio of HP/ kW = 1.341, meaning 1 HP = 1.341 kW. This shows that the HP and the kW are of nearly the same magnitude as measures of power.

The table also shows that 1 BTU/hr is a very small amount of power relative to the HP and kW, because it takes 3,412 BTU/hr to equal 1 kW.

Table 2.7 *Power conversion factors*

Entries are the column unit divided by the row unit	Kilowatt (kW)	Horse-power (HP)	British thermal units/per hour (BTU/hr)
1 kW =	1	1.341	3412.14
1 HP =	0.7457	1	2545
1 BTU/hr =	0.00029307	0.0003929	1

Tech Focus: Measures of Energy

We formed the power measure for a water heater by looking at the energy use (BTU) per unit of time (per hour). Thus, BTU is a measure of energy, and BTU/hr is a measure of power. One therm is defined to be 100,000 BTU, so the therm is a measure of energy, and therms/hour is a measure of power.

The kilowatt is a unit of power, but it is not expressed as energy per unit of time. *What, then, is the unit of energy that corresponds to a kilowatt?* The answer is not particularly satisfying to students of the subject. The unit of energy is the *kilowatt-hour* (kWh).

The kilowatt-hour is a measure of energy, because if you divide it by the unit of time (per hour), you get the measure of power, kilowatt. Thus, for electric energy, it is helpful to *base one's understanding on the kilowatt as a unit of power* and to think of electric energy as the result of running that power over a particular length of time.

The measure of energy in the International Scientific (SI) system is the *joule*. Examples later in this chapter show how to use the joule as a measure, but the important point here is that the watt, as a measure of power, is defined directly from the joule as a measure of energy:

$$1 \text{ Watt} = 1 \frac{\text{Joule}}{\text{Second}}$$

Example 7   Electric Power and Electric Energy

(a) How much energy, expressed in kilowatt-hours, is used when a hair dryer is run on the low setting (500 W) for 12 minutes? (b) How much energy is used by a 60-watt light bulb that is left on for eight hours? (c) If a household's monthly electric bill shows that 953 kWh of electric energy were used during a 33-day billing period, what was the average power draw of the house during that period?

Solution

The basic concept to apply is

$$\frac{Energy}{Time} = Power$$

We can also write this relationship as

$$Energy = Power \times Time$$

(a) Convert 12 minutes to hours: 12 min/60 (min/hr) = 12/60 hr = 0.2 hr. Now multiply the power rate by time to get the energy used

$$Energy = 500 \ (W) \times 0.2 \ (hr)$$
$$Energy = 500 \times 0.2 \ watt\text{-}hours$$
$$Energy = 100 \ watt\text{-}hours$$

Divide 100 watt-hours by 1,000 to convert it to kilowatt-hour,

$$Energy = 0.100 \ kWh$$

(b) A 60 W bulb run for eight hours consumes

$$Energy = 60 \ (W) \times 8 \ (hr)$$
$$Energy = 60 \times 8 \ (watt\text{-}hours)$$
$$Energy = 480 \ watt\text{-}hours$$
$$Energy = 0.48 \ kWh$$

(c) The household's average power consumption, expressed in kilowatts, will be the total energy used (kWh) divided by the number of hours in the billing period. Thirty-three days translates to $33 \times 24 = 792$ hr. So 953 kWh divided by 792 hr is

$$= 1.203 \text{ kW}$$

1.2 kW is only a little more than the power drawn by running one hair dryer on the maximum setting. So how might a household draw only 1.2 kW in power when there are many more electric devices in the house? The reason is that the 1.2 kW is the *average* power draw of the house, averaging daytime and nighttime use over all the hours of the month. During the daytime, the maximum power drawn at any point in time could be as high as 3.0 kW, whereas at night, with only a few lights and an electric fan blowing heated air, the power draw might be less than 0.5 kW at a particular point in time.

The Capacity Factor of a Device in Operation

When the actual usage of a device (per year) is divided by its rated capacity (output per year), the result is called the *capacity factor* of the device under the stated conditions of usage. For example, consider a wind turbine that has a rated capacity of 50 kW and produces 158,000 kWh of electric energy in a year. The maximum production of the wind turbine would be 50 kW $\times$ 24 (hr/day) $\times$ 365 (days/year) = 438,000 kWh. The actual production, as a percentage of its maximum would be $\dfrac{158,000}{438,000}$ = 0.36, meaning 36 percent.

The actual output of a solar power system or a wind system depends on the amount of insolation or the amount of wind at its location. Thus, the capacity factor of a solar or wind power system is a statement about the technology *in its particular location*, not about the device per se.

Capacity Factors for Wind Turbines

A significant determinant of the capacity factor of a wind turbine is the variability of wind speed at the site, because variability diminishes the

capacity factor significantly. The power output of a wind turbine is proportional to the cube of the wind speed, so when the rated capacity is
reached at wind speeds near the maximum tolerance of the device, wind
speeds lower than the maximum produce far less output than at the maximum tolerable wind speed.

Commercial wind turbines, under typical weather conditions at favorable sites, have had capacity factors between 20 and 40 percent.[2] Some
studies put the estimate closer to 20 percent.[3] Recent designs, which permit the turbine to reach its peak capacity over a wider range of wind
speeds, may reach 50 percent in onshore locations.[4] However, wind turbines that are sited for convenience (as on a college campus) rather than
for the stability of wind speed can have capacity factors below 10 percent.

Take-aways

The engineer's input–process–output perspective on technology enables
us to describe technologies, and the various devices that use or represent
the technologies, in several important ways. A basic but important concept in the description of technology is capacity, which conveys a sense
of how *big* a device is. The description of devices of different sizes led us
in this chapter to study the various ways that power and energy can be
measured. The key points from the chapter are the following:

- *Capacity* describes the size of a device, how big or small it is
  in relation to its purpose, which is the production of output.
  Capacity is almost always measured as the *output rate* of
  the device, such as watts, kilowatts, or megawatts for power
  systems.
- The exceptions to the rule are devices whose purpose is
  storage. Water tanks, hydrogen fuel tanks, and batteries have
  their capacities measured in the units of output that they
  store, for example, gallons, kilograms, or kilowatt-hours.
- Measures of energy and power are commonly expressed in
  different units according to the context (the type of energy),
  although all units are related mathematically through standard
  conversion formulas.

- The unit of measurement can be scaled up by using the prefixes kilo (× 1,000) or mega (× 1,000,000).
- Common measures of energy include the kilowatt-hour (electrical), the British Thermal Unit (heat), therm (heat), and the calorie (heat).
- Common measures of power include kW (electrical), the BTU/hr (heat), and HP (automotive).
- The *capacity factor* of a device indicates how much the device is being used, as a percentage of its maximum annual output.

CHAPTER 3

Efficiency

Overview

Efficiency is one of the defining characteristics of sustainability. In the later chapters of this book, efficiency will be a key concept in the economic evaluation of technologies as sustainable or unsustainable. The efficiency of a technology is a measure of its *output per unit of input*. This calculation can also be derived as the rate of output production divided by the rate of input usage. Efficiency can therefore be measured only in relation to *one* input. When a technology has several inputs, each input will have its own efficiency measure.

This chapter addresses several important questions:

- How do you measure the efficiency of a device?
- What makes one device more efficient than another?
- What is the Energy Star rating program in the United States, and how is the concept of efficiency used in rating various devices?
- When a device is really a system consisting of several processes in sequence, how can one calculate the efficiency of the system from knowledge of the efficiency of its components?
- What forms of energy are there in addition to heat (measured in British thermal units, BTUs) and electrical energy (measured in kilowatt hours, kWh), and what types of power technology use those forms?
- How does a process flow diagram depict the key characteristics of a technology's processes?

Examples of How Efficiency May Be Defined

The key to describing the efficiency of a device within a technology class is to be clear about the inputs and outputs of the technology and how they are measured. Table 3.1 shows some examples.

Notice that when the input and output are measured in the same units (energy in an engine or furnace, or water in a treatment plant, or patients in a hospital), the efficiency can be expressed as a *percentage* of output in relation to the input. That measure of efficiency is dimensionless, a number without units, because the units cancel in the calculation of output divided by input. Efficiency is commonly expressed as a percentage for power technologies, which transform one type of energy into another.

Table 3.1 Inputs, output, and efficiency of technologies

Technology	Inputs	Output	Efficiency
Solar thermal	Solar radiation	Heated water	*Percentage* of solar energy absorbed and retained (versus reflected or lost)
Automobile (engine, transmission, tire pressure)	Gasoline	Motion (kinetic energy)	Miles per gallon
Hydroelectric generation	Potential energy (water at height)	Electrical energy	*Percentage* of potential energy converted to electrical energy
Agriculture	Seeds, sun, water, land, fertilizer, pesticide	Fruits and vegetables	Land: bushels per acre
Home furnace	Fuel (oil or natural gas)	Heat	*Percentage* of fuel energy converted to heat energy in the home (not lost in failed combustion or exhausted to the outside)
Wastewater treatment	Sewage	Usable water, fertilizer	Gallons of usable water per gallon of sewage (a *percentage*)
Healthcare	Sick person, medicine, rest	Healthy person	*Percentage* of people cured (cure rate)
Light bulb	Electricity	Light	Lumens per kilowatt

The Efficiency of Power Technologies

The efficiency of a power technology is the amount of output energy per unit of input energy. It is usually expressed as the ratio of power output to power input.

Several power technologies are based on the *combustion* (burning) of fuel.

- Steam engines (transforming heat energy to rotational energy) have an efficiency up to 41 percent.[1]
- Large-scale coal-fired electric power plants convert fuel to electrical energy in a three-step process. First, they use a burner to convert fuel to heat energy in the form of steam. Second, they use a steam engine to convert heat into rotational energy. Third, they use an electrical turbine to convert the rotational energy of the turbine into electric energy. The combined efficiency of the second and third stages is as high as 40 percent.[2] The lost energy takes the form of heat, dissipated from the steam into the environment and from friction in the turbine. Efficiency is greater at higher temperatures, so research is now pursuing turbines that can get 50 percent efficiency at 700°C.[3]
- Gasoline engines (converting fuel energy to rotational energy) have efficiencies of only 26 to 28 percent.[4] The lost energy takes the form of heat (during combustion) and friction (internal to the operation of the engine). The automobile as a transportation system has even lower fuel efficiency, losing yet more energy due to friction in the drive train and wheels and friction with the air and road.

In contrast, *hydroelectric* turbines convert the potential energy of falling water into the rotational energy of a turbine shaft that is converted to electric energy. Large hydro systems can be 95 percent efficient, and smaller systems in the 5 MW range can have efficiencies of 80 to 85 percent.[5]

Solar photovoltaic (SPV) systems transform solar radiation into electric energy. Commercial SPV panels are only 10 to 15 percent efficient.

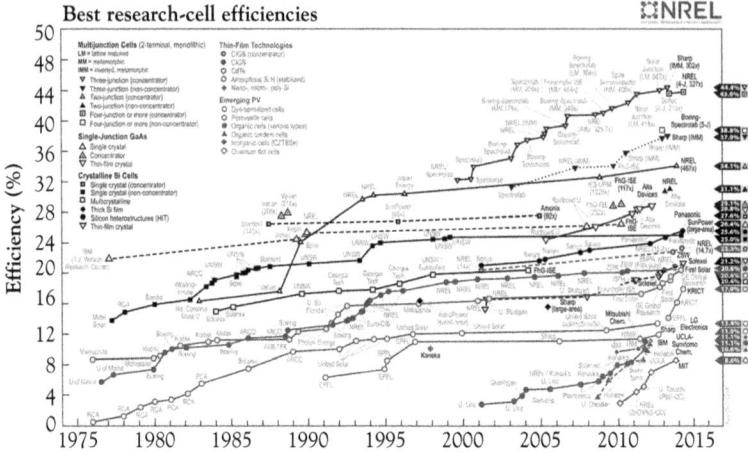

Figure 3.1 Efficiencies of SPV technologies over time

Source: This graphic was created by the National Renewable Energy Laboratory for the U.S. Department of Energy and is used with permission.

Technologies that are still being tested in laboratories are showing efficiencies of 20 percent or more. The lost energy is reflected as sunlight or dissipated as heat (Figure 3.1).

Water and Air Heating

- Electric water heating is 90 to 95 percent efficient, because the electric heating element is immersed in the water.
- Older natural gas burning water heaters are only 60 to 65 percent efficient, due to the loss of some heat as exhaust.
- *High-efficiency* natural-gas water heaters are 91 to 95 percent efficient in burning and 80 percent efficient overall.
- Wood stoves can be up to 40 percent efficient if they put exhaust gasses through a second burning cycle. Most of the heat from a wood stove goes up the chimney as waste.
- Solar thermal collectors convert sunlight to heat energy. When the temperature inside the collector is similar to that of the environment, solar thermal collectors have efficiencies in the range of 40 to 90 percent, depending on the type of technology.[6] When the ambient temperature is much lower than that inside the collector, much of the thermal energy gets lost to the environment.

Tech Focus: Water Heaters

We have seen that water heaters are rated both in terms of their maximum rate of fuel energy use (the BTU rating, which is really BTU/hr) and in terms of their *recovery rate*, which is the rate at which heat energy is imparted to the water. These measures of the rate of energy input and energy output permit us to calculate the efficiency of the heater.

Example 1

A Richmond 38-gal *high-efficiency* gas-fired water heater is rated at 40,000 BTU and has a recovery factor of 48.5 gallons per hour for a 90°F rise in temperature. What is the efficiency of this device?

Solution

The heat output of the device is calculated as the heat energy imparted to 48.5 gallons of water that rise in temperature by 90°F in 1 hour. The density of water is 8.34 lb./gal, so the energy output is $48.5 \times 8.34 \times 90 = 36,404$ BTU/hr. The energy input is 40,000 BTU/hr. Therefore, the efficiency of the device is

$$\frac{36,404}{40,000} = 0.91.$$

So the device has an efficiency of 91 percent.

The Energy Factor of a Gas-Fired Water Heater

Water heaters are also rated by an *energy factor* (EF). The U.S. Environmental Protection Agency's (EPA's) Energy Star website for water heaters describes the EF as a form of efficiency, "A measure of water heater overall efficiency, (EF) is the ratio of useful energy output from the water heater to the total amount of energy delivered to the water heater" (U.S. Environmental Protection Agency). However, that statement is not entirely correct. The EF for the Richmond 38-gal high-efficiency gas-fired water heater of example 1 is listed in the technical specifications for that product as 0.80. But we found in example 1 that its efficiency is

0.91. What, then, is the difference between the EF and the efficiency of a water heater?

A better explanation of the EF appears on the private Arico Plumbing website.[7]

The EF indicates a water heater's overall energy efficiency based on the amount of hot water produced per unit of fuel consumed over a typical day. This includes the following:

- Recovery efficiency—How efficiently the heat from the energy source is transferred to the water.
- Standby losses—The percentage of heat loss per hour from the stored water compared with the heat content of the water (water heaters with storage tanks).
- Cycling losses—The loss of heat as the water circulates through a water heater tank or inlet and outlet pipes.

This explanation shows that the efficiency measure that we calculate as energy output divided by energy input is known in the water heater business as the recovery efficiency. The EF also takes into consideration the loss of heat from the water heater and from related piping. This explains why the Richmond 38-gal heater could have a recovery efficiency of 91 percent but an EF of only 80 percent.

In closing this example, we note that this 0.80 EF means that a *high-efficiency* gas-fired water heater still loses 20 percent of its energy to the environment. In addition to those losses, there will be heat loss when the hot water circulates in the pipes of the house on its way to the sinks and bathtubs where it will be used. The designs that improve the EF of the heating system and reduce the energy losses in circulation are the electric heaters and tankless heaters.

The Efficiency of Electric Water Heaters

Gas-fired water heaters lose some energy to the environment, because the process of burning the natural gas fuel creates hot exhaust gases, some of which are released into the environment. A more efficient technology uses electric energy as the input and transforms the electric energy into heat energy through a resistor (heating element) that is immersed in cold water. In this design, almost all of the heat in the resistor gets transferred to the water, so its recovery efficiency is nearly 100 percent. If electric water heaters are more efficient than gas-fired heaters, why aren't they used universally? The answer lies in the economics of the technology, which is the subject of this chapter. Electric energy tends to be more expensive than the energy in natural gas, so the economic analysis considers the trade-off between greater efficiency and higher expense.

The Efficiency of Tankless Water Heaters

In example 1, the Richmond 38-gal gas-fired heater had a recovery efficiency of 91 percent but an EF of only 80 percent. This means that about 11 percent of the input energy was being lost to the environment through hot water cooling down in a collection tank or in the piping of the system. One improvement to that technology is a tankless design, which heats water precisely when it is needed.

A tankless heater can be positioned in a bathroom, within a few feet of the sink or shower where it is needed. This eliminates the loss of heat that occurs when water circulates through a system of pipes between the heater and its place of use.

Tankless water heaters come in several varieties according to their energy source: electricity, natural gas, or propane. An electric water heater in general has a recovery efficiency of nearly 100 percent, because the heating element is immersed in the water. A tankless electric water heater eliminates the standby losses, so its only loss of efficiency is in cycling losses, making its efficiency factor nearly 100 percent.

The efficiency factor of a heater examines heat losses associated with the design of the heater itself. It does not consider heat losses in the plumbing of the building as hot water travels from the heater to its points of use. However, a tankless water heater located at the point of use eliminates even these heat losses from circulation. Whole-house tankless water heaters do not have that advantage.

The gas-fired and propane-fired tankless heaters have a lower recovery efficiency, because they lose some energy in the exhaust gasses from combustion. A gas-fired tankless whole-house water heater that meets an Energy Star rating by the U.S. EPA has an EF of 0.83.

Tech Focus: Air Conditioning and Refrigeration

Air conditioning accounts for the largest share of the consumption of electric energy by home appliances. An air conditioner works like a refrigerator. Its engine draws heat out of a working fluid and exhausts the extracted heat by vent to the outside of the room, leaving the cooling effect of the fluid on the inside. (Refrigerators exhaust their heat into the kitchen. Yes, the effect of a refrigerator is to *warm up* the kitchen.)

The capacity of a residential air conditioner is usually expressed in BTU per hour, which measures the rate at which the air conditioner can extract heat from the house. A window-mounted air conditioning unit, to cool a single room, might have a capacity of 5,000 BTU/hr. A house might require 40,000 BTU/hr. The capacity of large, commercial air conditioners is usually described in terms of *tons of refrigeration*. One ton is equal to 12,000 BTU/hr. Residential central air systems are usually from one to five tons (3 to 20 kW) in capacity.

Table 3.2 shows the power consumption and the refrigerating capacity of two models of refrigerating unit.

In the United States, one measure of the efficiency of air conditioners is the *energy efficiency ratio* (EER). The EER calculation is the ratio of the maximum cooling output (in BTU/hr) to the required electric power input (in kW) under standard test conditions. Table 3.2 shows that the Soleus model, which is Energy Star certified, has a higher EER than the Comfort Aire model.

Table 3.2 Air conditioner characteristics I

	Soleus	Comfort Aire
Cooling capacity (BTU/hr)	10,000	10,000
Power consumption (kW)	0.989	1.150
Energy efficiency ratio (BTU/hr/W)	10.1	8.70
Energy Star	Yes	No

A related measure of efficiency is the seasonal energy efficiency ratio (SEER), which is the ratio of the *total* cooling output (in BTU) over a year to the consumed electric energy input (in kWh) during the normal annual usage of the air conditioner. SEER reflects the average efficiency of the device under a range of operating conditions, whereas EER reflects the efficiency at maximum output under standard test conditions. These may differ, because an air conditioner's efficiency depends on the temperature of the air that it takes in from the environment, a topic we discuss further in Chapter 4.

An interesting feature of air conditioning technology emerges when the cooling power of each air conditioner is expressed in kilowatts rather than in BTU. We convert BTU to kilowatts by the conversion factor 1 BTU/hr = 0.2931 kW. With the cooling power (output) and electric power input measured in the same units, we can calculate the efficiency of each model as output power divided by input power, which yields a measure of efficiency as a percentage. The resulting efficiency ratio is called the coefficient of performance (COP) of the air conditioner. Table 3.2 augmented with the kilowatts and COP data appears as Table 3.3.

Notice that, when the cooling power is measured in kilowatts, the cooling effect of an air conditioner is two to three times as great as the power it draws. How can this be possible? How can an air conditioner produce more cooling effect (output) than it draws in electric power (input)? The answer comes from insight into the technology of the air conditioner itself. The technology of air conditioning is very different

Table 3.3 Air conditioner characteristics II

	Soleus	Comfort Aire
Cooling capacity (BTU/hr)	10,000	10,000
Power consumption (kW)	0.989	1.150
Energy efficiency ratio (BTU/hr/W)	10.1	8.70
Energy Star	Yes	No
Cooling capacity (kW)	2.931	2.931
Coefficient of performance (kW/kW, %)	296% or 2.96	255% or 2.55

from a conventional electric heater, which uses electric energy to create heat energy in a one-to-one ratio. Air conditioners achieve this one-to-three ratio of input to output because the work they do is only to *separate* cold and hot from room temperature, not to *create* cold. A geothermal heat pump works the same way, but in reverse, which is why the geothermal heat pump is more efficient than ordinary heating systems.

Example 2   Energy-Efficient AC Unit

Consider the Soleus and Comfort Aire models described above in Table 3.3. Assume that in a summer month of 31 days, the device needs to be run at its maximum capacity for 12 hr/day. (a) How much electric energy would be consumed by each device in the month? (b) How much electric energy is saved by the Soleus model, compared with the Comfort Aire model? (c) If electric energy costs $0.08 per kWh, how much does the Soleus model save in the summer month compared with the Comfort Aire model?

Solution

(a) Operated for 12 hr/day and 31 days, the Soleus model uses 0.989 kW × 12 hr/day × 31 days = 367.9 kWh. The Comfort Aire model uses 1.15 × 12 × 31 = 427.8 kWh.

(b) The savings in energy is the difference 427.8 − 367.9 = 59.9 kWh.

(c) At a cost of $0.08 per kWh, the savings is 59.9 × 0.08 = $4.79 in the month.

Composite Efficiency and the Multiplication Rule

When a production process consists of several stages, and each stage has its own efficiency, the composite efficiency of the system is the product of the efficiencies of its components. This principle is illustrated well in SPV systems. The sun's energy is converted to direct current electric energy by a solar panel, but that energy must be transmitted through wires to an inverter and a transformer that produce alternating current at 110 volts for household use. Dust on the solar panels will reduce their efficiency.

Table 3.4 Component efficiencies in SPV

Component	Loss (%)	Efficiency (%)
PV module nameplate rating (relative to a 1 kW standard)	5	95
System downtime	2	98
Soiling (dust)	5	95
Wiring, diodes, and connections	3.5	96.5
Inverter and transformer	8	92
Mismatch of current–voltage characteristics between panels	2	98
Composite System		77

If the energy must be stored in a battery bank and recovered for use at night, that too will involve some loss. Downtime for maintenance reduces the amount of output that can be harvested from the available solar input. The U.S. Department of Energy's PVWatts solar energy calculator uses the default values for these component efficiencies shown in Table 3.4.[8] In solar power engineering, the composite efficiency of the system is called the *derate factor*. The standard 1 kW solar panel would yield 0.77 kW of AC power under the assumptions in this table.

Notice that the sum of the losses is 25.5 percent, but the composite efficiency is not 74.5 percent. It is 77 percent. This is a consequence of the multiplication rule for the efficiency of components that function in series, each taking the output of the other. Efficiencies multiply. Losses do not add.

Tech Focus: Potential Energy and Kinetic Energy

A hydroelectric power generator uses the pressure of water coming down from a dam to rotate a turbine that generates electric energy. The energy of the falling water is transformed into electric energy by the turbine. The energy of motion is called *kinetic energy*. The energy of a mass held at a height is called *potential energy*. When an object falls from a height due to gravity, its potential energy becomes transformed into kinetic energy. So, ultimately, it is the potential energy of water at a height above the turbine that becomes the kinetic energy of the rotating turbine, which becomes the electric energy output of the generator.

Let us now see how energy is measured in its potential and kinetic forms, because this will enable us to answer questions about the efficiency of devices that transform potential energy or kinetic energy into electric energy.

Potential Energy (Joules)

Potential energy is typically measured using the metric system. In that system, the unit of energy is *joule* (J). The equation for the potential energy of a mass of M (kg) held at a height H (m) is the mass multiplied by the height, multiplied by the force of gravity on earth, whose constant is 9.8,

$$E = M \times H \times 9.8 \text{ (joules)}$$

Example 3

How much energy does it take to lift a 10 kg (22 lb.) suitcase up 1.8 m (5′ 11″) into an aircraft carry-on bin? Measure the energy in joules.

Solution

$M = 10$ kg, $H = 1.8$ m, so $E = 10 \times 1.8 \times 9.8 = 176.4$ J.

The joule is a very small amount of energy. The conversion factors in Table 3.5 shows how the mega joule (1 million joules) compares to other units of energy.

Table 3.5 Conversion factors for energy measures

	kWh	BTU	kCal	MJ
1 kWh =	1	3412.14	860.44	3.6
1 BTU =	0.00029307	1	0.25217	0.001055
1 kCal =	0.0011622	3.9657	1	0.0041868
1 MJ =	0.27778	947.82	239.01	1

Notice that a million joules is still only a fraction (27.8 percent) of a kilowatt-hour. That shows how large a unit of energy the kilowatt-hour is. Another perspective on the joule helps us see its relationship with the unit of electric energy. The unit of power associated with joule is *joule per second*. Another name for joule per second is *watt* (W). Over one hour there are $60 \times 60 = 3,600$ seconds, so one *watt-hour* is 3,600 watt-seconds $= 3,600 \dfrac{\text{joule}}{\text{second}}$ seconds $= 3,600$ joules. Therefore, a kilo-watt-hour is $1,000 \times 3,600 = 3.6$ million joules. This fact appears in Table 3.5, where 1 kWh = 3.6 MJ (mega joules).

Example 4   A Low-Head Hydro

A *low-head* hydroelectric power station is defined as a dam (power station) that has up to a 65-ft. drop (called the head) and generates less than 1,500 kW of power. What is the power of a small river? As an example, calculate the power of a river that is 30-ft. wide, has an average depth of 5 ft., and flows at 1 ft./sec, over a 10-ft. fall or dam.

Solution

In this problem, power is measured as the flow of potential energy per unit of time as the mass of the water goes over a 10-ft. fall. So our first task is to determine the rate of flow of the water, expressed as kilograms per second. Then we will multiply that by 9.8 and by the height in meters (10 ft. = 3.05 m) to get the power.

The volume of water flow is $30 \times 5 \times 1 = 150$ cubic feet per second. We must now convert that to mass per second using information about the density of water. An Internet search for kilograms per cubic foot of water will prove futile, so take it in two steps. Either convert to pounds per second using the weight of one cubic foot of water and then convert from pounds to kilograms, or convert feet to meters and use the fact that one cubic meter of water weighs exactly 1,000 kg. By the first method, an Internet search shows that one cubic foot is 7.48 U.S. gallons. We saw in our examples of water heaters that one gallon of water weighs 8.34 pounds. So a water flow of 150 ft³/sec corresponds to $150 \times 7.48 \times 8.34 = 9,357.5$ pounds/sec flow. Translate that into kilograms per second using the fact that 1 lb. = 0.4536 kg. So 150 ft³/sec is 9,357.5 × 0.4536 = 4,245 kg/sec. That is the rate of flow of mass. Now look how far the mass is falling.

The water is falling down 3.05 m, so the release of potential energy is energy per unit time = 9.8 × M × H per second. Here, 9.8 × 4,245 × 3.05 = 126,883 joules/sec = 126,883 watts, which we round to 127 kW.

That is the power output of a small river, only 30-ft. wide and 5-ft. deep, flowing slowly (1 ft./sec) over a 10-ft. dam. If that kinetic power were converted with 100 percent efficiency to electric power, how many houses would it be able to supply? Recall that a typical house has a power requirement of approximately 2.5 kW. The 127 kW from the river would supply approximately 50 houses.

Hydroelectric generators are not perfectly efficient. Some water from a dam may be released intentionally, so the dam does not overflow. Some hydroelectric systems are designed without dams at all, which allows fish to swim freely upstream. Those are called run-of-the-river systems. They use large pipes to take a portion of the river's water and run it a long way down a steep portion of a river, so there is a large pressure at the bottom of the pipe where the turbine is placed. Very large hydroelectric generators can be 80 to 90 percent efficient. Smaller systems may be only 50 percent efficient.

Kinetic Energy

Automotive Systems

Kinetic energy is the energy of motion. Like potential energy, it is commonly measured using the metric system, so the unit of energy is joule. Motion can be translational (in a straight line) or rotational. For translational motion, the kinetic energy of a moving object is a function of the mass (M, kg) and the velocity (V, m/sec) of the object.

$$E = \frac{1}{2} M \times V^2 \qquad \text{(joules, J)}$$

Example 5

How much energy do you put into a 1 kg (2.2 lb.) brick when you throw it horizontally at a velocity of 10 m/sec (22.38 mph)?

Solution

The statement of the problem tells us that $M = 1$ kg and $V = 10$ m/sec. So we use the equation for kinetic energy to find that

$$E = \frac{1}{2} \times 1 \times 10^2 = 0.5 \times 1 \times 100 = 50 \text{ J}$$

The joule is a rather small unit of energy, as shown in this example where throwing a brick requires approximately 50 J. But now let us look at a problem on a different scale, braking a car.

Example 6

How much kinetic energy must be extracted, by the process of braking, to bring a compact car weighing 3,000 pounds to a halt from a speed of 70 mph?

Solution

The data are given in American units, so we must first convert them to metric. 3,000 pounds divided by 2.2 pounds/kg = 1,364 kg (mass, *M*). The speed of 70 m/hr converts mph to m/sec using the facts that 1 mile = 1609 m (holding four significant digits of accuracy) and 1 hour = 3600 seconds. So $70 \, \frac{miles}{hour} = 70 \times \frac{1609\,m}{3600\,s} = 31.29 \, \frac{m}{s}$. Now we use the kinetic energy formula with $M = 1,364$ and $V = 31.29$, so that

$$E = \frac{1}{2} \times 1,364 \times 31.29^2 = 0.5 \times 1,364 \times 979.06 = 667,719 \text{ J}$$

Thus, the energy that must be removed from a car to bring it to a stop from 70 mph is less than a million joules, rounding to 0.668 megajoules. As a sequel to Example 6, we might ask how that 0.668 MJ of energy compares to the energy used to run a 60-watt light bulb. How many watt-hours (Wh) is 0.668 MJ?

The table of conversion factors for units of energy shows that 1 MJ = 0.27778 kWh. So 0.668 MJ is 0.668 MJ × 0.27778 kWh/MJ = 0.186 kWh or 186 Wh. It is the same amount of energy needed to run a 60-W bulb for about three hours.

Wind Power Generation

A wind turbine converts the kinetic energy of a moving mass of air into
the rotational energy of the blades and turbine, which is then converted
to electric energy by the process of electrical induction in the turbine. In
this respect, the wind power system is like a hydroelectric power system.
However, hydroelectric systems hold water at a height and capture the
potential energy of that water as it falls through a pipe and runs into a
turbine. The wind power system can capture the energy of only the air
that is passing through the sweep area of its blades, and much of that
air passes through without putting any force on the blades. Thus, wind
turbines cannot be perfectly efficient, but given their limitations, they
are surprisingly efficient. Their theoretical maximum efficiency is the
Betz limit, which is 59 percent. However, some commercial turbines can
deliver about 75 percent of the Betz limit at their rated operating speed,[9]
which puts their efficiency at about 44 percent.

The kinetic energy of a mass M (kg) of air moving at a velocity V (m/
sec) follows the standard formula for kinetic energy,

$$E = \frac{1}{2} M \times V^2$$

The sweep area of a windmill whose blades have a radial length of L is
given by the familiar formula *pi times the radius squared*, $A = \pi L^2$. The
volume of air passing through the sweep area is $A \times V$. If the density of
the air is D (kg/m³), then the mass of air passing through the sweep area
in one second is

$$M = \pi L^2 VD \text{ (kg/sec)}$$

The energy of that moving mass is given by the kinetic energy formula
$E = \frac{1}{2} MV^2$. Substituting the formula for M above into kinetic energy
formula gives the energy (measured in joules) of the entire air mass that
passes through the swept area of the blades in one second. The result is a
measure of energy per unit time, which means power, so we denote it as
P. That power has the formula,

$$P = \frac{1}{2} (\pi L^2 VD) \times V^2$$

A little algebraic simplification results in the formula,

$$P = (\pi/2) \times D \times L^2 V^3 \text{ (J/sec or W)}$$

This equation shows that the power of the moving air mass is proportional to the *cube* of the velocity of the air. For this reason, small increases in the wind velocity result in large increases in the power available to a wind generator.

The output of the wind system will be the kinetic energy input, from the moving air, multiplied by the efficiency of the system, which we write here as a small *e*,

$$P = (\pi/2) \times D \times L^2 V^3 \times e \text{ (J/sec or W)}$$

The only constants in the power formula are $\pi = 3.1416$ (often rounded to three significant digits as 3.14) and the density of air. Air density varies with temperature, altitude, and humidity. The density calculator at DeNysschen LLC accounts for each of these variables. For example, at a temperature of 15°C (59°F), an altitude of 200 m (656 ft.) above sea level, and a relative humidity of 50 percent, the density of air is 1.189 kg/m³.

Example 7

A small wind power system has blades that are 3 m (10 ft.) long. Suppose that the system is 30 percent efficient, and the density of air at a particular point in time is 1.2 kg/m³. (a) If the wind is blowing at 5 m/sec (11 mph), what is the power output of the system? (b) What if the wind is blowing at 10 m/sec (22 mph)?

Solution

(a) Use the power equation with the metric measurements, $D = 1.2$, $L = 3$, and $V = 5$, to get the total kinetic energy *input* to the wind system,

$$P = (\pi/2) \times D \times L^2 V^3 \times e$$

$$P = (3.14/2 \times 1.2 \times 3^2 5^3 \times 30\%$$
$$P = (3.14/2 \times 1.2 \times 3^2 5^3 \times 30\%$$
$$P = 1.57 \times 1.2 \times 9 \times 125 \times 30\%$$
$$P = 635.85 \ (\text{watts})$$

(b) So, at a speed of 5 m/sec (11 mph), the wind system generates less than 1 kW of power.

Now change the V from 5 to 10,

$$P = (3.14/2) \times 1.2 \times 3^2 10^3 \times 30\%$$
$$P = 1.57 \times 1.2 \times 9 \times 1000 \times 30\%$$
$$P = 5,086.8 \ (\text{watts})$$

At a wind speed of 10 m/sec (22 mph), the system generates more than 5 kW of power. That shows the effect of the *cube law* in the wind speed. The doubling of wind speed creates an eightfold increase in the power output.

The Rated Capacity of a Wind Power System.   Wind systems need a minimum wind speed, called the *cut-in* speed, to overcome the resistive forces in the turbine and gears. Likewise, too high a wind speed could damage the rotors and turbine, so the system is designed to spill wind higher than its *cut-out* speed. Over a range of wind speeds below the cut-out speed, the system is designed to yield approximately a constant level of power. Therefore, the rated (maximum) capacity of a wind power system is based on the power output at the wind speed where power is first maximized. In some Danish models, for example, the cut-out speed is 25 m/sec, but the rated capacity is reached around 12 m/sec.[10]

Efficiency of a Wind Power System.   The efficiency of a wind power system in practice is less than the theoretical maximum (59 percent) expressed in the Betz limit. Friction in the hub of the blades and in the gearbox causes some loss of energy to heat. The generation process has some heat loss, as does the process of transforming the current to the right voltage level for distribution to buyers. Still, it is impressive that utility-scale wind turbines can deliver about 75 percent of the Betz limit.

Process Flow Diagrams

As the final topic of this chapter, we look at how a complex transformation process can be described succinctly in a *process flow diagram*, which distinguishes the various subprocesses and reveals their efficiencies and other useful data for calculating the output of the process. From the process flow diagram, it is easy to set up a spreadsheet model that performs the necessary calculations. We motivate this discussion with an example from the production of biodiesel fuel.

Example 8   Algae Biodiesel

Common green pond scum is a form of algae that has the potential to be used in the production of biodiesel fuel for vehicles. There are more than 100,000 strains of algae, and they differ in their rate of growth (propagation), their oil production, and their ability to tolerate temperature changes and invasive biological organisms. Algae use sunlight, together with carbon dioxide, water, and other nutrients to photosynthesize vegetable oil. Algae grow quickly, some strains doubling their mass in 48 hours. A method of algae propagation that works well in hot, sunny environments is the *open pond system* in which the algae grow in a pond that is open to the air and sun.

Algae that is drawn wet from the pond needs to be filtered and dried before it can be processed further. An open-pond system can produce for harvest 30 kg of dry algae per pond acre per day. Common pond scum, when dried, is 20 percent oil by weight. A vegetable oil press can capture 75 percent of the available oil. The oil has a volume of 0.30 gal/kg. The vegetable oil is transformed into biodiesel by a process called transesterification, which yields 0.95 gallons of biodiesel per gallon of vegetable oil, the remainder being 0.05 gallon of glycerol.

(a) Draw an input–output diagram for this process.

(b) Draw a process flow diagram for this process.

(c) What is the output of this process per acre, expressed as gallons of biodiesel per day and per year?

(d) The city of Logan, Utah, has a 460-acre lagoon in which it grows algae using municipal wastewater. How much biodiesel fuel can they produce per year?

Solution

(a) Our task here is to represent in a diagram this description of the chain of processes that lead up to the production of biodiesel. As a simple input–output diagram, which has processes within boxes and material or energy flows on arrows, the biodiesel production process would appear as shown in Figure 3.2.

(b) A *process flow diagram* reveals quantitative information about the transformation process at each step and is the basis for creating a spreadsheet model that calculates the entire process. The essential information about a process (each box in Figure 3.2) is its efficiency, which is the ratio of output quantity to input quantity. The efficiency data also reveal the units of measurement intended for the output and the input. In addition to the efficiency data, it may be useful to include unit conversion data that are relevant to the calculation. We write these in italic type to distinguish them from the efficiency data.

The statement of example 8 does not describe the processes of open pond cultivation, harvesting, or desiccation. The description begins with the result of all three processes as the stated 30 kg of dry algae per pond acre per day. The input–output diagram in Figure 3.2 becomes the *process flow diagram* (Figure 3.3) when we add these data.

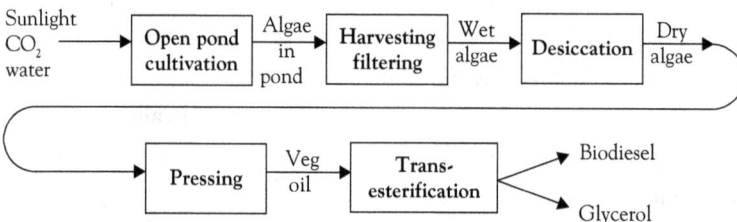

Figure 3.2 Biodiesel input–output diagram

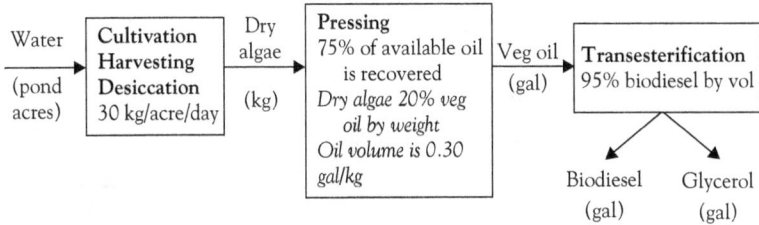

Figure 3.3 Biodiesel process flow diagram

(c) This diagram shows us how to write equations for each process, leading to the daily output of biodiesel from an open pond.

Desiccation   Dry algae (kg) = 30 × Pond acres

Pressing   Veg oil (gal) = Dry algae (kg) × 20% (kg oil/kg dry) × 75% × 0.30 (gal/kg)

Transesterification   Biodiesel (gal) = 95% × Veg oil (gal)

On a per-acre basis, we use the parameters shown in the process flow diagram to calculate the system's output rate:

30 × 20% × 75% × 0.30 × 95% = 1.2825 gallons of biodiesel per acre per day.

Expressed in annual terms, the output rate would be 1.2825 gal/acre/day × 365 days/year = 468 gallons of biodiesel per acre per year.

(d) If the Logan, Utah, open pond is 460 acres in size, it should be able to produce 460 (acres) × 468 (gal biodiesel/acre) = 215,280 gallons of biodiesel per year.

Take-aways

Efficiency is a vital concept in the engineering description of a technology. A key feature of the evolution of energy technologies is the steady improvement in the efficiency of devices, and efficiency is a key point of comparison among the various types or capacities of devices within a technology. The main ideas worth taking away from this chapter are as follows:

- The *efficiency* of a device that has one input is measured as its output (or output rate) divided by its input (or input rate).

- A device that uses more than one input has an efficiency defined for each input.
- Efficiencies are sometimes known by other names, such as the *energy factor* of a hot water heater or the EER of an air conditioner, but they are recognizable in any definition that divides an output rate by an input rate.
- Power technologies transform one type of energy into another type of energy, so the ratio of output rate to input rate results in a percentage. For example, a fuel cell may be 40 percent efficient in converting the chemical energy of hydrogen gas into electrical energy.
- Some technologies are composites of several processes in series, as in the example of SPVs, where the system includes a solar panel, wiring, a battery, and an inverter. The efficiency of a composite system is given by the product of the efficiencies of its components.
- A *process flow diagram* not only shows the inputs, outputs, and processes of a composite technology, it shows numerically the efficiencies of the processes and indicates the units of measurement for each material in the flow.

CHAPTER 4

Constraints

Overview

The constraints of a technology are the limitations on the environmental conditions or internal operating conditions under which its transformation process can function efficiently or effectively. The varieties of a technology (in various devices) often differ in how well they can handle changing environmental or internal operating conditions. Thus, for the description of technologies, it is essential to have a terminology that describes these limitations. We use the term *constraints* in this sense.

The analysis of constraints focuses our attention on the environmental and internal operating conditions of a technology. We describe constraints by showing, in a graph or equation, how the efficiency or effectiveness of a device varies with the particular condition. This question addresses the following important questions:

- How do we identify the factors that might affect the efficiency or capacity of a technology?
- What factors affect the efficiency of technologies in the sustainable energy arena, such as solar water heating, solar photovoltaics (SPVs), wind turbines, and hydroelectric turbines?
- How much does temperature affect the efficiency of an air conditioner?
- What attributes of a technology, other than efficiency, may be affected by environmental or internal operating conditions?

Examples of Constraints

Some technologies perform differently in different environmental or internal operating conditions.

Example 1

What environmental and operating factors affect the fuel efficiency of a car? Think of as many factors as you can.

Solution

- Operating speed (wind resistance decreases fuel efficiency);
- Wind direction and speed (headwind reduces fuel efficiency and tailwind increases it);
- Load in the car (increases friction between the tire and the road);
- Tire pressure (low pressure creates more deformation of the tire on each rotation, which results in heat to the tire and thus waste of energy; low pressure also creates more of a surface of the tire touching the road, increasing friction).
- Driving style (stop-and-go driving in the city has lower fuel efficiency than highway driving, because energy is wasted in braking);
- Design of the vehicle, for lower air resistance (e.g., tractor–trailer systems eventually got deflectors on their cabs to reduce air resistance on the trailer);
- Design for energy conservation (regenerative braking systems in hybrid vehicles use the brakes to recharge the car battery and the battery to drive the vehicle);
- Type of fuel used (gasoline mixed with ethanol gets fewer miles to the gallon).

The number of miles per gallon that a car gets is a measure of its efficiency. Each of these factors is a constraint on the operation of the car, because each affects the efficiency of the device.

Environmental conditions that might limit the effectiveness of a technology's process for converting inputs into outputs include the following:

- Temperature of the environment (solar water heating is poor in cold climates);
- Atmospheric pressure (cooking takes longer at high altitudes);

- Humidity (affects SPV systems);
- Salinity (salt infusion in soil can damage crops);
- Acidity (many crops do poorly in acid soil).

Internal operating conditions also can limit the effectiveness of a technology's process for converting inputs into outputs. Some of these conditions are as follows:

- Temperature at which the process operates. A lithium-ion battery in an electric vehicle should be kept between 14°F and 86°F (−10°C and +30°C). It loses its power at cold temperatures, and its capacity degrades faster at high temperatures.[1]
- Speed at which the process operates. An automobile engine can be ruined if it is run at a speed that takes the engine above its *red line*. A wind generator needs a minimum wind speed to overcome internal resistance, and above a certain wind speed its rotors and gears can be damaged.

Table 4.1 gives examples of the constraints that limit the performance of several *green* technologies.

Tech Focus: Constraints on Power Technologies

Every technology has limits to the conditions under which it can operate efficiently. These are the constraints on the technology. The types of environmental and operating conditions that might constrain the efficiency of a power technology are seen in the following examples.

- A wind turbine may not function well unless the wind speed is at least 9 mph, and it might break apart if it rotated fully under a 75 mph wind.
- The current voltage generated by an SPV panel decreases at high temperatures.
- Hydroelectric turbines are built for a particular flow rate of water. Lower or higher flow rates result in less efficiency.

Table 4.1 Constraints on various technologies

Technology	Inputs	Output	Process	Constraints
Crystalline SPV	Solar radiation	Electric energy	Photoelectric	Ambient temperature −20°C to +40°C humidity<85%
Solar water heating	Solar radiation	Hot water	Absorption of radiation	Ambient temperature cannot be too cold
Hydroelectric generation	Potential energy (water at height) → Mechanical energy (spinning turbine)	Electrical energy	Electromotive technology	Water quality (suspended particles) Water pressure
Steam turbine	Steam	Mechanical energy (rotary)	Impact (transfer of kinetic energy)	Steam at temperatures up to 600°F
Wind turbine	Wind	Mechanical energy (rotary)	Impact and Bernoulli effect	Wind 9–75 mph
Air conditioner	Electric energy	Reduction of heat energy	Compression and evaporation	Outside temperature cannot be too high
Agriculture	Seeds, sun, water, labor, land, fertilizer, equipment	Fruits and vegetables	Cultivation, growth	Temperature, soil acidity, moisture
Algae bioreactor	Sunlight, CO_2, algae	Diesel fuel	Propagation, transesterification	Temperature, water acidity, moisture content of oil
Biomass digester	Organic compounds	Methane (CH_4)	Digestion (bacterial)	Temperature, toxicity
Ethanol production	Sugars	Ethanol (alcohol)	Fermentation	Temperature

- The efficiency of a solar thermal collector becomes less when the environmental temperature is much lower than that inside the collector, and even less when the wind is blowing.
- The efficiency of a solar thermal electric generator is higher when the temperature in the solar collector is higher.

Solar Water Heating Technologies

A solar thermal collector is a device that absorbs heat energy from the sun's radiation. The technology can be as simple as black piping coiled on the roof of a house and carrying water. As the sun's rays warm the pipes, the water heats up and is drawn off for bathing or washing dishes or for use in a swimming pool.

The power input to the solar thermal collector depends on the angle of the sun and the orientation of the collector. A collector that is maintained at a right angle to the sun's rays, on a cloudless day, will receive the highest amount of insolation. A collector in a fixed position will maximize the insolation when it is tilted at an angle equal to its latitude.

Irradiance Versus Insolation

The power (energy/time) received from the sun at a given instant in time is called *irradiance*, and it is typically measured per unit of surface area. The sun produces electromagnetic radiation, so the common unit of power for irradiance is the watt. On a per-area basis, irradiance is measured in watts per square meter (W/m^2).

A square meter of area that is oriented directly at the sun in space above the earth's atmosphere receives about 1,360 W of solar radiation power (irradiance) according to NASA.[2] The earth's atmosphere reflects some of the sun's light and power, so at the surface of the earth, a square meter oriented directly at the sun at midday on the equator receives about 1,000 W of power. At other locations and times, the sun's rays pass through more of the earth's atmosphere, where oxygen, nitrogen, water vapor, and atmospheric pollutants reduce the intensity of the radiation received at the earth's surface. That is why at sunrise or sunset, it is possible to look directly at the sun, although you cannot do so at midday.

In contrast to irradiance, which is an instantaneous measure of the intensity of radiation, *insolation* is the amount of energy received from the sun over a period of time. It is measured as energy per time, so it is a power measure as irradiance is, but it expresses the average of the irradiance over a period of time, such as a day, month, or year.

At any location, the maximum insolation is captured by putting the collector on a device that tracks the sun, but tracking mechanisms are expensive, so the next best solution is to put the collector on a rack facing directly south (in the northern hemisphere) and tilted at an angle to collect the maximum amount of solar energy over a year, which depends on the latitude of its location. Even so, a fixed collector will have the perfect orientation only at midday on the spring and fall equinoxes. At all other times, the sun's rays will strike the collector at an angle, reducing the power that the collector receives. Adjusting the angle of the collector monthly is one way to improve the performance of the collector, albeit only slightly. According to the Solar Energy Handbook calculator,[3] a collector on a fixed tilted rack facing south, at a latitude of 40° (such as New York City), would receive an average amount of solar energy across a year of 4.47 kWh/m^2/day. If the solar rack were adjusted monthly to an optimal angle to the sun, the yearly insolation would average to 4.70 kWh/m^2/day, reaching a maximum of 6.05 in June and its minimum of 3.34 in January.

Notice that *average* power (insolation) rate is described as kilowatt-hours of energy per day, whereas the instantaneous (irradiance) rate is watts per square meter. To convert kWh/m^2/day to an average W/m^2, we need to make an assumption about the duration of daylight. In a 12-hour day, the fixed rack's 4,470 Wh/m^2/day corresponds to an average of 4,470/12 = 372.5 W/m^2. The adjustable rack, reoriented monthly to an optimal angle to the sun, would average 392 W/m^2 over a year. That is a 5 percent improvement over the fixed rack, but it is still substantially less than the maximum of 1,000 W/m^2 that reaches the surface of the earth at midday on the equator.

Much of the difference between the actual average of 392 and the maximum 1,000 is accounted for by climate. The sun's energy can pass through clouds, but a cloud cover will reflect or absorb about half of the sun's energy. Thus, the number of sunny days at a location significantly affects its annual insolation.

The chart below shows the amount of solar energy received by a collector tiled at an angle equal to its latitude, on average across a year, expressed (as insolation) in kilowatt-hours per square meter per day (kWh/m^2/day). The chart shows, for example, that such a collector in New York would receive an average of about 4.4 kWh/m^2/day, consistent with the data from the Solar Energy Handbook cited previously. Notice

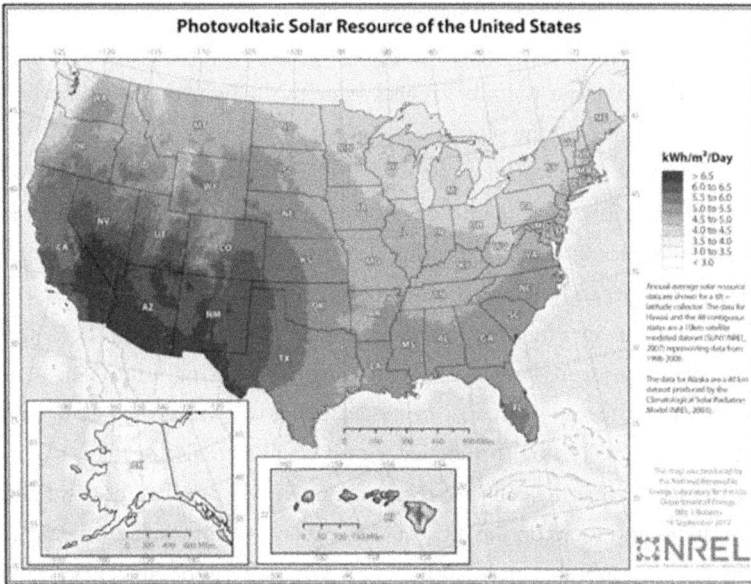

Photovoltaic Solar Resource of the United States

Figure 4.1 Insolation (kWh/m²/day) in the United States

also how much higher the insolation is in the American Southwest, which has many more sunny days than elsewhere (Figure 4.1).

In the American system, solar irradiance is measured in BTU per hour per square foot rather than in watts per square meter. The conversion between these units is based on the facts that 1 meter is 3.281 feet and 1 watt is 3.412 BTU per hour:

$$\frac{1\,\text{Watt}}{(1\,\text{meter})^2} = \frac{3.412\,\text{BTU/hr}}{(3.281\,\text{feet})^2} = \frac{3.412}{(3.281)^2}\frac{\text{BTU/hr}}{\text{ft}^2} = 0.3170\frac{\text{BTU/hr}}{\text{ft}^2}.$$

The measure of insolation converts from metric to American in a similar way that reflects the factor of 1,000 in a kilowatt versus a watt:

$$\frac{1\,\text{kWh}}{(1\,\text{meter})^2\,\text{day}} = \frac{3.412\,\text{BTU}}{(3.281\,\text{feet})^2\,\text{day}} = \frac{3.412\,\text{BTU}}{10.765\,\text{ft}^2\,\text{day}} = 317\frac{\text{BTU}}{\text{ft}^2}\,\text{per day}.$$

Efficiencies of Solar Water Heating Technologies

Solar thermal collectors are not very efficient. Even a black collector will reflect some of the sun's radiation, and when it does capture the radiation as heat, it may lose some of that heat to the environment as the pipes cool to the air. Sealing the collecting pipes in a vacuum tube is one way to reduce that loss, but the tubes reflect some of the light that would otherwise be captured by the pipes.

The efficiency of a solar hot water system depends on the design of the collector. The three main types of design are the unglazed uninsulated collector typically used for heating water for swimming pools, the flat-plate collector, and the evacuated-tube collector.

The efficiency of a solar hot water system also depends on the difference in temperature between the hot water or working fluid (T_i) in the collector and the ambient air (T_a), because that will affect the rate of heat loss from the collector. The efficiency of the collector also depends on the irradiance (I) that the collector receives, but we will put that idea aside for a moment and focus on the difference between the hot water temperature and the atmospheric temperature $T_i - T_a$ as the driver of efficiency.

The maximum efficiency of an unglazed collector is about 90 percent. The maximum efficiency for a flat-plate collector is about 70 to 75 percent depending on its design, and the maximum efficiency for an evacuated-tube collector is about 50 percent. However, as Figure 4.2 shows, the unglazed collector loses its efficiency rapidly as the atmospheric temperature T_a decreases relative to the desired hot water temperature T_i. The graph shows that the flat-plate collector loses its efficiency less rapidly than the unglazed pool collector, as a function of the temperature difference, and the evacuated-tube collector is least affected by the temperature difference. (These graphs assume an irradiance of 530 W/m^2 or 168 BTU/hr/ft^2. We address the role of irradiance in the next paragraphs.)

The lines in Figure 4.2 show that the efficiencies of the four types of solar water heating technology respond differently to the temperature difference, so the choice of solar-thermal collecting technology should depend on the environmental conditions in which it will operate. The unglazed, uninsulated collector (which is usually black piping coiled on a roof to heat water) is best when the output hot water temperature is less than 10°F above the ambient temperature, and that is why its common application is for heating a swimming pool. An article in *Home Power* reports that the flat-plate collector tends to be the most efficient design when the environmental temperature is 36°F to 90°F below the temperature of the water or

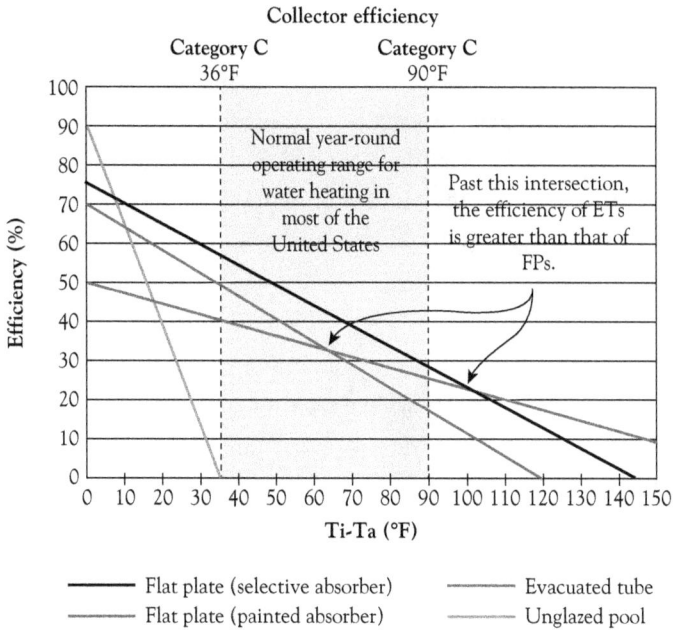

Figure 4.2 Efficiency graphs for solar hot water technologies

Source: Reprinted with permission. © 2014 Home Power Inc., www.homepower.com

working fluid, and only an evacuated collector can work well when you want very hot water on a cold winter day.[4]

The efficiency of a solar hot water collector depends not only on the difference between the hot water temperature and the atmospheric temperature ($T_i - T_a$) but on the intensity of the sun's radiation, its irradiance (I). For a flat-plate collector, with temperature measured in degree Celsius and irradiance measured in watt per square meter, an equation that calculates a collector's efficiency is given by the National Institute for Building Sciences' *Whole Building Design Guide*,[5]

$$\text{Efficiency} = 0.70 - 4\frac{T_w - T_a}{I}, \text{ (metric units)}$$

When the temperature is given in degrees Fahrenheit, and the irradiance is expressed in BTU per hour per square foot, the equation, to two significant digits, takes the form

$$\text{Efficiency} = 0.70 - 0.70\frac{T_w - T_a}{I}, \text{ (American units)}$$

Example 2   Flat-plate Solar Hot Water Efficiency

A four-by-eight foot flat-plate solar hot water collector located in Chicago is tilted at an angle equal to the latitude of its location. For the month of April, the insolation reported at the PVWatts website is an average of 5.11 kWh/m²/day, and the number of hours of daylight is 13.5 per day. The collector's output water temperature is to be maintained at 120°F, and the air temperature is 50°F.

(a) What is the efficiency of the collector?
(b) How much heat energy will be transferred to the water in one day?
(c) How many gallons of water at 120°F will the collector produce in one day, if the inflowing water is at 55°F?

Solution

(a) To calculate the efficiency, we need to know the sun's intensity (irradiance) in Chicago in BTU per hour per square foot. The insolation over an entire day is 5.11 kWh/m². We divide that by the number of hours of daylight to get an average of the irradiance across the day, 5.11/13.5 = 0.378 in kW/m², which is 378 W/m². We convert this number to BTU per hour per square foot using the conversion factor 1 W/m² = 0.3170 BTU/hr/ft²,

$$378 \, \frac{W}{m^2} = 378 \times 0.3170 \, \frac{W}{m^2} = 119.8 \, \frac{BTU/hr}{ft^2}$$

Now use the American efficiency equation with a water temperature of 120°F and ambient temperature of 50°F.

Efficiency = $0.70 - 0.70 \dfrac{120 - 50}{119.8}$

Efficiency = $0.70 - 0.70 \times 0.584$

Efficiency = $0.70 - 0.41$

Efficiency = 0.29

Efficiency = 29 percent.

(b) The amount of heat energy transferred to the water *in one day* can be calculated from the *insolation* rate multiplied by the efficiency of the collector and multiplied by the area of the collector. The insolation in Chicago in April is 5.11 kWh/m²/day. Convert that to $\frac{BTU/hr}{ft^2}$ per day using the conversion factor, $5.11 \times 317 = 1{,}620 \frac{BTU/hr}{ft^2}$ per day. The four-by-eight collector has 32 square feet of area, so in total the insolation is $1{,}620 \times 32 = 51{,}840$ BTU/day. At an efficiency of 29 percent, the amount of heat energy captured will be $51{,}840 \times 29\% = 15{,}033$ BTU/day.

(c) If the cold water flows into the collector at 55°F and is raised to 120°F, the rise of temperature is 65°F. Recall that one BTU will raise one pound of water by one degree Fahrenheit, so divide the 15,033 BTU of heat energy by the 65°F rise to get the number of pounds of water that can be heated: $15{,}033/65 = 231.3$ lb. One gallon of water weighs 8.34 pounds, so the number of gallons raised to that temperature is $231.3/8.34 = 27.7$ gal. That number is the output of heated water from this collector on that day in April.

This is a low quantity of hot water, because the efficiency of the collector is only 29 percent when the collector has to produce 120°F water against an environmental temperature of 50°F. If the collector could be made more efficient, it would produce a lot more hot water.

Solar Photovoltaic Technologies

The standard testing condition for rating a solar panel's power output is 25°C (77°F). Above that temperature, the panel's output will be less than its rated capacity, but below that temperature its output will be better. The effect of temperature on efficiency is given by the *temperature coefficient* of the SPV panel. Solar cells based on crystalline technology typically have temperature coefficients in the range of 0.44 to 0.50 percent per degree Celsius above 25°C. Amorphous silicon cells can have a temperature coefficient as low as 0.35 percent, and cadmium telluride panels can get down to 0.25 percent.[6] On a hot summer day, a solar cell can reach a temperature of 70°C (158°F),[7] so the efficiency of a crystalline SPV module can be reduced by as much as 22.5 percent.

Wind and Hydroelectric Power Technologies

Both wind and hydroelectric power technologies convert kinetic energy into electric energy using a generator. Generators tend to be designed for a specific power output and therefore for a specific level of kinetic energy inflow. In wind power, the inflow characteristic is *wind speed*. For hydroelectric power, it is the *flow rate* of water through the turbine. The most efficient devices are designed for a specific rate of energy inflow, meaning a specific wind speed or flow rate. When a device must be designed to operate under varying conditions of energy inflow, that flexibility tends to come at some sacrifice of overall efficiency.

Wind and hydro systems demark their energy inflow characteristics at three points. The *cut-in point* is the wind speed or flow rate needed to overcome the internal resistance in the device and start the process of generating electric energy. The *rating point* is the inflow rate at which the device reaches its rated output capacity. The *cut-out point* is the inflow rate at which the device must shut itself off to avoid internal damage to the generator. The *survival point* is the maximum inflow rate at which the device can survive without external damage, such as blades breaking on a wind turbine.

Between the rating point and the cut-out point, wind and hydro systems are designed to throw off some of the inflow of energy. A horizontal-axis windmill will spill some of its wind by feathering its blades (adjusting the pitch of the blades by pointing the back end of the blade further downwind) or by having blades constructed of a flexible material that can bend downwind. A water turbine would adjust the pitch of its blades. Such designs deliberately sacrifice efficiency at those high inflow rates in order to preserve the functioning of the system at a level near its rated capacity. As a result, the device is best described not by its efficiency as a function of the inflow but by its power output as a function of the inflow characteristic. It is this *power curve* for the device that best describes its operation under diverse conditions of inflow.

Wind Power Efficiency

Variable wind speed is the bane of the wind farm owner. The power output of a wind system is proportional to the *cube* of the wind speed, meaning that if the wind speed reduces to half, the power output reduces to one-eighth. High, consistent winds are the best resource, but such locations are rare. Until recently, most wind turbines were designed for Class 4 wind environments (average wind speed 7.0 to 7.5 m/sec or 15.7 to 16.8 mph at 50 m height). Owing to the cube law, lower average wind speed means substantially less power, making Class 3 winds (average wind speed 6.4 to 7.0 m/sec or 14.3 to 15.7 mph) less economical for wind power development. However, researchers and engineers have recently found ways to build commercial-scale wind turbines that function better at low wind speeds.[8] These systems have larger swept areas for the same capacity of generator, and some use direct-drive generation rather than gearboxes.[9]

The graph in Figure 4.3 shows the efficiency curve (humped, right axis) and the power curve (rising, left axis) for the Vestas V90 turbine that has a rated capacity of 3 MW.[10] The graphs show that the V90 achieves its rated capacity at a wind speed of 14 m/sec, but its peak efficiency is at 9 m/sec. The efficiency decreases significantly below its rating point,

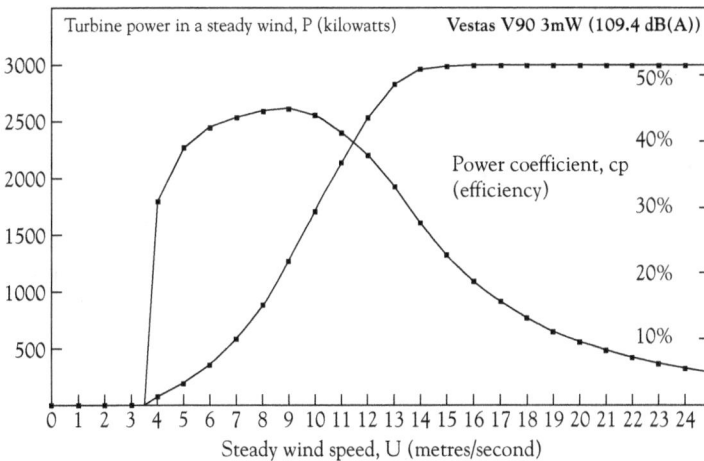

Figure 4.3 Wind turbine power and efficiency
Source: Wind Power Program (www.wind-power-program.com).

because the wind power system is designed to spill wind so it can maintain its rated power output over a range of wind speeds, here 14 to 25 m/sec.

Hydroelectric Power Efficiency

Hydroelectric systems of the larger sizes, designed for high heads (water-fall heights) and high flow rates, tend to be built behind large dams where the head and flow rate can be controlled to a narrow range. Thus, large-head systems can reach efficiencies as high as 90 percent.[11] In contrast, low-head systems, whether they are run-of-the-river systems or dammed systems, all tend to depend on the water flow in a river, which is subject to seasonal variations.

One response is to design a hydroelectric turbine system that has a fairly flat power curve even if that means sacrificing some efficiency over-all. The U.S. EPA reports that Canyon's hydro-Kaplan turbine can main-tain its efficiency, by adjusting the pitch of its blades and its wicket gates even with a flow as low as 35 percent of its rating point.[12]

The chart below shows the shape of the power curves for several types of hydroelectric turbines. The maximum efficiencies have been normalized to 100 percent, so the chart shows only the shape of the power curve, not its height. However, it shows that the propeller turbines have a narrower range of high-power output than the Pelton and Kaplan types, which can maintain as much as 95 percent of their maximum efficiency for flow rates (power output) as little as 25 percent of their capacity (Figure 4.4).[13]

Air Conditioning and Refrigeration Technologies

The efficiency of a cooling system is greater when the difference between the ambient (outside) temperature and the desired (inside) temperature is small. Thus, like SPV systems, they are not very efficient at high environ-mental temperatures. Unfortunately, that is when cooling technologies are needed the most (Figure 4.5).

The graph above shows the power line for an AHP-6250 air condi-tioner made by TECA Corp.[14] It shows that when the inside and outside temperatures are the same, the unit has a cooling power of 4,433 BTU/hr or 1,300 W. However, when the outside temperature is 10°C (18°F)

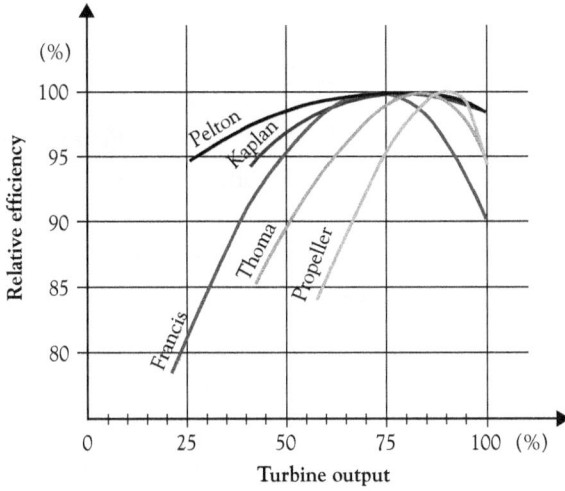

Figure 4.4 Hydroelectric turbine efficiency curves

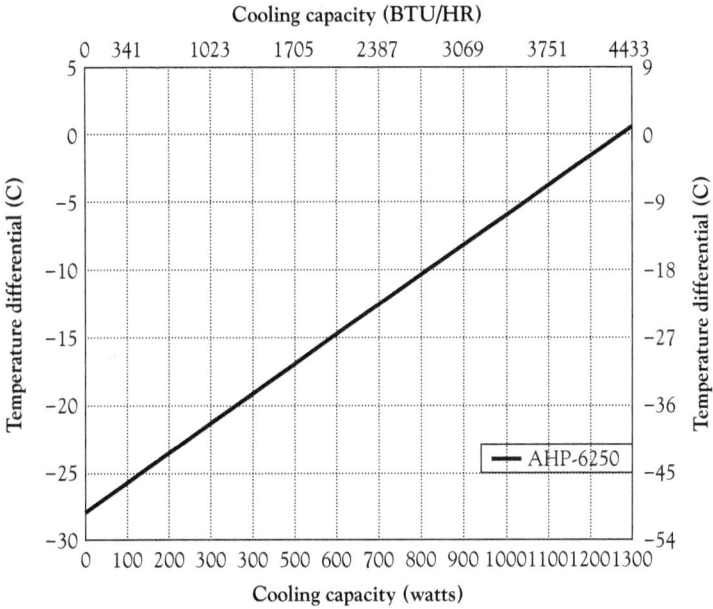

Figure 4.5 Effect of ambient temperature differential on AC cooling capacity

Source: TECA Corporation (2010).

higher than the inside temperature, the cooling power is only 2,730 BTU/hr (800 W), meaning 38 percent lower than under the equal-temperatures condition.

The standard testing condition for the energy efficiency ratio (EER) rating of an air conditioner is an outside temperature of 95°F and an inside temperature of 80°F with a relative humidity of 50 percent.[15] At that 15°F (8.3°C) difference, the AHP-6250 unit described in Figure 4.5 would have a cooling power of 913 W or 3,116 BTU/hr. Thus, air conditioners can have a cooling power higher than their EER when the actual environmental conditions are more favorable (lower temperature difference) than the standard testing condition. The seasonal energy efficiency ratio (SEER) rating captures the effect of changing temperature differences over a year, and because those conditions are often more favorable than the standard testing condition for the EER, the SEER rating is higher than the EER rating.

Constraints Affecting Other Qualities of Performance

The examples given to this point in the chapter show how attributes of the environment or of internal operating conditions affect the efficiency of a device. Other aspects of the performance of a device can also be affected by these conditions.

Constraints Affecting Lifespan

Chapter 5 treats the subject of durability in greater detail, but it is worth noting here that any factor affecting the useful life of a device may well be considered to be a constraint on its operation. Several examples relate to sustainable technologies.

- The age of an SPV panel affects its maximum possible output, which may be interpreted as a change in its capacity or in its efficiency. This effect of time is called the *age derating* of an SPV unit.
- The number of on and off cycles to which a light bulb, battery, or fuel cell is put affects its useful life.

Constraints Affecting Capacity

Some technologies lose capacity over time or with use.

- The ability of a battery to store electric energy degrades over time due to chemical processes within the battery.
- The capacity of a rechargeable battery degrades with use according to the number of charge–discharge cycles that the battery has experienced and according to the depth of discharge in each cycle.

Take-aways

Efficiency is an important concept in the description of technologies precisely because it can vary according to the environmental or internal operating conditions of a device. The different sensitivities of devices to these conditions determine which types of devices are best suited to the conditions. In many important examples, the choice of technology is affected significantly by these conditions.

- A *constraint* is an attribute of the environment or internal operating condition of a device that changes either its efficiency or another aspect of the performance of the device, such as its lifespan or capacity.
- Solar hot water systems and air conditioning systems are each sensitive to the ambient air temperature (specifically, the air temperature in relation to the desired water or air temperature) but in different ways. For water heating, higher air temperatures are closer to the desired water temperature, so higher air temperatures yield higher efficiency. For air conditioning, higher air temperatures are farther from the desired air temperature, so higher air temperatures yield lower efficiency.
- SPV devices are sensitive to the temperature of the solar panel. Higher temperature results in lower efficiency.
- Wind power systems have an efficiency that is greatest at an intermediate wind speed. Below that, efficiency falls due to

internal resistance in the turbine. Above that, efficiency falls as the system has to spill wind by feathering the rotors to avoid damage to the turbine.

- Some devices, such as water turbines, are designed for a specific output rate and become less efficient at rates higher or lower than the standard.
- Constraints may affect the performance of a device in terms of its lifespan or its capacity, not just its efficiency.

CHAPTER 5

Dependability

Overview

In this chapter, we describe a device in terms that relate to its functional lifetime. As defined by the IEEE, dependability, or reliability, describes the ability of a device to function under stated conditions for a specified period of time.[1] That *specified period of time* is the lifespan of the device. Such a concept applies clearly to devices that fail precipitously, such as a light bulb that burns out, but the *stated conditions* are meant to be broader than that. They may include performance characteristics, such as capacity or efficiency, so the concept of dependability also applies to devices that lose some of their functionality over time or with use, rather than precipitously. In the latter case, it is common to establish a standard for performance that defines the useful life of the device, so the device is deemed to have expired when its performance drops below the specified level.

We will see in Chapter 6 that assumptions about the lifespan of a device—and the factors that determine lifespan—are crucial to the financial analysis of technology, where we will want to *spread* the purchase price of a device over its expected useful life.

In engineering, the study of dependability or reliability is typically conducted by looking at the complementary concepts, namely, degradation and failure. In that analysis, we distinguish devices as nonrepairable or repairable. A light bulb is the standard example of a nonrepairable device; when the light bulb fails or becomes too dim, we throw it out and buy a new one. Devices that can be repaired after a failure are more complex to study in terms of reliability, but even those have a finite life, the automobile being a familiar example.

Reliability engineers use the mathematics of probability theory to quantify concepts such as reliability. However, our treatment of the subject will not reach to that level of analysis. This chapter addresses, for the most part without mathematics, important questions such as:

- What affects the lifespan of a device that cannot be repaired?
- In which contexts does calendar time affect the lifespan of a device, and in which does lifespan depend on usage? (This question will become very important in Chapter 7, where we compare two or more technologies using break-even analysis.)
- Which three failure processes account for the *bathtub curve* in reliability theory?
- Which types of failure account for the lifespan of a solar photovoltaic (SPV) panel, and how long can an SPV panel be expected to last?
- How is the availability of a repairable device measured?

This chapter ends with a Tech Focus on energy storage that lays the groundwork for examples related to hydroelectric systems, heating systems, batteries, and hydrogen fuel cells in the chapters to come.

The Lifespan of Nonrepairable Devices

Whether a device can be repaired or not is a matter of economics as much as it is of design and engineering. Even a device that is designed with replaceable parts can fail if a failed part is too expensive to replace. Our analysis of nonrepairable systems therefore applies not only to light bulbs but to the *long-term perspective* on devices that might go through a series of repairs (wind turbines, automobiles) or degradation of performance (solar cells, batteries) before finally being discarded as useless.

The principal issues in the analysis of durability are how to quantify the lifespan of a device and how to predict its failure.

Durability: The Useful Life of a Device

Some devices do not fail precipitously. Their performance degrades over time or use. A light-emitting diode (LED) bulb will fail completely when the solid state junction that produces the light fails due to heat fatigue, but the significant feature about the performance of LEDs is that they degrade—lose their intensity with use. All bulbs have that problem, but LEDs lose intensity much faster than incandescent or halogen bulbs.

For such devices, dependability is described by the pattern of degradation of performance over time or with usage. The concept that expresses this idea is the *durability* of a device, measured as a rate of degradation of performance. Durability, as a rate of performance decline, together with a *standard of performance* relative to the original level of performance, yields a prediction of the *useful life* of the device. For example, in consumer marketing, the *effective rated life* of an LED is defined as the time at which the intensity has decreased to 70 percent of its original value.[2] In a similar way, but with a significant difference, the life-rating criterion for high-intensity discharge (HID) bulbs is that the bulb is producing 40 percent of its original light output.[3]

Batteries in electric vehicles have rated lifetimes that are defined in this manner. For lithium–manganese batteries, a reduction of storage capacity to 70 percent of the original value is said to be a typical definition of *end of life*.[4] More conservatively, Apple Computer describes the lifespan of its batteries as the number of recharge cycles that the battery can take before its storage capacity is reduced to 80 percent of its original value.[5]

The decrease in battery storage capacity is a function of several variables. A battery degrades over time according to both the temperature at which it is stored and the state of charge at which it is stored. A battery also degrades with usage as a function of both the number of discharge cycles and the depth of the discharge in each cycle. As a function of the number of discharge cycles, the degradation appears to be linear. A study of lithium–polymer batteries showed that their actual storage capacity begins at approximately 90 to 95 percent of their rated capacity, and that the durability of the battery is described by a linear decline in capacity at a rate of about 1 percentage point for every 20 discharges.[6]

In SPVs, it is well understood that the durability of a solar panel is described by an exponential decrease in power output over time at a rate between 0.5 and 1.0 percent per year. Manufacturers estimating the useful life of a crystalline SPV unit use an estimate of 0.8 percent per year. The standard for performance, defining the useful life of a solar panel, is

80 percent of the original power output.[7] Thus, most solar panels have a rated life of approximately 25 years.

Quantifying Lifespan

The expected lifetime of a nonrepairable device is known formally in engineering statistics as the *mean time to failure* (MTTF), but the measure of time must be understood properly and the factors that cause the failure should be recognized.

Calendar Time for Continuous Operation

For devices that operate continuously, such as turbine in a hydroelectric power system, calendar time is a good measure for the lifespan of the device. Calendar time affects the performance of a device due to fatigue arising from the operation of the device or due to exposure to persistent environmental conditions. Cars rust over time. Batteries degrade with time. Solar cells are subject to *age derating*, which can be interpreted either as a loss of capacity or as a loss of efficiency. Windmills are exposed to nature whose thermal cycles and solar radiation cause material deterioration. Elastic components, critical to some devices, dry out predictably over time.

Usage Time for Periodic Operation

For devices that operate periodically, starting and stopping, the best way to quantify durability is cumulative usage, which may be measured by time of use or by quantity of output. Examples of the former are the number of hours that a light bulb has been on or that an aircraft engine has been running. Examples of the latter are the mileage on a car or a tire.

Usage may be the most accurate predictor of the time to failure for a device, but as we shall see in Chapter 7, the financial analysis of a device is usually based on an estimate of the calendar life of the device. The two concepts are related through an assumption about the rate at which the device will be used over its calendar life,

$$\text{Usage life} = \text{Average usage rate} \times \text{Calendar life}$$

Example 1   Incandescent Bulb

An average incandescent bulb has a usage life of 1,000 hours. If the bulb is used four hours per day, what will be its expected calendar life?

Solution

Usage life = Average usage rate × Calendar life
1,000 hours = 4 hr/day × Calendar life
$$\text{Calendar life} = \frac{1000}{4}$$
Calendar life = 250 days.

Example 2   Vehicular Lifespan as Age or Miles Driven

The useful life of a vehicle depends on both environmental and operating conditions. Environmental conditions cause metallic components to rust and corrode and rubber components to dry out and stiffen, giving vehicles a useful life that depends on age and location. In contrast, the moving parts—the engine and drive train—tend to age more with usage than with time. A transmission may have a life of 100,000 miles. An engine may be expected to last 150,000 miles. To illustrate the relationship between usage rate and calendar life, consider a vehicle that has a useful life of 150,000 miles. Calculate its calendar life for usages of 6,000 miles/year, 12,000 miles/year, 20,000 miles/year, and 30,000 miles/year.

Solution

The mathematical relationship is (Usage Rate) × (Calendar Life) = 150,000 miles, so the calendar life is equal to 150,000 divided by the usage rate. Thus,

6,000 miles/year → 150,000/6,000 = 25 years
12,000 miles/year → 150,000/12,000 = 12.5 years
20,000 miles/year → 150,000/20,000 = 7.5 years
30,000 miles/year → 150,000/30,000 = 5 years.

In Chapter 6, we will look in some detail at the cost of battery electric vehicles and fuel-cell electric vehicles. As of 2014, the durability of a fuel cell, in the sense of useful life, is about 75,000 miles, not the 150,000 needed to be commercially competitive.[8] When we study the economics of sustainable transportation, we will see that the assumption about what determines a vehicle's life—calendar time or usage—yields very different conclusions about the relative costs of these two types of sustainable transportation.

Operating Cycles in Periodic Operation

The life of most electromechanical devices is affected by the operating cycle of their use, meaning how long they are run for each start. Even within a technology group, the standard cycle for testing product life may depend on the type of device. For fluorescent bulbs, the testing conditions established by the Illuminating Engineering Society of North America is three hours per start, and the rated life is the point at which 50 percent of the bulbs have failed.[9] For HID (metal halide) bulbs, the standard test cycle is 10 hours per start.[10]

The life of a fluorescent bulb is particularly sensitive to its operating cycle. The standard operating cycle for rating compact fluorescent light (CFL) bulbs is three hours on and 20 minutes off. A study conducted at the Lighting Research Center of Rensselaer Polytechnic Institute found that the bulb life at one hour per start was 80 percent of the rated life, but at 15 minutes per start it was only 30 percent of the rated life, and at five minutes per start the bulbs lasted only 15 percent of the rated life.[11] A power equation that approximates these data is

$$H = R \times (S / 3)^{0.5}$$

where H is the number of hours of useful life, R is the number of hours in the rated lifetime of the bulb, and S is the number of hours of use per start in the operating cycle of the bulb.

Example 3   Calendar Life of a CFL bulb

Many CFL bulbs have a rated life of 10,000 hours. What will be the expected calendar life of the CFL bulb for each of the usage conditions shown in Table 5.1, which all correspond to eight hours use per day?

Table 5.1 Usage conditions

Starts per day	Hours used per start	Hours used per day
1	8	8
2	4	8
4	2	8
8	1	8

Table 5.2 Calculation of calendar life

Starts per day	Hours of use per start	Hours use per day	Hours of useful life	Calendar life (yr)
1	8	8	16,330	5.59
2	4	8	11,547	3.95
4	2	8	8,165	2.80
8	1	8	5,774	1.98

Solution

We get the calendar life in two steps. First, we use the equation $H = R \times (S/3)^{0.5}$ to compute the hours of useful life (H) given the stated number of hours of use per start (S), then we calculate the calendar life using the useful life H and the number of hours of use per day. In all cases, the rated life is $R = 10,000$ hours.

For the first line in the Table 5.2, $S = 8$ hours per start. Therefore, the total hours of useful life is predicted to be $H = 10,000 \times (8/3)^{0.5} = 16,330$ hours. Divide that by 365 times the number of hours of use per day to get the calendar life, $16,330/(365 \times 8) = 5.59$ years.

This example shows how dramatically the operating cycle of a CFL bulb can affect its calendar life, even when the usage rate in hours per day is held constant.

Reliability, Lifespan, and Processes of Failure

Even when failure is discrete or precipitous, it nevertheless occurs unpredictably. The study of such failure processes is the domain of *reliability theory* in engineering. The task of the reliability engineer is to determine the form of the probability distribution that describes the device's time to failure and to understand the features of the device, its operation, or its environmental conditions that influence the probability of failure.

For example, under a *Poisson failure process*, there is a constant probability of failure over any interval of time. Such a process is described by a single number, the half-life or median time to failure. The decay of carbon-14 for radioactive dating is the best example. Under the more general *Weibull failure process*, the relative probability of failure is a *power function* of time described by a parameter or constant k. Specifically, $k - 1$ is the power of time used in the Weibull power function formula. For many devices, the probability of failure is low when the device is new (i.e., in the early years of life but *after* a short period in which defects in manufacturing are typically discovered), and then the probability of failure in any given time interval increases over time as the device is used or exposed to environmental conditions. As an example, if the relative probability of failure were to increase linearly with time, the probability distribution for the time to failure would be described by a Weibull distribution with parameter $k = 2$. If the probability of failure were relatively flat and then increased quickly near the wear-out point of a device, the relative probability of failure would be cubic ($k = 4$) or higher. It is not our task in this book to go into the details of failure processes, but they are an interesting extension of the topics in this chapter.

The general model for failure is depicted by the *bathtub curve* for the relative probability of failure over the lifetime of a device, shown above.[12] In the earliest period of the device's life, it is subject to significant *infant mortality* due to defects arising from poor quality in the manufacturing process. Once the device has passed the point at which manufacturing problems tend to cause failure, and throughout its expected operational lifespan, the device has a stable probability of failure from random causes. When it reaches its wear-out point, its probability of failure rises quickly (Figure 5.1).

Failure Modes of SPV Cells

SPV panels have the advantage of no moving parts, so they avoid many of the typical failure modes associated with mechanical systems. SPV

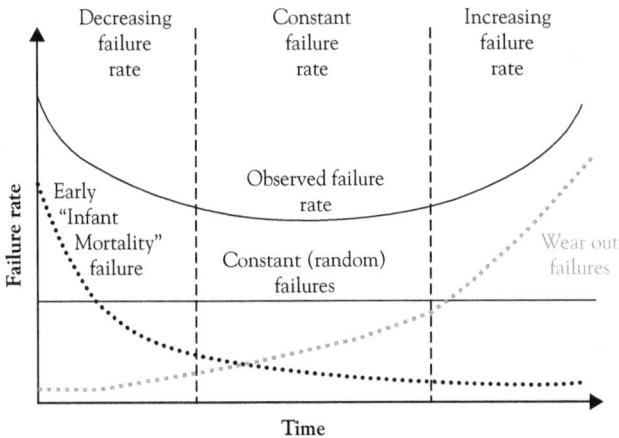

Figure 5.1 The bathtub curve for the observed failure rate

systems ultimately fail mainly due to the deterioration or corrosion of their materials owing to the environmental effects of solar radiation, thermal stress, and water vapor intrusion.

The antireflective coating of a cell can deteriorate due to radiation. Water vapor intruding a cell can cause corrosion of the metal contacts in a cell. PV cells can crack, causing an open circuit that stops the flow of electricity, due to thermal stress, hail, or *latent cracks* that occur during processing or assembly but are not detectable in manufacturing quality control and appear only later. The interconnects between cells can be broken due to thermal stress and wind loading. Short circuits in the PV module can occur due to the degradation of insulation from weathering, which results in delamination, cracking, or electrochemical corrosion.[13]

The actual failure rate for solar panels is difficult to determine. *The New York Times* published an article in May, 2013, describing a spectacular failure in an SPV array and noting that there is no industrywide information on the reliability of solar panels. The reporter quoted a source, "'We have inspectors in a lot of factories, and it's not rare to see some big brands being produced in those smaller workshops where they have no control over quality,' said Thibaut Lemoine, general manager of STS Certified, a French-owned testing service. When STS evaluated 215,000 photovoltaic modules at its Shanghai laboratory in 2011 and 2012, it found the defect rate had jumped from 7.8 percent to 13 percent."[14]

The press about SPV failures was exaggerated, according to a writer at the Rocky Mountain Institute, first because a defect may cause only a small loss in the power of a module, not a complete failure and second, because quality depends on quality control, "Modules that are qualified to [International Electrotechnical Commission] standards are much more likely to survive in the field and not have design flaws leading to premature failure, or 'infant mortality,' as it is known in the industry. A National Renewable Energy Laboratory (NREL) study, reporting on ten years of field results, showed that unqualified modules suffered from 45 percent field failure rates while qualified modules suffered from a less than 0.1 percent field failure rate."[15]

Another article reported a study at Sandia National Labs showing a failure rate in SPV modules of 0.05 percent per year and concluded, "Module reliability and durability are separate issues that a potential investor must consider independently. PV modules can fail in many ways, but the risk seems relatively low based on module reliability studies. However, little public data is available on actual field results to verify the studies. A project with narrow margins could be impacted by even very small losses in generation or increased O&M. Even when backed by a warranty, failure rates drive lost revenue for investors, developers, and plant operators. As such, a potential investor should carefully consider a module manufacturer's track record, qualification tests, reliability forecasts, and warranty coverage before investing in a project."[16]

Reliability and Lifespan

The reliability of a device, at a point in time, is the complement to the annual probability of failure. The typical pattern for the failure rate of a well-engineered device over a long span of time is illustrated by the *bathtub curve*. The probability of failure is high in the first year due to the *infant mortality* problem that originates in defects of manufacturing. Then the probability of failure tends to be low and constant for a long period of time. Then the probability of failure rises sharply as the components of the device wear out more or less around the same time, which is the engineered life of the device.

After the period in which manufacturing defects can cause failure, the probability of failure becomes more or less constant. During that period, there is a rather simple mathematical formula that relates the annual probability of failure to the *cumulative* probability of failure—the probability that the device will have failed by a particular point in time. If we write r for the annual rate or probability of failure of the device during the middle period of the bathtub curve, the probability that the device will survive each year is the complementary probability, $1 - r$. The probability that the device will have survived after T years is the probability that it survived in each of T years, which is given by the exponential formula,

$$S = (1 - r)^T \qquad \text{(Survival Equation)}$$

The probability of failure (F) by time T is the complementary probability,

$$F = 1 - S$$
$$F = 1 - (1 - r)^T$$

Often, the reliability of a device is described indirectly by the long-term probability of failure (F) after some specific number of years, as the following example shows.

Example 4   Failure Rate of an SPV Module

Suppose that accelerated laboratory testing of SPV modules results in a prediction that 95 percent of the modules will survive after 20 years of use.

(a) What is the annual failure rate of the SPV modules?
(b) If it costs $3,500 to replace a 1 kW SPV module, what is the expected cost of replacing failed modules each year?

Solution

(a) The 95 percent survival rate is denoted by the letter S in our formulas above. The time of use is $T = 20$ years. Therefore, the survival equation for this problem is

$$95 \text{ percent} = (1 - r)^{20}$$

Our task is to solve this equation for the annual failure rate, r. First, for clarity in computation, we write 95 percent as a decimal. Then, using the rules of algebra, we raise both sides to the 1/20 power,

$$0.95^{1/20} = (1 - r)^{20/20}$$

Calculate the number on the left side using a scientific calculator or spreadsheet, and recognize that $20/20 = 1$,

$$0.99744 = (1 - r)^1$$
$$0.99744 = 1 - r$$

Add r to both sides and subtract 0.99744

$$r = 1 - 0.99744$$
$$r = 0.00256$$

So the annual probability of failure of an SPV module is 0.256 percent per year.

(b) If it costs \$3,500 to replace a failed 1 kW SPV module, then the expected cost of replacements each year is the probability of failure multiplied by that replacement cost,

$$= 0.00256 \times 3,500$$
$$= \$8.96 \text{ per kW per year}$$

Estimates of the cost of maintaining and repairing an SPV installation run between \$20 and \$60 per kW per year. This example shows that less than \$10 of that can be attributed to the failure of the SPV module. Inverters are much more likely to fail, and their replacement tends to account for more of the annual cost of an SPV installation than that of the modules.

Conditions on Useful Life

Just as the conditions of usage and of the ambient environment can affect the efficiency of a device, they also affect the life of a device. The lifespan of an incandescent light bulb depends on its position (vertical or horizontal), the ambient temperature (not too cold or too hot), the degree of vibration to which it is subject. The example of the position of a bulb is interesting, because it can be a significant factor in the life of a lamp.

> Position-oriented lamps (designed to burn in a certain position) are tested and rated based on their designated position. Burning these lamps in other positions can dramatically shorten life, lumen output, and color. Universal lamps can be burned in any position, but as a result, they sacrifice life expectancy and lumen output in some operating positions. Published *rated life* for universal lamps is based on the lamps being burned in the vertical position. The *rated life* for lamps burned in the horizontal position is 75 percent of the published rating for the vertical application.[17]

The useful life of a lithium-ion battery, measured in discharge cycles, depends on the depth of discharge in a nonlinear manner, which shows that there is a level of discharge that optimizes the amount of energy that can be drawn from the battery over its life. Here, a 100 percent discharge refers to the maximum recommended discharge for the battery, which for deep-cycle batteries is about 80 percent of their entire capacity and is the level at which a laptop is programmed to shut down. Even a rechargeable battery would not be able to recharge if it were discharged of its entire capacity. Battery University publishes the following account of the relationship between the depth of discharge and the number of discharge cycles. To that, we add a calculation of the number of full-discharge equivalents for the average of the low and high estimates.

Table 5.3 shows that a partial discharge prolongs the useful life of the battery, with a 50 percent discharge being the best.

Designing for Long Life

The *Three Rs* of sustainability are reduce, reuse, and recycle.[18] There should be a fourth R in that list, reduce, reuse, *restore*, and recycle. Much waste is produced in our society, and much created value is lost, because people do not know when a device can be repaired economically.

Table 5.3 Battery performance and depth of discharge

Depth of discharge (%)	Discharge cycles (lowest)	Discharge cycles (highest)	Full-discharge equivalents
100	300	500	400
50	1,200	1,500	675
25	2,000	2,500	562
10	3,750	4,700	422

Repairability Through Interchangeable Parts

The development of interchangeable parts was the foundation of the assembly-line system of production, but it is also the foundation of repairability. The key to repairability is that the components of a device can be replaced, so the failure of a component does not cause the entire device to fail irreversibly. However, the repair process depends on an active market in component parts. If manufacturers do not sell the parts, the devices cannot be repaired. An unfortunate example is Hewlett-Packard's (HP's) laser printer. HP is known for its excellence in engineering, so its laser printers tend to last a long time. However, the mechanism that feeds paper into the printer consists of a rotating bar with two small wheels called pickup rollers that are wrapped by an elastic band that grabs the paper. The elastic predictably dries out after about five years and ceases to grab the paper. HP users have posted a temporary solution to the problem on the company's website—turn the elastic bands inside-out to expose the inner side that had not been dried. That enables the printer to work for a few more years. But when the second side has dried and stops grabbing the paper, the only recourse is to replace the elastic, and HP does not sell that component. A fully functional laser printer then goes to a recycling center.

Planned Obsolescence

The antithesis of design for durability is design for obsolescence. In 1960, author Vance Packard exposed the practice of planned obsolescence in his book *The Waste Makers*. Planned obsolescence had been common in the automobile industry since the 1930s, but Packard found it in many industries where companies sought to shorten the replacement cycle of their products. In the modern economy, where the conservation of resources is a key element of the transition to sustainability, planned obsolescence is obsolete.

The Availability of Repairable Devices

When a device can be repaired after a failure, its performance can be described by its uptime or *reliability*. The concept of MTTF for a non-repairable system is replaced by mean time *between* failures (MTBF). To characterize the reliability of a device, we must also account for the mean time to repair (MTTR), because the potential operating time of a device is the sum of its MTBF and its MTTR.

$$\text{Reliability} = \frac{\text{MTBF}}{\text{MTBF} + \text{MTTR}}$$

Computer servers, computer networks, electric power generators, and electric power distribution networks are often described in terms of their reliability.

The *availability* of the device is the percentage of time that it is operational, which is also affected by the amount of scheduled maintenance required each year. Availability, as the percentage of uptime relative to the potential operating time, is therefore calculated as the probability of being available despite failures (its reliability) multiplied by the probability of being available despite maintenance,

$$\text{Availability} = \frac{\text{MTBF}}{\text{MTBF} + \text{MTTR}} \times (1 - \frac{\text{Days Maintenance}}{365}).$$

Example 5   Availability of a Wind Turbine

Consider a wind turbine that has an MTBF of 150 days, an MTTR of 8 days, and regularly scheduled maintenance of 2 days per year.

(a) Calculate the availability of the wind turbine.
(b) If the system has a rated capacity of 1.5 MW, and the wind conditions would allow a capacity factor of 0.35, what will be the annual output from the wind turbine?

Solution

(a) Availability $= \dfrac{150}{150+8} \times (1 - \dfrac{2}{365})$

   Availability $= 0.9494 \times 0.9945$
   Availability $= 0.944$

   This wind turbine is available 94.4 percent of the year, to three significant digits.

(b) With a rated capacity of 1.5 MW and the wind conditions permitting production at 35 percent of capacity, the energy (in megawatt-hours) generated during a year of full-time operation would be $1.5 \times 24 \times 365 \times 0.35 = 4,599$ MWh. However, the system is available only 94.4 percent of the time, so the actual amount of energy generated will be $4,599 \times 0.944 = 4,340$ MWh, reported to three significant digits.

The familiar commercial wind turbine has a capacity of about 1.5 MW and has blades or rotors oriented with a horizontal axis to the wind. Its rotors turn a shaft at 15 to 20 revolutions per minute (rpm) that is connected to a gearbox that scales up the rotational speed to 3,000 or 3,600 rpm (50 or 60 cycles per second) to drive an electric generator to create alternating-current electric energy at a frequency of 50 (in Europe) or 60 (in America) cycles per second. That energy then passes by wire to a transformer on the ground where it is converted to high-voltage current for transmission to customers. A typical availability for commercial wind systems is 93 to 95 percent.[19] However, the availability depends on the design of the system.

Turbulence in the wind puts tremendous stress on the wheels and bearings in a wind turbine's gearbox. A small defect in any one component, such as a worn or broken ball bearing, can bring the turbine to a halt. This makes the gearbox the most high-maintenance part of a turbine. Gearboxes in offshore turbines, which face higher wind speeds, are even more vulnerable than those in onshore turbines,[20] and offshore wind generators are much more expensive to maintain than onshore systems. As a result, researchers at NREL have been looking for ways to improve the reliability of the wind-generating system. They found that wind turbines that were supposed to last 20 years were often failing after 7 to 10 years, and the cause was usually in the gearbox. A reporter described the outcome, "After years of experiments and changes, the solution to the problem turned out to be remarkably simple: get rid of the gearbox. In other words, Butterfield and his peers were advocating a transition to direct-drive turbine designs."[21]

The direct-drive wind turbine has a generator that runs at the rotational speed of the blades, 15 to 20 rpm. This design, however, requires a much larger and heavier generator, making the system more expensive. The permanent-magnet generator in General Electric's 4.1 MW turbine is six meters in diameter. Siemens has a 6 MW direct-drive turbine used for offshore placements. Northern Power builds a 100 kW direct-drive turbine, and their tests have demonstrated a reliability of 98.7 percent, which is better than the typical 93 to 95 percent of geared turbines.[22]

The newly emerging competition from direct-drive systems has spurred engineers to improve the reliability of their geared systems, too. One report holds that contemporary geared turbines have availability in the high 98 to 99 percent range.[23]

An article in *Wikipedia* illustrates several designs for wind power systems, including systems that spin around a vertical pole. The article notes that *eggbeater* turbines, known as Darrieus turbines, "have good efficiency but produce large torque ripple and cyclical stress on the tower, which contributes to poor reliability."[24]

Tech Focus: Energy Storage

Energy storage is a vital component of nonfirm power systems, such as those that depend on sun or wind. Here, we look at several ways to store energy from renewable sources.

The Energy Content of Fuels

Chemical energy is the energy contained in the atomic bonds that holds a molecule together. Chemical energy is released, in the form of heat, when a molecule is altered through a chemical reaction, such as oxidation (burning). For that reason, the chemical energy *contained in fuels* is usually measured in the same way as heat energy, using the kilocalorie (kCal) or the British thermal unit (BTU).

Example 6   Heat Energy in Methane

The energy content of methane (natural gas) is 930 BTU per cubic foot. How many cubic feet of natural gas would have to be burned to raise the 60-gallon water tank by 50°F, assuming that all the heat from combustion is transferred to the water? (It is not generally true that all the chemical energy from combustion goes into the heat of the water, due to inefficiency in the combustion process, but here you may ignore that complication.)

Solution

We saw above that the heating problem requires 30,060 BTU of energy. The amount of methane required is the X that satisfies the equation

$$30,060 = (930 \text{ BTU/ft}^3) \times X \text{ ft}^3$$

Solve this to find $X = 30,060/930 = 32.32 \text{ ft}^3$, if combustion were perfectly efficient.

The other context in which chemical energy is found is food and exercise. Your body *burns* (metabolizes) sugars and stores energy in the form of fat, which is a type of oil. The chemical energy in food and fat becomes the mechanical energy of bodily motion and the heat energy that keeps your insides at 98°F. In food and exercise, energy content is measured in *food calories*, which are known scientifically as kilocalories. Here, we use *calorie* to mean food calories. As a point of comparison, we saw previously, in the description of heat energy, that a scientific calorie (Cal) is the amount of heat energy required to raise 1 kg of water by 1°C.

Example 7   Electric Energy Stored in a Battery

A common 12-volt car battery used to store energy from an SPV system can deliver a power of 200 W for five hours. How much energy is stored in the battery?

Solution

$$200 \text{ W} \times 5 \text{ hr} = 1{,}000 \text{ Wh} = 1.0 \text{ kWh}$$

The Storage of Heat Energy, Part 1 (Thermal Mass)

Heat energy is stored in different amounts in different materials. A *thermal mass* is any mass that holds heat energy, and the calculation of energy in thermal mass is an important element in *passive solar design*.

The physical concept that helps us understand the heat content of a mass is the *specific heat capacity* of the material. The specific heat capacity of water is defined to be one. The specific heat capacity of any other material reflects the amount of heat that one unit of mass of that material can hold, relative to water. For example, the specific heat capacity of a common red brick is 0.84. This means that it takes 0.84 BTU of heat energy to raise a one-pound brick by one degree Fahrenheit. Likewise, looking at the definition of heat energy in the metric system, it would take 0.84 kCal (*food calories*) to raise one kilogram of brick material by one degree centigrade.

The heat contained in a thermal mass is calculated as the mass (M), multiplied by its specific heat capacity (s), multiplied by the difference between the temperature of the mass T_m and the temperature of the environment, T_e:

$$\text{Heat available} = M \times s \times (T_m - T_e)$$

The density and specific heat capacity of some common building materials are shown in relation to water in Table 5.4.[25]

Example 8   Thermal Mass

A brick wall has become hot in the day's sunlight. Now in the evening, the air temperature is 75°F but the brick wall is still 90°F. The wall is six feet tall, 20 feet long, and one foot thick. The air will stay at 75°F throughout the night. How much heat energy will the wall give off to the air as it cools down?

Table 5.4 Densities and specific heats of materials

Material	Density (lb./ft³)	Density (kg/m³)	Specific heat capacity
Water (liquid)	16.02	1,000	1.00
Paraffin wax (solid)	13.30	830	0.58
Paraffin wax (liquid)	12.50	780	0.57
Vegetable oil			0.48
Wood	8.81	550	0.40
Brick	30.79	1,922	0.22
Concrete	36.85	2,300	0.21
Stone	27.23	1,700	0.20
Iron	126.08	7,870	0.11

Solution

The amount of heat energy that the wall will give off depends in part on the temperature difference (D), which here is $90 - 75 = 15°F$. The mass of this wall must be calculated as the product of its volume and its density. The description of the wall shows that it has a volume of $6 \times 20 \times 1 = 120$ ft.³ The density of brick is 30.79 pounds per cubic foot, so the mass of the wall is $120 \times 30.79 = 3{,}694.8$ lb. The heat energy to be given to the environment is the product of the mass, the specific heat capacity of brick, and the temperature difference,

$$\text{Heat energy} = 3{,}694.8 \times 0.22 \times 15 \text{ (BTU)}$$
$$\text{Heat energy} = 12{,}193 \text{ BTU}$$

Solar thermal electric (STE) systems, also called concentrating solar power (CSP) system, concentrate the sun's energy using mirrors or parabolic troughs to achieve very high temperatures (up to 400°C) in a working fluid that generates electric energy using a heat engine. The feature that distinguishes STE from SPV is that the heat energy from an STE system can be stored, at least for a while. The 250-MW Solana plant in Gila Bend, Arizona, uses a parabolic trough system to collect the sun's heat energy, but some of that energy can be stored for as long as six hours in molten salt (50 percent KNO_3, 40 percent $NaNO_2$, and 7 percent

$NaNO_3$ by weight) at temperatures between 142°C and 540°C so that it can be used to power the heat engine even after the sun has gone down, especially in the early evening when household electric power demand is at its peak. Molten salt has a specific heat capacity of only 0.372, but its density (1.68 times that of water) and high temperature capability make it useful for STE systems. The fact that the STE system can store energy means that it can be called upon when needed. In the language of the electric power industry, it is *dispatchable*, and can therefore be integrated into utility planning in ways that SPV and wind power cannot. This feature of the Gila Bend project is said to have been critical in the decision of the Arizona Public Service power company to agree to buy all of the project's electric power for 30 years.[26]

The Storage of Heat Energy, Part 2 (Latent Heat)

The heat that is released as a material cools is called its *sensible heat*. Another form of heat storage in materials reflects the fact that when a material undergoes a change from gas to liquid or liquid to solid, even while maintaining its temperature at the boiling or melting point, it must release heat to permit the reorganization of its physical structure. Correspondingly, when a material passes from solid to liquid or liquid to gas, it must gain an extra amount of heat. The heat required to effect the phase transition is called the *latent heat capacity* of the material and is quantified in units of energy per unit of mass, for example, BTU/lb. or kCal/kg or MJ/kg.

Materials that are used to store energy in this way are called phase-change materials. The material must have a melting point higher than the temperature of the input heat. For example, a flat-panel device for collecting solar heat can produce hot water at temperatures of up to 170°F to 180°F (77°C to 82°C), so the phase-change material should have a melting point below that.

One such material is paraffin wax. The varieties of paraffin wax melt at temperatures of 116°F to 149°F (47°C to 65°C),[27] so they can be melted by the output of a flat-panel solar water heater. Paraffin has a latent heat capacity of 63.2 BTU/lb.

In California and the American Southwest, the days can be very hot and the nights cold. On a hot day, a solar water heating system may have much more capacity than is needed for heating water. Its excess heating capacity can be used to store heat in the form of melted paraffin. At night, the heat from the paraffin can be transferred to air or to water for distribution around the house. The following example compares water and paraffin for the purpose of storing heat.

Example 9   Heat Storage by Water Versus Paraffin

A solar hot water system with more heating capacity than is needed for the hot water requirements of a household can be used to store heat during the day for release at night. Suppose that in the daytime, a flat-panel solar water heater can deliver water at 140°F, and at night the house is kept at 60°F.

(a) How much heat can be stored in a 100-gal hot water storage tank for distribution to the house at night through a system of radiators?

(b) How much heat would be stored in the same weight of paraffin wax, assuming the following parameters for a commercial-grade paraffin[28]: melting point 54.3°C (130°F), specific heat capacity (solid and liquid) 0.58, and latent heat capacity 184.5 kJ/kg (79 BTU/lb.).

Solution

(a) Water has a density of 8.34 lb./gal, so the 100-gallon hot water tank stores $100 \times 8.34 = 834$ pounds of water. At a temperature difference of $140 - 60 = 80$ degrees from the nighttime temperature, the tank stores $834 \times 80 = 66{,}720$ BTU of heat energy.

(b) After the paraffin is heated to 140°F by the solar heating system, its heat will be released *both* as sensible heat when the paraffin cools *and* as latent heat when the paraffin solidifies. It will cool from 140°F to 60°F, a difference of 80°F. Having a specific heat capacity of 0.58 in both liquid and solid phases, it will release $834 \times 0.58 \times 80 = 38{,}700$ BTU as sensible heat when it cools. The paraffin has a latent heat capacity of 79 BTU/lb., so when it changes phase from liquid to solid, it will release $834 \times 79 = 65{,}900$ BTU. The total release of heat energy is therefore $38{,}700 + 65{,}900 = 104{,}600$ BTU.

In this example, the paraffin stores about 50 percent more heat energy than the water, due mostly to its phase change from solid to liquid as it absorbs heat.

Flywheels for Regenerative Braking: The Storage of Kinetic Energy

A *flywheel* is a disk that spins at high speed to store *rotational energy*. For rotational motion, the kinetic energy depends on the shape of the rotating object. For a solid disk rotating about its center, the kinetic energy contained in the rotating disk is a function of the disk's mass (M, kg), its radius (r, meters), and its spinning frequency (w, cycles per second) according to the equation,

$$E = \frac{1}{2} M \times (\pi \times r \times w)^2$$

where π is the Greek letter *pi* equal to 3.1416.

Example 10   Energy Stored in a Flywheel

How much energy is in a 100 kg lead flywheel, one meter in diameter, which is rotating at 50 cycles per second?

Solution

The mass is $M = 100$ kg. The radius of the flywheel is half of its diameter, so $r = 0.5$. The rotational speed $w = 50$ cycles/sec. So

$$E = \frac{1}{2} \times 100 \times (3.1416 \times 0.5 \times 50)^2 = 50 \times (15.708)^2 = 308{,}425 \text{ joules}$$

Compare that answer to the amount of energy in the car going at 70 mph (example 2). This flywheel, spinning at 50 rotations per second, has about one-half of the kinetic energy needed to accelerate a heavy car to 70 mph. Some attempts to make cars more energy efficient have considered putting a flywheel into a car, to be accelerated when the car brakes, as a way to conserve the energy required to move the car.

Example 11   Flywheel, Continued

To what speed could the flywheel of example 3 accelerate the car of example 2 if the car started from a motionless position, assuming perfect efficiency and no resistance from wind or road? How many miles per hour is that?

Solution

The flywheel contains 308,425 joules of kinetic energy. Translating this into the kinetic energy of the car brings the car to a velocity that is given by the equation for kinetic energy,

$$\frac{1}{2} \times 1400 \times V^2 = 308,425 \text{ (joules)}$$
$$V^2 = 440.607$$
$$V = \sqrt{440.607} = 20.1 \text{ (m/sec)}$$

Convert that to miles per hour using the conversion factor:

$$1 \text{ meter/sec} = \frac{\left(\dfrac{1}{1,609}\right) \text{mile}}{\left(\dfrac{1}{3600}\right) \text{hour}} = 2.2374 \text{ miles/hour.}$$

So 20.1 meter/second is $20.1 \times 2.2374 = 45.0$ miles per hour.

Pumped Water: The Storage of Electric Energy in the Dam above a Hydroelectric Plant

Hydroelectric turbines can be designed to run in reverse, using electric energy to pump water up to the top of a dam. When the water is released back through the hydroelectric turbine, it generates electric energy again. According to the Electricity Storage Association,[29] pumped hydroelectric storage can have a round-trip efficiency as high as 80 percent.

The Storage of Renewable Electric Energy in Hydrogen

Hydrogen is the fuel from which a fuel cell generates electric energy, so if hydrogen can be produced by renewable means, the fuel cell would have a zero-carbon footprint. Hydrogen gas has a very high chemical energy content per unit of weight, 120 MJ/kg (33.3 kWh/kg), almost three times higher than gasoline (43.5 MJ/kg), but hydrogen is a gas over a wide range of temperatures and pressures, so it is not easy to hold large quantities of hydrogen in a small volume of space.

Hydrogen can be produced by several methods. The most common method at present is the steam reformation of methane, which uses a hydrocarbon (methane) as its source of hydrogen atoms, so it generates carbon compounds as a byproduct. The other method is the electrolysis of water (H_2O), which is a much more expensive process at present, but it involves no carbon emissions at all. In the renewable energy arena, there is interest in both methods as sources of hydrogen for fuel cells.

Electrolysis of Water

The mature technology for the electrolysis of water is the alkaline electrolysis of liquid water at temperatures of 70°C to 100°C and pressures of 1 to 30 atmospheres (bars). The process is more efficient at higher pressure and at higher temperature. The energy efficiency can reach 70 to 80 percent in commercial applications.[30]

Steam Methane Reforming

The steam methane reforming (SMR) process is used for 95 percent of the hydrogen produced in the United States.[31] In the SMR process, steam (H_2O) reacts with a hydrocarbon feedstock such as methane (CH_4) at high temperature (850°C) and in the presence of a metal catalyst to produce hydrogen gas (H_2) and carbon monoxide (CO). That is followed by a lower-temperature reaction, called the water–gas shift, in which CO combines with steam to produce carbon dioxide (CO_2) and more hydrogen. In a final step, CO_2 is removed from the gas stream to leave pure hydrogen. At high capacity, the process operates at a composite energy efficiency of 70 to 85 percent.[32] Commercial SMR plants have capacities as high as 10,000 kg of hydrogen per hour. There are significant economies of capacity in the SMR process.

Take-aways

- The *durability* (lifespan) of a device may be a function of calendar time, as when a device rusts, corrodes, or desiccates due to environmental conditions.

- The durability (lifespan) of a device may also be a function of the usage of the device, measured in hours of operation, or miles driven, or on and off cycles.

- The *reliability* of repairable devices is measured by the percentage of time in a year that the device is available for use (its *availability*), which is 100 percent minus the *downtime* percentage of the device.

- The *reliability* of nonrepairable devices is measured as the probability that the device will continue to operate after X hours of operation or years of calendar time. Hundred percent minus the probability that failure will occur within X hours of operation or calendar years. When the device's failure is independent of time or usage—when failure is due entirely to random causes—the reliability of the device may be expressed as the probability of failure within any one-year time span.

The distinction between lifespan in *calendar time* and lifespan in *operational time* is worth remembering, because it will make a significant difference in the economics of a technology. We will see this in the comparison of battery electric vehicles and fuel cell electric vehicles in Chapter 6.

CHAPTER 6

Cost Structure

Overview

In the engineering perspective on technology, we look at the process by which inputs are transformed into outputs (Figure 6.1).

A new perspective on technology reveals to us when we study the cost of the technology rather than its input–output structure. In the economic perspective, we add information about the prices of each input, from which we can calculate the total cost of all inputs together, but we suppress the details about the process of transforming inputs into outputs. The economic perspective is therefore pictured as in Figure 6.2.

In Chapter 2, we studied how to measure the capacity of a device as an indicator of size. The interesting economic question about capacity is whether large devices are cheaper than small devices *per unit of capacity*. The study of *economies of capacity* and *economies of scale* in this chapter will answer that question.

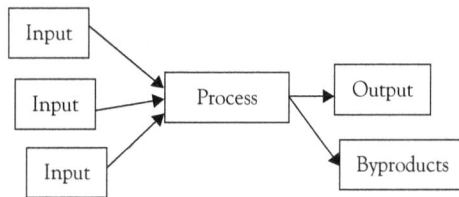

Figure 6.1 Input–output diagram

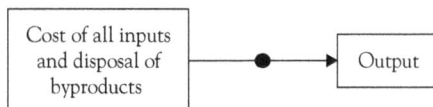

Figure 6.2 The economic perspective on technology

The cost to purchase or build a device is only one aspect of the economics of technology. The operation of a device uses costly inputs, so we must also study the operational cost of the device, known in economics as its *variable cost* per unit of output. To put these two ideas together—the cost of acquisition and the cost of operation—we express the cost of owning the device as an equivalent annual cost over the expected lifespan of the device, like an annual lease payment, then divide that *annualized* or *levelized* cost of the device by the annual output of the device to get an *average annualized cost* per unit of output. Adding this average annualized purchase price per unit to the variable cost per unit gives a *levelized total cost* per unit. The examples in this chapter show that these concepts explain why one technology is economically superior to another, and they lay the foundation for our study of break-even analysis in Chapter 7.

The key questions addressed in this chapter are as follows:

- In which technologies does *bigger* mean *better* (*cheaper*)?
- Why is it necessary to distinguish the cost of operating a device from the cost of owning a device? In what units are those two types of cost measured?
- What does the *levelized cost* of a device refer to, and how is it measured or calculated?

In a Tech Focus at the end of this chapter, we apply these ideas to compare the use of batteries versus fuel cells in electric vehicles.

Economies of Capacity

The capacity of a device is its maximum rate of output. Two devices of different capacities may be compared according to their *price per unit of capacity*. This concept is often abbreviated as the *cost of capacity* or *capacity cost* of the device.

A technology exhibits *economies of capacity* when larger devices have a lower price *per unit of capacity*. This concept is measured empirically by looking at the market prices for devices of different capacities.

Table 6.1 Calculations of capacity cost revealing economies of capacity

Type	Capacity (kW)	Installed cost ($)	Capacity cost ($/W)
Small scale	10	50,000–80,000	5–8
Medium scale	100	300,000–500,000	3–5
Utility scale	2,000	3–4 million	1.5–2

Economies of Capacity in Wind Power

Consider the example of wind power devices. Table 6.1 shows the typical installed cost of wind turbines of various capacities in 2012.[1] Installed includes the purchase price and all expenses of installing the device and making it ready for use. Table 6.1 also shows the installed cost per unit of capacity, which is the capacity cost of the device.

Notice that the capacity cost is lower for devices with higher capacities. This indicates *economies of capacity* in the wind turbine technology.

Economies of Capacity and Economies of Scale

In many popular writings about technology, the reduction in capacity cost at higher levels of capacity is referred to as economies of scale or scale economies. That usage is not consistent with the definition that economists use for *economies of scale*. In economics, *economies of scale* exist for a technology when the long-run average total cost (ATC) of producing output using the technology declines with the scale of output. This is similar to our concept of economies of capacity, but it includes a consideration of the cost of producing output from the technology. A larger device or production system, usually thought of in economics as a factory, might be able to use its higher output rate and thus higher rate of input use to get volume discounts in the purchase of raw materials, or it might achieve efficiencies in production that are not possible for technologies that are designed for lower output rates. Either of those effects would contribute to economies of scale under its proper definition. In summary, both economies of capacity and economies in production at higher capacities contribute to economies of scale.

Economies of Capacity in Solar Photovoltaics

The way to make a larger installation of solar photovoltaic (SPV) technology is to put together a large number of SPV modules, each of which consists of SPV panels. A common configuration for an SPV module is eight panels of 125 watts output each, for a total of 1,000 W or 1 kW in the module. A larger installation means having a larger number of modules. With that kind of technology, assembling a large facility from many small components, the cost of a large facility should be near the sum of the costs of its modules and the labor necessary to install and connect them. There would be no decrease in the total cost of the large installation *per kilowatt of capacity* under these conditions.

However, an SPV system is more than its panels. It consists of panels mounted on a frame and connected by wires to a battery bank and an inverter that converts the direct current (DC) output of the panels into alternating current (AC) output that can be used by home appliances. This entire system has to be installed by workers who are familiar with the technology. Batteries and inverters may be subject to economies of scale. The installation process may likewise show economies of scale. Data on the median installed price of SPV systems supports a claim to economies of scale. Table 6.2 shows data on the price of SPV systems during the first half of 2012 as published in a November 2012 report from the National Renewable Energy Laboratory (NREL).[2] The declining price per unit of capacity demonstrates economies of scale.

According to the Solar Energy Industries Association, the median 5-kW residential system had an installed cost of $4,800 per kilowatt in mid-2013, but commercial systems on the order of 100 kW had a median installed cost of $3,700 per kW, and utility-scale systems (1,000 kW and

Table 6.2 Solar photovoltaics

Capacity (kW)	Price ($/W)
<10	5.94
10–100	5.44
>100	5.05

up) had an average installed cost of $2,100 per kW.[3] These data indicate economies of capacity in SPV.

Economies of Capacity in Solar Thermal Electric Systems

Solar thermal electric (STE) technology, also called concentrating solar power (CSP) concentrates solar radiation to heat water into steam, which then drives a steam turbine to run a generator that produces electric energy. The typical structure of an STE installation is a tower at the top of which is a container holding the working fluid (water) toward which many mirrors on the ground are pointed to concentrate the solar radiation. The heat from the concentrated radiation converts the water to steam, which is conveyed by pipes to ground level where it can run a turbine generator to produce electricity.

The large mirrored STE installations are therefore *not* just a collection of smaller installations as in the case of SPV. Instead, like the hydroelectric technology, larger installations can be more efficient and less expensive per unit of capacity, than small ones. The largest system operating in 2012 was a 100 MW plant in Abu Dhabi. Another STE installation is Brightsource Energy's Ivanpah Solar Electric Generating System in the Mojave desert, which started operations in 2013 and cost $2.2 billion. It uses 170,000 mirrors to focus the sun's energy on a tower's boiler and generate 370 MW of AC power,[4] meaning a capacity cost of $5.95 per AC watt. The world's largest STE installation will be a 1,000 MW system being built near Blythe, California, at an estimated cost of approximately $2.1 billion,[5] which if realized would amount to $2.10 per watt.

The reported capacities and costs of various STE installations indicate widely varying capacity costs (Table 6.3). These may be due to differences in land cost, labor cost, distance to existing electric power transmission lines, and amount of thermal storage capacity built into the project. As a result, commercial-scale STE plants do not appear to indicate consistent economies of capacity.

A different design of STE system is to use parabolic troughs as collectors. The individual collectors can be as small as 0.5 kW each but are strung together to feed a single steam turbine. The collectors will not

Table 6.3 Reported capacity and cost of STE systems

Project	Capacity (MW AC)	Total cost ($M)	Capacity cost ($/W)
Spain	100	560	5.60
Solar reserve	110	921 (est)	8.34
Solana (Gila bend)	280	2,000 (est)	7.14
Ivanpah	370	2,200	5.95
Blythe, California	1,000	2,100	2.10

show any economies of capacity, but the generator that they feed might have economies of capacity, which would contribute to economies of capacity for the whole system. Even so, the International Energy Agency reported in 2009 that the installed cost of trough-type solar thermal electric concentrating solar power (STE/CSP) systems was $4.2 to $8.4 per watt, depending on land and labor costs, the amount of storage capacity with the system.[6]

The Costs of Operation (Variable and Fixed)

Every technology produces an output and requires an expenditure on inputs. The total cost of all inputs used to produce a specific amount of output is called the *total variable cost* (TVC) of that output level. When the TVC is divided by the output level, it gives the *average variable cost* (AVC) per unit of output.

Technology with Constant Average Variable Cost

The simplest type of technology has one input and one output, an example being a natural gas water heater. Its input is an amount of natural gas, X, measured in therms (100,000 BTU). Its output is a quantity of heated water, Q, also measured in therms. (It is common in economics to represent an output quantity by the letter Q and an input quantity by the letter X.) Its input–output equation reflects the efficiency of the process.

If a gas-fired water heater is 91 percent efficient, then its input–output equation would be

$$Q = 0.91 \times X \text{ (Output = Efficiency} \times \text{Input)}$$

If natural gas costs \$0.80 per therm, then the quantity X therms would cost $X \times 0.80$. The number of therms of gas input needed to produce Q therms of heated water is found by dividing both sides of the input–output equation by 0.91, $X = \dfrac{Q}{0.91}$.

The TVC of producing Q therms of heated water would therefore be this input quantity X multiplied by its price, \$0.80 per therm.

$$\text{TVC} = \frac{Q}{0.91} \times 0.80$$

$$\text{TVC} = 0.88 \times Q \text{ (measured in \$)}$$

This equation shows how the TVC depends on the output quantity Q. Because the input price \$0.80/therm is assumed not to change at higher levels of output, and the efficiency 0.91 is assumed not to change with output, the result is a (total) variable cost that is a fixed dollar amount (\$0.88) per unit of output.

The total variable cost depends on the amount of output produced. What we are looking for in this analysis is a characteristic of the technology itself, not dependent on the level at which the technology is used. The present example shows that if you divide the TVC by the output quantity Q, you get a single number \$0.88, which we call the AVC (averaged per unit of output). Economists abbreviate this as AVC but often call it simply the *variable cost* of production (per unit),

$$\text{AVC} = \frac{TVC}{Q} \qquad \text{(definition of AVC)}$$

$$\text{AVC} = \frac{0.88 \times Q}{Q} \qquad \text{(using the TVC equation)}$$

$$\text{AVC} = 0.88(\$/\text{therm of heated water})$$

This equation says that, for this technology, the AVC of heated water is $0.88 per 100,000 BTU. In this simple one-input, one-output example, the TVC formula was proportional to the output Q, and the constant of proportionality 0.88 was the AVC per unit of output.

A one-input, one-output technology is the simplest kind imaginable. In the next simplest case, the technology has one output, but it may have many inputs, and it uses all inputs in fixed proportions. In this case, any increase in output requires a proportional increase in the use of all inputs. Assuming that the prices of all inputs remain the same irrespective of the output level (no volume discounts), the TVC will be proportional to the output level, as in the equation TVC = 0.88 × Q, and that constant of proportionality will be the AVC per unit of output.

Example 1   AVC of a Car

Suppose that a car gets 25 miles per gallon of gasoline, and gasoline costs four dollars per gallon. Suppose also that the car must be taken in for maintenance at a cost of $250 every 10,000 miles. Calculate the AVC of the car in dollars per mile driven.

Solution

The output of the car is miles driven, so the AVC will be expressed in dollars per mile. Four dollars for one gallon of gas takes the car 25 miles, so the average cost of the gasoline input is 4.00/25 = $0.16 per mile. The maintenance input costs $250 per 10,000 miles, so it adds 250/10,000 = $0.025 per mile to the variable operating cost of the car, for a total of $0.16 + $0.025 = $0.185 per mile driven.

Technology with Fixed and Variable Costs

One step more general, and more realistic, is a technology that has some costs of operation that must be paid whether or not the device is operating. That is, a cost in addition to the variable operating costs that arise from expenditures on inputs. Such a cost is called a *fixed cost* of operation, because it does not depend on the amount of output. The money you spend each year on the registration and insurance of your car is a fixed cost of operation, because the expenditure does not depend on how many miles you drive.

Another common example of a fixed cost is the expense to rent a device, which must be paid whether or not the device is used to produce output. We will see in example 3(c) below that the cost to purchase a device can be translated into an equivalent rental cost using the methods of financial analysis, so the purchase price is related to the fixed cost of operation.

Our analysis of the costs of production focuses on the output and expenses in a particular time period, such as a year. Thus, the quantity Q of output is meant as a rate of output, such as Q units per year. If we write F for the fixed cost of a device (per year) and v for the variable operating costs per unit produced, then the total operating cost TC has the equation

$$TC = F + v \times Q \qquad \text{(Total Cost Equation)}$$

For example, if the car in example 1 had an annual registration fee of $60 and an annual insurance cost of $500 (and it was a gift to the owner, so we don't consider the purchase price here), then the total annual cost of driving the car Q miles per year would be

$$TC = 560 + 0.185 \times Q \text{ (dollars per year)}$$

The average total cost (in $ per mile) is always the total cost TC divided by the output rate Q. In this model equation, which considers both fixed and variable operating costs, the ATC is not a constant. It depends on the annual usage rate Q, because the fixed costs of operation have to be spread out, on average, across the Q units of usage,

$$\text{ATC} = \frac{TC}{Q} \qquad \text{(definition of average cost)}$$

Substitute the formula for TC, $\text{ATC} = \dfrac{560 + 0.185 \times Q}{Q}$

$$\text{ATC} = \frac{560}{Q} + 0.185 \text{ ($ per mile)}$$

We saw above that the total cost is the sum of the fixed cost and the total variable cost, $TC = F + v \times Q$. Dividing both sides of that equation by Q shows that the ATC is the sum of the average fixed cost (AFC) and the average variable cost (AVC).

$$\frac{TC}{Q} = \frac{F}{Q} + v$$

$$ATC = AFC + AVC$$

These concepts will be helpful in the break-even analysis that follows in Chapter 7. A technology *breaks even* at the output rate where the average total cost of production is equal to the price that the output can sell for. The variable cost per unit may not depend on the output level (in the simple technology model used here), but the AFC will always depend on the output quantity Q. It is often very revealing to see how the ATC of using a technology breaks down into its average fixed and variable costs.

Example 2   ATC of a Car

Continuing example 1, suppose that the cost of registration and insurance is $560 per year. Calculate the ATC of the car if it is driven 2,000 miles per year, 5,000 miles per year, or 10,000 miles per year.

Solution

The output of the car is miles driven, we must calculate the ATC for three cases, $Q = 2,000$, $Q = 5,000$, and $Q = 10,000$ miles per year, using the ATC equation above.

Case 1. $Q = 2,000$ miles per year.

$$ATC = \frac{560}{2,000} + 0.185$$

$$ATC = 0.28 + 0.185 = 0.465 \ (\$ \text{ per mile})$$

Case 2. $Q = 5,000$

$$\text{ATC} = \frac{560}{5,000} + 0.185 = 0.112 + 0.185$$

$$\text{ATC} = 0.295 \; (\$ \text{ per mile})$$

Case 3. $Q = 10,000$

$$\text{ATC} = \frac{560}{10,000} + 0.185 = 0.056 + 0.185$$

$$\text{ATC} = 0.241 \; (\$ \text{ per mile})$$

This example shows that, because of the fixed cost of $560 per year, the average cost of operating the vehicle is $0.465 per mile when used 2,000 miles per year, but it drops to $0.295 per mile at 5,000 miles usage and $0.241 per mile at 10,000 miles usage.

Levelized Cost of Capacity

Examples 1 and 2 assumed that the car was a gift, so those examples did not consider the purchase price of the car as part of its average cost of operation. A realistic consideration of total and average cost must account for the purchase price of a device.

The purchase price is paid only once, not every year like the car registration and insurance, so the purchase price itself cannot be related to a cost per mile *per year*. However, in the theory of finance, any amount of value paid today (a *present value*) can be made equivalent to a series of equal payments spread out over a known period of time. For example, suppose that the car in examples 1 and 2 is a used car that has a present value of $6,000 and that has an estimated five years of useful life remaining. You might think to divide the $6,000 price by the five years remaining and allocate the expense as $1,200 per year for five years. However, that method does not give proper consideration to the interest that an investor could earn on $6,000. It is more appropriate to think of an investor who would buy the car for $6,000 and then lease it to you for five years at a constant lease payment each year.

The annual lease payment that should be charged for the use of a device can be calculated in Microsoft Excel using the *payment* function PMT. Its syntax is

$$=PMT(rate, nper, pv)$$

where *rate* is the discount rate that the decision-maker uses to evaluate cash flows over time; in similar contexts it may be called a rate of interest or expected rate of return. It is written as a percentage per period (here, per year), such as 10 percent. The *nper* in the PMT function is the number of periods (here, years), and *pv* is the present value of the investment, which here is the purchase price of the car.

Suppose that an auto leasing company wants to get a return on its investments of 9 percent per year. We find the annual lease payment by giving the formula to Excel as

$$=PMT(9\%, 5, 6000)$$

The = symbol is necessary in this expression to tell Excel that one of its financial functions follows. Excel uses commas to separate numbers in its functional formulas, which means that Excel cannot interpret commas *within* a number, such as in 6,000. Typing 6,000 as the third number in the formula would appear to Excel as the two numbers 6 and 000 separated by a comma. The spreadsheet program in OpenOffice uses the same financial function names and syntax as Excel, but OpenOffice uses semicolons to separate its numbers, so it does permit a price to be entered as 6,000.

Using the Excel formula given above, we find that the annual lease payment that is equivalent to a single present payment of $6,000 is $1,542.55 per year. The fact that this is more than the simple $1,200 per year accounts for the 9 percent interest per year that the leasing company is getting.

In Excel, the number that results from the formula $=PMT(9\%, 5, 6000)$ appears as (1,542.55) and is colored red. The parentheses and red color are Excel's way of indicating a negative number. In Excel's financial functions, a positive number for the *pmt* or *pv* quantities indicates a cash inflow, and a negative number means an outflow. Our use of 6000 for the *pv* represents the perspective of the car owner, who received (inflow, positive) $6,000 in the form of a car and who must therefore pay (outflow, negative) $1,542.55 per year under a lease contract.

The PMT function *annualizes* or *levelizes* the $6,000 payment into a series of five payments of $1,542.55 each. Thus, the lease payment that is equivalent to a present value, under a specific assumption about the interest rate received by the investor, is called the *annualized cost* or *levelized cost* of the device. Whereas the price paid for a car is expressed in dollars, the lease payment or annualized cost is expressed in dollars *per year*.

Example 3   Natural-Gas Fired Electric Generator

A factory is considering the purchase of a supplemental electric generator that has a capacity of 50 kW, costs $75,000, and would have a useful life of 15 years. The generator is 35 percent efficient in converting the chemical energy of the natural gas into electric energy. The current price of natural gas is $0.80 per therm. Maintenance expense is expected to be $1,000 per year. Investors who are in the business of leasing such equipment would expect a rate of return of 9 percent per year, so the factory will use that as its discount rate for the evaluation of this investment decision.

(a) What is the capacity cost of the generator?
(b) Considering only the use of natural gas as a fuel, what is the AVC per kWh generated?
(c) Considering both the maintenance expense and the annualized cost of purchasing the generator, what are the fixed costs of operation per year? *For simplicity, ignore depreciation and other tax-related aspects of the purchase.*
(d) If the generator operates for 2,000 hours per year what is the ATC of the electric energy produced, per kilowatt-hour?

Solution

(a) The capacity cost of the generator is the purchase price of the generator divided by its capacity, $75,000/50K = $1.50 per watt of capacity.

(b) To find the cost of output, we must first look at the technology from the engineering perspective and perform an input–output analysis. Its input is natural gas (in therms, 100,000 BTU) and its output is electric energy (in kilowatt-hours, kWh), but the process is only 35 percent efficient. The conversion factor from BTU to kWh is 1 BTU = 0.00029307 kWh, so 1 therm = 29.307 kWh. At 35 percent efficiency, the output from the generator will be only 29.307 × 35 percent = 10.26 kWh per therm of natural gas input. Now use the input-price information to determine the AVC of the output: each therm costs $0.80, so the 10.26 kWh produced from 1 therm costs $0.80/10.26 = $0.078. In other words, the AVC of production is 7.8 cents per kWh.

(c) The maintenance expense is a fixed cost of $1,000 per year. The purchase price of $75,000, levelized over 15 years at a discount rate of 9 percent per year has an annualized cost given by the Excel formula =PMT(9%,15,75000), which is a fixed cost of $9,304.42 per year.

(d) If the generator operates at a rate of 50 kW for 2,000 hours per year, it will produce 50 × 2,000 = 100,000 kWh of electric energy. At that level of output, the maintenance cost of $1,000 per year contributes $1,000/100,000 = $0.01 per kWh to the AFC of the electric energy. Dividing the annualized purchase price, $9,304.42 by 100,000 kWh output per year adds $0.093/kWh or 9.3 cents per kWh to the AFC of using the generator for 2,000 hours per year. Thus, the maintenance cost and the annualized purchase price add $0.01 + $0.093 = $0.103 or 10.3 cents per kWh to the ATC of production. Together with the AVC of 7.8 cents per kWh found in part (a), this gives an ATC of $0.181 or 18.1 cents per kWh of electric energy output, when the generator is run for 2,000 hours per year.

The previous example uses several important concepts in the analysis of power systems. The *cost of capacity* is expressed as $/W (dollars per watt). The *cost of energy* is expressed as $/kWh. The *annualized purchase price* is expressed in $/year, but it can be converted to $/kWh by assuming a particular rate of output (kWh/year): the annualized purchase price ($/yr) *divided* by the output rate (kWh/yr) results in a measure of $/kWh, the average annual fixed cost per kilowatt-hour. When that is added to the variable cost per kilowatt-hour ($/kWh), the result is known in the electric power industry as the *levelized cost of electricity* (LCOE). In economic terms, LCOE would be called the annualized average total cost (ATC).

Tech Focus: Energy Supply for Electric Vehicles

Electric vehicles use electric energy to drive an electric motor that turns the wheels of the car. This is in contrast to internal combustion vehicles, which use gasoline or diesel fuel in an internal combustion engine (ICE) that turns the wheels of the car. In electric vehicles, the electric energy can come either from a battery or from a fuel cell. At present, purely electric vehicles in the United States are almost all battery powered. These battery electric vehicles (BEVs) are sold commercially by Nissan, Renault, Mitsubishi, and the American firm Tesla. Hybrid vehicles that have plug-in chargeable batteries along with an ICE are known as plug-in electric vehicles (PEVs) and are available from many manufacturers.

As of 2014, there have been only a few hundred fuel cell electric vehicles (FCEVs) on lease in the United States from Toyota, Hyundai, Honda, Ford, and BMW. In 2015, Toyota is expected to release an FCEV for sale at a price under $70,000, pushing this technology further into the attention of the American public. However, the common perception is that the FCEV technology has a way to go before it will be competitive with the BEV. The CEO of Tesla, a maker of BEVs, has even called fuel cells *fool cells*. In the following three examples, we investigate the economics of the battery and fuel-cell technologies as power supplies for electric vehicles.

Battery Storage for Electric Vehicles

Batteries are heavy, and they have a low ability to store energy per unit of weight in the battery, but they are perceived to be safe to operate, and their zero emissions *at the tailpipe* (in fact, there is no tailpipe in a BEV) give them an appeal to environmentally conscious consumers.

Example 4   Battery Storage in a BEV

The Nissan Leaf is a BEV that has an engine power of 80 kW and gets up to 3.5 miles per kWh. Its battery can hold 24 kWh of energy of which the recommended discharge in each round of use is not more than 80 percent. The replacement battery pack weighs 300 kg (660 lb.), costs $5,500 plus $200 for installation, and is warranted for five years or 60,000 miles, whichever comes first. A home charging station for the Leaf costs $1,000, and for the purpose of this example we assume a useful life of 10 years. Nissan does not publish the efficiency losses of its battery upon charging or during storage or discharge, but we may conservatively assume the battery loses 5 percent of the energy taken in when it is charged, and it loses 5 percent of its stored energy during storage or when it is being discharged. For financial purposes, assume a personal discount rate of 6 percent per year. Consider the following questions for an owner who drives the Nissan Leaf 12,000 miles per year.

(a) What is the capacity cost of the Leaf battery?
(b) What is the expected driving range of the Leaf on one charge of the battery?
(c) What is the levelized cost of the battery, and what is the levelized cost of the charging station? What is therefore the total levelized cost of the system?
(d) How much energy does an owner use when driving 12,000 miles per year?
(e) What is the AFC of the energy delivered to the motor over 12,000 miles per year?
(f) If the price of residential electric energy is $0.12 per kWh, and the user always charges the Leaf at home using the charging station, what is the effective price of the electric energy, recognizing the one-way efficiency loss of the system?
(g) What is the ATC of electric energy delivered to the motor for the owner who drives the Leaf 12,000 miles per year?
(h) How does the answer to (g) change if the Leaf goes 20,000 miles per year?

Solution

(a) Recall that batteries are unusual as a technology in their definition of capacity. For batteries, the meaning of capacity follows the familiar use of the word as an amount that can be stored, not the main definition as output rate per unit of time. The capacity cost of the Leaf battery is therefore its installed cost $5,700 divided by its capacity of 24 kWh, giving 238 $/kWh.

(b) The expected range of the Leaf will be the dischargeable capacity of the battery, which is 80% of 24 kWh, discounted for a one-way loss of electric energy in storage and discharge equal to 5 percent, then multiplied by the efficiency of the Leaf in miles/kWh. We get 80% $\times$ 24 $\times$ (1–5%) $\times$ 3.5 = 64 miles.

(c) The life of a BEV battery is limited by its usage, not by the passage of time. We use the warrantied 60,000 miles as the useful range, so at a usage of 12,000 miles per year, the Leaf battery will last five years. The levelized cost of the $5,700 battery over this five-year calendar life is given by the spreadsheet function =PMT(6%,5,–5700), which returns the number $1,353 per year. The levelized cost of the $1,000 charging station over its 10-year warranted life is given by the spreadsheet function =PMT(6%,10,–1000), which returns the number $136 per year. The total of these is $1,489 per year.

(d) The amount of energy that must go into the electric motor, when the owner drives 12,000 miles per year is 12,000 (miles/year) divided by 3.5 (miles/kWh) = 3,429 kWh per year.

(e) The average fixed cost (AFC) of the energy delivered to the motor in a year is the levelized system cost $1,489 divided by the 3,429 kWh delivered per year, which is $0.434 per kWh.

(f) The amount of (input) energy that needs to be drawn from the owner's house, through the charging station, into the battery is equal to the (output) energy stored in the battery divided by the 95 percent efficiency of the charging process. Therefore, the effective price of the stored energy is $0.1200/95% = $0.1263. This stored energy is subject to another 5 percent efficiency loss when it is discharged from the battery, causing the effective price of the energy delivered to the motor to be $0.1263/95% = $0.133 per kWh.

(g) The total average cost of energy delivered to the motor, assuming 12,000 miles driven per year, is therefore $0.434 + $0.133 = $0.567 per kWh. It is interesting to see that the effective price of the energy delivered to the motor is so much higher than the price paid at the plug (the $0.12 per kWh).

(h) When these calculations are set up in a spreadsheet model, it is a simple matter to change the annual mileage from 12,000 to 20,000 and see how the answers change. Doing so, one sees that the levelized cost of the device (now over three years, not five) goes up to $2,132 per year, AFC per kWh falls only a little, from $0.434 to $0.397. The variable cost of the energy is not affected by the annual usage, so it remains $0.133, so the total average cost of delivered energy is $0.530.

This analysis reveals an important consequence of the manner by which a device exhausts its useful life. The life of the charging station is defined by calendar time, 10 years. The life of the battery depends on how much it is used. When the useful life depends on calendar time alone, then the levelized fixed cost gets spread over more miles of use, so the AFC per year goes down. But when the lifespan is defined by usage, a higher usage rate simply exhausts the device sooner, so there is little change in the AFC per year.

The conclusions of this analysis will be an important point of comparison between the BEV and the FCEV that follows in examples 5 and 6. Four calculated costs of the electric energy delivered to the motor of the electric vehicle—the annual (levelized) fixed cost, the average annual fixed cost per kWh, the variable cost (per kWh), and the ATC per kWh—will be important points of reference as we study the delivery of electric energy to an FCEV.

Hydrogen Storage for FCEVs

Hydrogen can be used as a fuel in vehicles, feeding a hydrogen fuel cell that produces electric power to drive an electric motor. Hydrogen cars and buses are a form of sustainable transportation for two reasons. One is that the hydrogen fuel can be produced either from water through the process of electrolysis using solar or wind systems for the required electric energy or from natural gas (methane) that is produced from renewable sources such as municipal waste. The second reason is that the byproduct of the use of hydrogen in either a combustion engine or a fuel cell is only water (H_2O). There are no *tailpipe emissions*.

At present, the most common commercial technology for electric vehicles is the BEV or the ICE–EV hybrid called a PEV rather than FCEV. There appear to be various reasons for the disadvantage of the FCEV, but we will focus on the economic reasons in the next two examples.

In vehicular applications, the key attributes of an energy storage system are its gravimetric and volumetric capacity. Gravimetric energy capacity is measured in energy storage per unit of weight of the system when it is filled to capacity. It is significant, because systems that are heavy, for the amount of energy they carry, make a vehicle less efficient overall. Volumetric energy capacity is measured as energy storage per unit of volume of the system when it is filled. It is significant, because a storage system that takes up too much space will compromise other uses of the vehicle. The next example gives some details about current and future hydrogen storage using compressed-gas technology using the fact that the energy density of hydrogen gas is 33.33 kWh per kg.

Example 5   Hydrogen Fuel Storage Systems

Current compressed-gas storage for hydrogen (H_2) can safely hold the fuel in a cylinder at a pressure of 700 atmospheres (10,000 lb./sq.in.). Its volumetric physical capacity of 0.0225 kg of H_2 per liter of storage unit space corresponds to a volumetric energy capacity of $0.0225 \times 33.33 = 0.75$ kWh per liter. Its gravimetric physical capacity, or *weight ratio*, of 3.5 percent (hydrogen weight to total system weight) corresponds to a gravimetric energy capacity of $0.035 \times 33.33 = 1.17$ kWh/kg.[7] The capacity cost of a 700-atmosphere system is $16 per kWh.[8] Assume that the hydrogen storage system can discharge 98.6 percent of its contents (the remainder being residual pressure in the tank when it is *empty*). Assume also that it has a useful life of 10 years, driven by calendar time, not by usage, and limited by the life of the vehicle as a whole. Create a spreadsheet model that answers the following questions about the hydrogen storage system.

(a) Current electric vehicles have an efficiency of approximately 3.5 miles/ kWh. What capacity of electric energy storage system (in kWh) would be needed to drive 300 miles?

(b) How large in volume would the storage system have to be? Compare that to a 20-gallon fuel tank in an ICE.

(c) How much would the storage system add to the weight of an electric vehicle? How does that compare to the battery in a Nissan Leaf (example 4)?

(d) How much would the hydrogen storage system cost?

(e) Assume a typical personal discount rate of 6 percent per year. What is the levelized cost of the storage system over its useful life?

(f) For a user who drives 12,000 miles per year, what is the AFC of the storage system, expressed in $ per kWh delivered to the motor?

(g) For a user who drives 20,000 miles per year, what is the AFC of the storage system, expressed in $ per kWh delivered to the motor?

(h) The U.S. Department of Energy's (DOE's) goal for 2015 was to achieve a volumetric physical capacity of 0.070 to 0.075 kg H_2 per liter of storage unit space and a weight ratio of 7.5 to 8.0 percent. Assume that such a system could be sold for eight dollars per kWh. How would that affect the AFC of the storage system?

(i) The U.S. DOE's long-term goal for hydrogen storage technology, which may have to be achieved by technologies other than compression, such as solid-state materials-based storage, is to achieve a volumetric physical capacity of 0.040 kg H_2 per liter of storage unit space and a weight ratio of 5.5 percent. Assume that such a system could be sold for six dollars per kWh. How would that affect the AFC of the storage system?

Solution

The reader should develop a spreadsheet solution using the logic presented in the following solution. Questions (g) and (h) can be answered as sensitivity analysis on the model by changing the assumptions about the gravimetric and volumetric capacities of the system.

(a) The storage system would need to deliver 300 (miles)/3.5 (miles/ kWh) = 85.7 kWh. But the system can discharge only 98.6 percent of its contents, so the capacity needed to go 300 miles will be 85.7/98.6% = 87 kWh.

(b) The system would have a volume of 87 kWh/0.75 (kWh/L) = 116 liters. One gallon is 3.785 liters, so that volume would be 116/3.785 = 30.6 gal. That would be about half again as large as a 20-gal gasoline tank in an ICE vehicle.

(c) The weight of the storage system would be 87 kWh/1.17 (kWh/kg) = 74.3 kg, which at 2.2 lb./kg corresponds to 164 lb.

(d) At a capacity cost of $16/kWh, the system would cost 16 × 87 = $1,391.

(e) The levelized cost of that system over a 10-year useful life would be given by the spreadsheet function =PMT(6%,10,–1391), which returns the answer $189.03 per year.

(f) A usage of 12,000 miles per year corresponds to 12,000/3.5 = 3,428.6 kWh per year. Divided into the $189.03 levelized cost, this gives an AFC of *$0.055 per kWh* of energy delivered from storage, meaning 5.5 cents per kWh.

(g) Replacing 12,000 by 20,000 as the annual mileage in a spreadsheet solution to this problem reveals a new AFC of delivered energy, *$0.033* per kWh. Percentagewise, this is a significant decrease in the per-kWh cost, and it is due to the life of the storage system being defined by calendar time, not by usage.

(h) Under the DOE's target for 2015, and the assumed capacity cost falling to $8/kWh, the AFC would fall to $0.028 per kWh, which is about half of the present value.

(i) Under the DOE's long-term target, and the assumed capacity cost falling to $6/kWh, the AFC would fall to $0.021 per kWh.

The system in an FCEV that corresponds to the battery in a BEV is the hydrogen storage system *together with* the fuel cell that converts the hydrogen to electric energy that can be delivered to the motor and a battery as a secondary power source used in acceleration and in regenerative braking. We studied the economics of the hydrogen storage system in example 5. The next example looks at the economics of the fuel cell itself.

Example 6   Delivered Energy Cost from a Fuel Cell

A hydrogen fuel cell uses hydrogen to create electric power that drives the electric motor of the vehicle. Automotive fuel cells in 2013 had a capacity cost of $55/kW. Their lifespan is defined by usage, as they are expected to last 75,000 miles.[9] The fuel cell has an electric-energy efficiency of 40 percent, the remainder of the energy in the hydrogen going into heat (about 50 percent) or other forms of waste. To power the vehicle, the fuel cell must have an output of 85 kW. Its hydrogen fuel costs five dollars per kg at experimental pumping stations in California. As with the BEV, assume that the FCEV has an overall efficiency of 3.5 miles per kWh of energy delivered to the motor. The FCEV has a battery, like a hybrid car's battery, which must be considered as part of the energy-delivery system. Hybrid batteries cost about $3,000 to replace, but here we will assume a $2,500 installed cost of the battery and a lifespan of 100,000 miles. Analyze the cost structure of this energy-delivery system assuming a usage of 12,000 miles per year.

(a) How much will the fuel cell cost?

(b) How much energy will the fuel cell need to deliver to the motor over one year of use?

(c) What is the levelized cost of the fuel cell, and what is the average annual fixed cost of the fuel cell per kWh at the stated usage level?

(d) Considering the efficiency of the fuel cell, how much energy must the hydrogen storage system deliver to the fuel cell over one year?

(e) Recalling that the energy density of hydrogen is 33.3 kWh/kg, how many kilograms of hydrogen must the user purchase each year, and how much will that cost?

(f) What is the variable energy cost of the fuel cell system, in dollars per kWh delivered to the motor?

(g) What is the levelized cost of the battery system, and what is its annual fixed cost per kWh, given the stated annual usage rate?

(h) Looking back at example 6, record the levelized cost of the hydrogen storage system and the corresponding ATC of hydrogen storage for 12,000 miles driven per year.

(i) What is the total levelized cost of the fuel cell, battery, and storage system ($/year), and what is the average annual fixed cost per kWh delivered to the motor?

(j) What is the ATC per kWh delivered to the motor? (Add the AFC and the variable cost per kWh.)

(k) If the vehicle were driven 20,000 miles per year, what would be the ATC per kWh delivered to the motor?

Solution

(a) The cost of the unit will be its capacity cost $55/kW multiplied by its capacity 85 kW = $4,675.

(b) The energy that must be delivered to the motor by the fuel cell over one year is the usage 12,000 miles/yr divided by the efficiency of the vehicle 3.5 miles/kWh = 3,429 kWh/yr.

(c) The calendar lifetime of the fuel cell will be 75,000 miles/12,000 miles/yr = 6.25 years. The annualized fixed cost of the fuel cell is =PMT(6%,6.25,–4675) = $918.97 per year. The average annual fixed cost of the fuel cell is therefore 918.97 ($/yr) divided by 3,429 (kWh/yr) = 0.268 $/kWh.

(d) The energy that must go into the fuel cell, to get 3,429 kWh/year out, is 3429/40% = 8,571 kWh/year.

(e) At 33.3 kWh/kg of hydrogen the physical input to the fuel cell must be 8571/33.3 = 257.4 kg/yr. At a price of $5/kg, this will cost $1,287/yr.

(f) The variable cost of the energy delivered to the motor is therefore $1,287 divided by 3,429 kWh = 0.375 $/kWh.

(g) At 12,000 miles per year, the 100,000-mile battery will last 8.33 years. Its annualized cost is therefore =PMT(6%,8.33,–2500) = 389.96 $/year. Its average cost per kWh delivered to the motor is 389.96/3429 = 0.114 $/kWh.

(h) From example 6, the annualized cost of the storage system was $189.03, and its average cost per kWh delivered to the motor was 0.055 $/kWh.

(i) The annualized costs of the fuel cell, battery, and storage systems sum to $918.97 + $389.96 + $189.03 = $1497.96. Averaged over the 3,429 kWh used per year, the AFC of all three systems is 0.437 $/kWh.

(j) The AFC of $0.437 per kWh plus the variable energy cost of $0.375 per kWh gives an ATC of $0.812 per kWh.

(k) With this solution set up in a spreadsheet (not shown here), it would be an easy matter to change the annual usage from 12,000 miles to 20,000 miles. The result is that the AFC of $0.437 per kWh at 12,000 miles goes down only a little to $0.387, and the ATC remains high at $0.762 per kWh.

This example gave another illustration that the cost per unit does not decrease very much at higher usage levels if the lifespan of the device depends on usage rather than on calendar time. We summarize the results for 12,000 mile usage as a comparison of the battery and the fuel cell as power delivery systems for electric vehicles in Table 6.4.

The lesson from Table 6.4 is that the total fixed cost per kWh is almost the same for the battery and the fuel cell systems. The disadvantage of the fuel cell comes not from the cost of the fuel cell, battery, or storage system. It comes from the *variable cost* of the fuel cell system, which is the cost (per kWh delivered to the motor) of the hydrogen needed to run the fuel cell. That variable cost is driven by two parameters, the price of hydrogen ($5/kg) and the efficiency of the fuel cell in converting hydrogen energy into electrical energy (40 percent). If we look at hydrogen for its energy content (33.3 kWh/kg in electrical terms), then the price of hydrogen at $5/kg corresponds to 5/33.3 = $0.15 per kWh. The relatively low efficiency of the fuel cell drives the price of energy delivered to the motor up to 0.15/40% = $0.375 per kWh. The nominal price of electric

Table 6.4 Comparison of battery and fuel cell costs

	Battery		Fuel cell	
Annual vehicle usage	12,000 mi.	20,000 mi.	12,000 mi.	20,000 mi.
Fixed cost, battery ($/yr)	1,353	2,132	390	390
Fixed cost, charging station ($)	136	136		
Fixed cost, fuel cell ($/yr)			919	919
Fixed cost, H$_2$ storage ($/yr)			189	189
Total fixed cost ($/yr)	1,489	2,268	1,498	2,212
Total fixed cost per kWh used ($)	0.434	0.397	0.437	0.387
Variable cost per kWh ($)	0.133	0.133	0.375	0.375
Average total cost per kWh ($)	0.554	0.530	0.812	0.762

energy at a home charging station, $0.12 per kWh is subject to the mere 5 percent inefficiency of the charging process, running its effective price up to 0.12/95% = $0.133 per kWh.

Both battery technology and fuel cell technology can be expected to improve over time, so their comparable total fixed costs will probably not change very much relative to each other. The hope for fuel cells is that the price of the hydrogen will decrease as a national distribution system for hydrogen develops, as producers of hydrogen gain economies of scale, and as fuel cell technologies become more efficient. If the price of hydrogen were to fall to two dollars per kg, and fuel cell efficiency were to rise to 45 percent, the variable cost of the fuel cell would fall to 2/33.3/45% = $0.133 per kWh, the same number used for the battery problem in example 5, and the fuel cell would be competitive with the battery.

Take-aways

This chapter has brought together two ideas that at first seem to be wholly unrelated, the cost of buying a device and the cost to operate the device. We had to frame these two types of cost in a way that permits them to be measured in the same units, because some devices are expensive to buy but cheap to operate, and others are cheap to buy but expensive to operate. A choice between the technologies must hinge on some unified concept of *cost* that permits a direct comparison of the technologies.

- A convenient way to compare the cost to purchase or build devices of different sizes is to divide the cost of a device by its size (capacity). This is the *capacity cost* of the device. The capacity cost of a fuel cell is $55 per kW, but the capacity cost of a solar or wind power system is approximately $2,000–$5,000 per kW.
- The cost to operate a device is expressed as the *variable cost* (per unit of output), which depends on the amount and price of inputs needed to produce 1 unit of output. For example, the variable cost of a fuel cell is the cost of the hydrogen it consumes to yield one unit of output, for example, $0.375 per kWh.

- The cost of owning a device can be expressed on a per-unit basis, like the variable cost per unit, but that requires two further assumptions: (1) a discount rate to levelize the purchase price on an annual basis, and (2) an annual output rate of the device. The calculation has two steps: (1) use the PMT spreadsheet function to calculate the annualized (levelized) cost of the device over its useful life, analogous to an annual rental payment, then (2) divide the annualized cost ($/year) by the output rate (units/year) to get the average levelized cost per unit ($/unit).
- The cost of owning and operating a device is expressed on a per-unit basis, for a given annual output, as the sum of the average levelized cost per unit and the variable cost per unit.

CHAPTER 7

Break-Even Analysis

Overview

Electric power technologies have electric energy as their single output. If we can describe the cost (in dollars) of producing any quantity Q of output (measured in kWh), *and if we know the price that the output can sell for,* we can ask the question, "What level of output per year would yield revenues sufficient to cover all the costs of production?" The answer to that question is the *break-even output rate* for the technology given the prices of all inputs and the selling price of the output. The break-even problem is quite general, applying to many types of technology.

A related question that we will take up in this chapter is the comparison of two devices that produce the same output. This question arises in the replacement of an old, inefficient device by a new, more efficient device. Using a variation on the theme of break-even analysis, we will see that the choice between the old and the new technology may depend on how much the device will be used—its output rate. In sum, this chapter takes up three questions that break-even analysis can address:

- How do you calculate the break-even usage level of a device?
- How do you make the decision about replacing an existing device by a more efficient device, and why is the decision often to hold onto an existing, inefficient device?
- Under what conditions is the choice between two devices driven by their relative costs of possession and costs of operation?

Pursuing these questions, we will see, in detailed examples about wind power and solar photovoltaic (SPV) power, how spreadsheet software makes it easy to analyze break-even problems.

The Break-Even Point for a Device

The break-even question is particularly significant, because all power devices have some costs that must be paid whether the device is producing power or not. These are the fixed costs and annualized purchase price or the cost of leasing the device. If the power device were to produce only a small quantity of energy, the sale of that energy would not be enough to cover the fixed costs. What quantity of output sold, then, will exactly cover the total cost of production? That is the break-even question.

To answer that question, we look back at the cost equation for the technology. The total cost function for a device must include the fixed costs and also the cost of raw materials, fuel, energy, and labor that are necessary to operate the equipment. These latter costs, which must increase in order to produce more energy from the technology, are the variable costs of production.

In a simple mathematical model of cost, we write F for the fixed cost that must be paid per unit of time (month or year) and v for the variable cost per unit of production. We write Q for the quantity of output from the technology per unit of time. The total cost function of the device can be written as sum of the fixed cost and the total variable cost,

$$C = F + v \times Q$$

Solar power technologies have little or no variable costs, because they do not require any fuel or energy input other than sunlight, which is free. What little maintenance they require is best considered a fixed cost of keeping the solar panel operational, paid on an annual schedule, rather than a variable cost per kilowatt-hour produced. The same can be said about the maintenance of wind and hydro technologies. However, ground-source heat pumps require some electric energy as input, and conventional fossil-fueled technologies require fuel and some labor. These latter technologies have variable costs that must be calculated in order to answer the question about a break-even level of output.

The revenue from the sale of a quantity Q of output at a price of p per unit of output has the equation $R = p \times Q$. The break-even equation says *revenue equals cost*,

$$R = C$$
$$p \times Q = F + v \times Q$$

Now solve this equation for the break-even quantity of output per year, Q:

$$p \times Q - v \times Q = F$$
$$(p - v) \times Q = F$$

$$Q = \frac{F}{p - v} \qquad \text{(Break-Even Quantity)}$$

The expression $p - v$ is the price minus the average variable cost of production, which is the *profit margin* of the device, expressed in dollars per unit. F is the fixed cost, so the second of the three break-even equations above tells us that the break-even quantity Q is the rate of output per year at which the profit from the sale $(p - v) \times Q$ is just enough to cover the fixed costs F of production during the year.

Note our interpretation of the break-even quantity as a zero-profit point. This means that the break-even output rate Q *can be used as a decision rule for investing* in the device. If the expected usage of the device is less than or equal to Q units of output per year, the device would not produce more revenue than it costs to own and operate, so it should not be purchased. On the other hand, if the device can be used at a rate higher than Q units per year, it will produce a profit and would be a financially viable investment.

Example 1   Break-Even Output Quantity for a 50 kW Wind Turbine

A 50 kW wind turbine might cost $200,000 and have a useful life of 20 years. Assume that the purchase of the turbine could be financed with a bank loan at a 9 percent interest rate. The amount of electric energy the turbine can produce will depend on the average wind speed where it is located, so our task here is to determine how much energy per year would be needed just to cover the costs of production. Two questions must be answered:

(a) If the wind turbine would be used to replace electricity from a public utility that would otherwise cost $0.11 per kWh, how many kilowatt-hours (or megawatt-hours) must the turbine generate in a year?

(b) What percentage of the maximum energy output from the wind turbine does that break-even quantity represent? (That is, what is the break-even capacity factor?)

Solution

(a) There is no variable cost to operating a wind turbine, so first we determine the levelized installed cost for the turbine. The levelized cost is given by Excel using the syntax =PMT(9%,20,–200000), which returns the number 21,909, meaning a levelized cost of $21,909 per year.

The number of kilowatt-hours needed to justify that annual cost is the quantity Q that satisfies

$$\text{Revenue per year} = \text{Total cost per year}$$
$$Q \times 0.11 = 21,909$$

So
$$Q = 21909/0.11$$
$$Q = 199,175 \ (\text{kWh per year})$$

(b) The maximum output of energy from a 50 kW wind turbine in one year is its power capacity (50 kW) multiplied by the number of hours in a year. 50 kW × 365 × 24 hours = 438,000 kWh of energy per year. So, as a percentage of the maximum output, the break-even output quantity is 199175/438000 = 45.5 percent.

For a wind turbine under common operating conditions, 45.5 percent would be a very high capacity factor.

Sensitivity Analysis on a Financial Model

Let us look back at the financial model of the wind turbine and see which parameters of the model affect the break-even capacity factor. These parameters are as follows:

1. Cost of the turbine (here assumed to be $200,000)
2. Discount rate for financial analysis (here 9 percent)
3. Sale price of electric energy (here $0.11/kWh)
4. Useful life of the turbine (here 20 years)

Changing *any one* of these assumptions would change the break-even capacity factor. The practice of examining the effects of changes in these assumptions is called *sensitivity analysis* or *What if?* analysis on the solution.

We will now perform a sensitivity analysis on each of the first three parameters, one by one, to see how specific changes in each parameter would affect the break-even capacity factor. Then we will consider a collection of changes simultaneously. Motivating this analysis is the fact that government policies have been designed in recent years to make renewable energies more financially attractive. These include a 30 percent tax credit that effectively reduces the cost of the device (parameter 1), low-interest loans that reduce the discount rate (parameter 2), and producer price subsidies that effectively increase the effective selling price of the energy (parameter 3).

Our focus in this analysis is on the break-even capacity factor, which essentially defines the geographic range in which a particular device will be economically viable. Locations that have consistently high wind speeds, the best for wind power, are rare. Most regions have more variable wind speeds and lower average wind speed. The lower the average speed, and the more variable the wind speed is at a location, the lower will be the capacity factor of the wind power system and the less economical it will be. Therefore, government policies that make wind power viable at lower capacity factors will motivate the use of wind power systems more widely in the country.

A sensitivity analysis requires a recalculation of the solution to the basic problem with a change in one or more of the parameters. That can mean a lot of arithmetic and algebra, unless one uses a spreadsheet to do the calculations. So let's first set up a spreadsheet solution to the basic problem and then see how easy it is to conduct the sensitivity analysis.

Setting Up a Spreadsheet for Financial Analysis

The remarkable feature of spreadsheet software is that it permits the user to enter basic data for a problem and then calculate other quantities from those data. A change to the basic data flows automatically into the calculated quantities. The art of constructing a financial model in a spreadsheet consists in putting the parameters of the model each in their own cell and calculating other cells from them. In Figure 7.1, cells B3 to B7 contain the basic data for the wind generator problem. Those cells were colored yellow cells to clearly demark them from the other cells, which contain textual explanations that make the spreadsheet easier to understand.

We solved the wind power problem using these data in four steps. First, we calculated the *annualized cost* of the power system using Excel's payment (PMT) function, then we calculated the *break-even output* of the system in kilowatt-hours per year using the break-even formula $Q = F/(p-v)$, then we calculated the *maximum annual output* of the wind power system based on its rated capacity, then we calculated the *break-even capacity factor* by dividing the break-even quantity Q by the maximum annual output. To solve the problem in the spreadsheet, we created four new lines, one for each of these calculated quantities. The following display shows the formulas that one would type into each cell of the spreadsheet to calculate these quantities. Writing those formulas using

◇	A	B	C
1			
2	**Wind Power Financial Viability Model**		
3	Rated capacity	50	kW
4	Installed cost	200,000	dollars
5	Useful life	20	years
6	Selling price (wholesale)	0.11	$/kWh
7	Discount rate	9%	per year
8			

Figure 7.1 Parameters of the wind power financial viability model

◇	A	B	C
1			
2	**Wind Power Financial Viability Model**		
3	Rated capacity	50	kW
4	Installed cost	200000	dollars
5	Useful life	20	years
6	Selling price (wholesale)	0.11	$/kWh
7	Discount rate	0.09	per year
8			
9	Annualized installed cost	=-PMT(B7,B5,B4)	per year
10	Break-even output rate	=B9/B6	kWh per year
11	Maximum output rate	=B3*365*24	kWh per year
12	Break-even capacity factor	=B10/B11	

Figure 7.2 Formulas for calculations in the wind power model

the cell addresses of the data, rather than retyping the numerical data in the formula, is what gives the spreadsheet the ability to recalculate all quantities automatically when you change any number in the basic data of the problem, which is what we have done in the sensitivity analysis seen in Figure 7.2. The formulas used for those four calculated quantities are displayed in the figure.

Notice the negative sign in front of the PMT function in cell B9. This is necessary to show a positive number in cell B9, because Excel's sign convention is to make the PMT number the opposite sign from the present value (PV) (the installed cost, cell B4). Excel's sign convention uses positive numbers for cash *inflows* and negative numbers for cash *outflows*. The interpretation of PMT and PV as quantities having opposite sign reflects the use of this function in banking: the payment by a borrower is a cash outflow (negative number) that pays back a loan that was received by the borrower as a cash inflow (positive number) when the present value amount was borrowed.

When those formulas are typed into those cells, the spreadsheet shows the calculated quantities, not the formulas (Figure 7.3).

Wind Power Break-Even Capacity Factor (Sensitivity Analysis)

We will now perform the sensitivity analysis on the three parameters of the model that affect the break-even capacity factor and that could vary due to location or government policy. The fourth parameter, the useful life of the wind turbine, like the capacity of this turbine, is a fixed

◇	A	B	C
1			
2	**Wind Power Financial Viability Model**		
3	Rated capacity	50	kW
4	Installed cost	200,000	dollars
5	Useful life	20	years
6	Selling price (wholesale)	0.11	$/kWh
7	Discount rate	9%	per year
8			
9	Annualized installed cost	$21,909	per year
10	Break-even output rate	199,175	kWh per year
11	Maximum output rate	438,000	kWh per year
12	Break-even capacity factor	45.5%	

Figure 7.3 Outcomes of calculations in the wind power model

characteristic of the device. The parameters for sensitivity analysis are as follows:

1. Installed cost of the turbine (was $200,000)
2. Discount rate for financial analysis (was 9 percent)
3. Sale price of electric energy (was $0.11/kWh)

1. **Installed Cost:** A 30 percent tax credit is available for wind power installations. How much would that tax credit reduce the break-even capacity factor for the wind turbine?

   The installed cost of the wind power system is $200,000, so the tax credit will be 30% × 200,000 = $60,000. The owner of the wind generator may deduct that $60,000 from the amount of taxes owed at the end of the year. So, essentially the U.S. government is paying $60,000 of the cost of the wind power system. The net payment from the system owner is therefore $140,000.* Typing the number 140,000 in cell B4 over the old number 200,000, we see immediately the effect of this change (Figure 7.4).

---

* In Chapter 8, we will look in more detail at federal tax credits for renewable energy and see that the net payment is affected by the owner's state tax rate. For the example here, we ignore that complication.

◇	A	B	C
1			
2	**Wind Power Financial Viability Model**		
3	Rated capacity	50	kW
4	Installed cost	140,000	dollars
5	Useful life	20	years
6	Selling price (wholesale)	0.11	$/kWh
7	Discount rate	9%	per year
8			
9	Annualized installed cost	$15,337	per year
10	Break-even output rate	139,423	kWh per year
11	Maximum output rate	438,000	kWh per year
12	Break-even capacity factor	31.8%	

Figure 7.4 Sensitivity analysis on installed cost in the wind power model

The annualized fixed cost of the wind power generator fell to $15,337 per year, reducing the break-even output rate to 139,423 kWh per year and the break-even capacity factor to 31.8 percent from the level of 45.5 percent in the original statement of the problem. The new capacity factor is in the middle of the range of 20 to 40 percent that wind power systems are said to achieve in the United States, so the 30 percent tax credit makes wind power financially viable in a much wider region of the country.

2. **Discount Rate for Financial Analysis:** Return now to the original example, with an installed cost of $200,000, but suppose that instead of the tax credit, the wind power project is eligible for a low-interest, 20-year loan at an interest rate of 5 percent per year from the U.S. government for the entire $200,000. What would be the new break-even capacity factor?

   We solve this by typing 5 percent over the 9 percent in the original spreadsheet and inspecting the result (Figure 7.5).

   The new break-even capacity factor is 33.3 percent, not quite as low as the effect of the 30 percent tax credit, but still within the range that is achievable in many parts of the United States.

3. **Selling Price of Electric Energy:** Some states give producers of renewable energy a production credit or subsidy of $0.02 per kWh.

◇	A	B	C
1			
2	**Wind Power Financial Viability Model**		
3	Rated capacity	50	kW
4	Installed cost	200,000	dollars
5	Useful life	20	years
6	Selling price (wholesale)	0.11	$/kWh
7	Discount rate	5%	per year
8			
9	Annualized installed cost	$16,049	per year
10	Break-even output rate	145,896	kWh per year
11	Maximum output rate	438,000	kWh per year
12	Break-even capacity factor	33.3%	

Figure 7.5 *Sensitivity analysis on discount rate in the wind power model*

◇	A	B	C
1			
2	**Wind Power Financial Viability Model**		
3	Rated capacity	50	kW
4	Installed cost	200,000	dollars
5	Useful life	20	years
6	Selling price (wholesale)	0.13	$/kWh
7	Discount rate	9%	per year
8			
9	Annualized installed cost	$21,909	per year
10	Break-even output rate	168,533	kWh per year
11	Maximum output rate	438,000	kWh per year
12	Break-even capacity factor	38.5%	

Figure 7.6 *Sensitivity analysis on energy price in the wind power model*

What effect would that have on the break-even capacity factor for this 50 kW wind power generator?

It would raise the selling price from $0.11 to $0.13 per kWh. Substituting that value in cell B6 of the spreadsheet gives a new result (Figure 7.6).

The production subsidy would reduce the break-even capacity factor from the original 45.5 to 38.5 percent, which is not as much as either the 30 percent tax credit or a 5 percent (low-interest) loan.

Sensitivity analysis can study the effect of simultaneous changes in several parameters of the model as easily as individual changes. The exercises in this chapter of the Study Guide for this book explore that type of extended sensitivity analysis.

Break-Even Analysis of an SPV Power System

Consider the costs and benefits of operating an SPV system. For convenience of calculation, we will consider an SPV module that has a 1 kW rated capacity. The output of the SPV system is electric energy, measured in kWh. That output depends on how much the sun shines, which varies a lot throughout the United States.*

Our basic model will analyze the economics of SPV for a homeowner living in California, where the benefit of solar power is that it saves the owner from paying $0.17 per kWh, which we take here to be the homeowner's retail price of electric energy plus any applicable state sales tax. That is the homeowner's *avoided cost* of electric energy.

Example 2   SPV Power

In 2011, the installed cost of SPV units for homes was about $6 per W, meaning $6,000 per kW.[1] Most units had a 25-year warrantied lifetime. The electric energy from the SPV system will supplant electric energy for which the homeowner is now paying $0.17 per kWh, including sales tax. Suppose, also, that the homeowner's alternative use for investment capital would yield a 9 percent return on investment. For this analysis, we assume that there are essentially no variable costs to producing electric energy with an SPV system.

(a) What is the break-even number of kilowatt-hours of electric energy that must be generated by the SPV unit per year?
(b) What percentage of the system's capacity is that? How many hours per day of sunshine, on average across the year, does that imply?

---

* For a great map of the solar incidence throughout the United States, see U.S. National Renewable Energy Laboratory, "Dynamic Maps, GIS Data, and Analysis Tools," www.nrel.gov/gis/solar.html

Solution

(a) **Break-Even Output:** The fixed cost of the SPV unit is only the level-ized installed cost of the device, which we can calculate in Excel using the syntax =PMT(9%,25,–6000) which returns the answer $611 per year (per kW). Write Q for the quantity of electric energy needed to break even on this purchase. According to the break-even equation,

$$\text{Revenue from energy savings per year} = \text{Cost per year}$$
$$0.17 \times Q = 611$$
$$Q = 611/0.17$$
$$Q = 3,593 \text{ (kWh/yr)}$$

(b) **Capacity Factor:** Because our SPV module has a rated power capac-ity of 1 kW, if we follow the example of the wind turbine, the SPV unit could in theory produce 1 kW $\times$ 24 hr/day $\times$ 365 days/yr = 8760 kWh of energy per year. The break-even output of 3,593 kWh/yr thereby corresponds to a capacity factor of 3593/8760 = 41 percent of its theoretical maximum output.

The capacity factor for an SPV unit has to be interpreted in light of the fact that *the sun does not shine 24 hours per day*. No SPV unit anywhere on earth can have an annual capacity factor greater than 50 percent.

When we studied the capacity factor of a wind turbine, the purpose was to identify geographic regions where wind power would be financially viable. We could do that with the capacity factor, because the distribution of wind speeds at any location can be used to calculate the energy pro-duction of a given wind turbine and hence its capacity factor. We were using the capacity factor as an indicator of the *wind energy resource* at a particular location. However, the measurement of solar energy resources is not quite as simple.

Rated Capacity of an SPV Unit

SPV systems are commonly described in terms of their rated capacity in kilowatts. The definition of that rated capacity is the key to understanding how to calculate the output of an SPV system. SPV panels have a *rated capacity* that is defined under the assumption that an irradiance of 1,000 W/m^2 is streaming onto the panel at a right angle to its tilt. Recall that the efficiency of an SPV unit indicates the percentage of its irradiance that is transformed into direct current (DC) electric energy. A 1 kW solar panel must therefore have a surface area in square meters equal to the inverse of its efficiency.

Measures of the Solar Resource in a Location

One approach to the break-even problem for SPVs is to translate the annual break-even output rate of the SPV device into a number of kilowatt-hours per day, because that will reveal the number of hours per day that the sun must shine at peak strength, on average across the year, on a 1 kW SPV unit. For example 2, that calculation is

$$3,593/365 = 9.84 \ (kWh/day/kW = sun \ hours \ per \ day)$$

This break-even measure for an SPV unit is called technically the *peak sun hours* per day. It is not the same as the number of daylight hours, because the sun does not shine with the same intensity at all times of the day or at all times of the year. *Solar irradiance* is the power inherent in the solar radiation falling on a surface facing the sun. Some of the sun's energy is reflected or absorbed by the atmosphere, so the greater the angle of the sun from directly overhead, the greater is the loss of solar irradiance. As a result of this effect, solar irradiance varies by time of day and by season of the year. The *peak sun-hours* at a particular location is the average number of hours of peak irradiance (defined as 1,000 W/m^2) that would result in an energy gain equal to the actual energy received by one square meter of surface area at that location. Measured in terms of peak sun hours, the solar resource of the United States appears as shown in the map in Figure 7.7.[2]

Our SPV unit in example 2 was located in California, and if we take that to be Southern California, it can get between five and six peak sun hours. However, our break-even requirement was 9.84 peak sun hours per day, so the parameters of example 2 do not imply a financially viable SPV system.

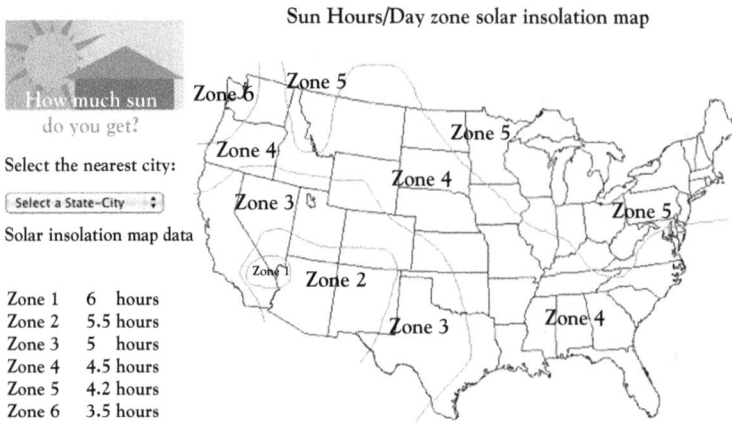

Figure 7.7 *U.S. solar resource data*

Before we continue with a sensitivity analysis on the solution to example 2, we should look a little deeper into the measurement of the solar resource at any particular location to better inform our break-even analysis.

Properly calculated, the peak sun hours include the effects of meteorological factors that affect the output of a solar power array. Clouds have a variable impact on solar irradiance at the earth's surface. Depending on how dark the clouds are, they can reduce the output of an SPV unit to as little as 10 to 25 percent of its rated capacity.[3] Similarly, smog can reduce direct solar irradiance by as much as 40 percent.[4] A direct measure of the solar resource available at a location, taking account of the meteorological factors, is the amount of solar energy received, on average across a year, by one square meter of surface area. This is termed *insolation* and is typically measured in kilowatt-hours per square meter per day, $kWh/m^2/day$. The National Renewable Energy Lab (NREL) has published maps of the United States and a calculator called PVWatts[5] that gives a location's solar energy resource in terms of insolation.

Any map or insolation calculator must state its assumptions about the orientation of the surface that is collecting the solar energy. There are four orientations that are typically used as benchmarks for insolation:

1. A surface lying flat on the ground.
2. A surface tilted at an angle equal to its latitude and facing south in the Northern Hemisphere or north in the Southern Hemisphere.

3. A surface mounted on a one-axis tracking system that follows the sun east to west during the day, tilted at a fixed angle.

4. A surface mounted on a two-axis tracking system that follows the sun both east-to-west and low-to-high during the day.

These orientations make a large difference in the amount of energy that a panel will collect during the day. In Los Angeles, the daily insolation, averaged over a year, for a panel lying flat on the ground is 5.04 kWh/m²/ day. That figure goes up to 5.63 for a surface tilted at latitude, to 6.92 for one-axis tracking and 7.27 for two-axis tracking.

Sources of insolation data on the Internet are not always clear about the orientation assumed in their data. The Gaisma database[6] reports that their data were obtained from the NASA Langley Research Center Atmospheric Science Data Center, but they do not make it clear that their data are for a panel lying flat on the ground.

The NREL map below shows the annual average daily insolation of a fixed surface facing south and tilted at an angle equal to its latitude (Figure 7.8).[7]

The values for inland Southern California and western Arizona shown on this map have a high of 6.5 to 7.0 kWh/m²/day. Los Angeles, being on the ocean and subject to clouds and rain, has an annually averaged insolation of 5.63 kWh/m²/day.

The insolation received by a solar panel depends on atmospheric and meteorological conditions as well as the path of the sun in the sky at a particular location. The NREL data are based on measures of solar radiation received at locations around the United States, so they account for factors such as smog and cloudy weather.[8] NREL's PVWatts calculator also accounts for the temperature at which the SPV device will operate, subtracting 0.5 percent in efficiency per degree Celsius above 25°C (called temperature derating), and it accounts for reflective losses off the surface of a solar panel when the sun's rays strike the panel at a more shallow angle.

The inclusion of climatic data with solar radiation data makes PVWatts a useful calculator. However, because climatic conditions vary from year to year, the PVWatts estimates of annual output from an SPV unit are still subject to an error of 10 to 12 percent.[9]

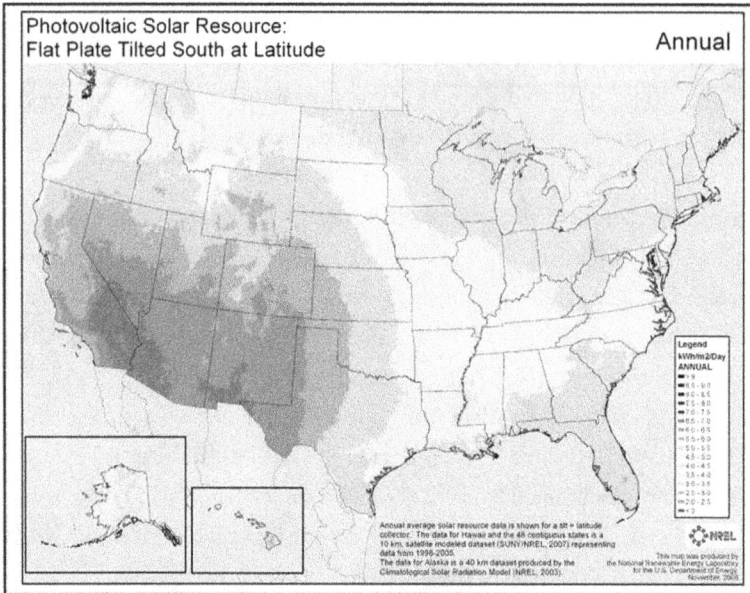

Figure 7.8 U.S. solar resource: flat plate tilted at latitude

Source: This map was created by the National Renewable Energy Laboratory for the U.S. Department of Energy.

Optimal Tilt Angle for a Fixed Solar Panel

There is no easy, accurate answer to the question of what angle a fixed solar panel should be tilted at to maximize its annual energy output. It will depend on the latitude where the panel is located, but it also depends on climatic factors such as the amount of time there is snow on the ground (reflecting the sun's rays upward, favoring a steeper angle) and clouds in the sky (diffusing the sun's radiation, favoring a shallower angle).[10] The following formula is an approximation based on latitude (L, degrees) alone, for latitudes between 25° and 50°.[11]

Approximation to Optimal Tilt: Angle = L × 0.76 + 3.1 (degrees)

For example, at 40° north latitude, the approximation to the optimal tilt would be 40 × 0.76 + 3.1 = 30.4 + 3.1 = 33.5° from horizontal.

NREL's PVWatts calculator uses a database of weather information, so one strategy using PVWatts would be to start with the approximation formula given above and try slightly higher and lower tilts to see if they improve the annual output.

Parity of Solar Power and Conventional Electric Power

Under what conditions would the SPV be at parity with conventional electric power production? To find out, we do some sensitivity analysis on the solution.

Sensitivity Analysis on the SPV Financial Model

Example 2   SPV Power (Continued)

Suppose that the buyer of the SPV unit can get a 30 percent federal tax credit.* Recalculate the effective cost of the unit and the break-even number of hours of operation per day.

Solution

With the 30 percent tax credit, the effective cost of the unit is $(1-30\%) \times 6000 = \$4,200$, and the levelized cost will be PMT(9%,25,–4200) = $428 per year. The new break-even point is $Q = 428/0.17 = 2,518$ hours of operation per year (for a 1 kW unit), meaning 6.9 peak sun hours per day. The sun hours map above shows that the best parts of California get just six hours of peak sun per day across the year, so while the tax credit helps the SPV unit get close to parity with the conventional power technologies, it is not quite there.

Break-Even Analysis in the Equipment Replacement Problem

In example 1, the point of reference for the revenue from the wind turbine was the price charged for electric energy by the public utility company, because that represents the savings that the owner of the wind turbine would realize by using the output of the wind turbine, even without selling

---

* The treatment of tax credits in this chapter is simplistic. A more realistic treatment appears in Chapter 9.

it to others. In the following example, we see that the reference point for revenue, as savings, can also be the operating characteristics of an existing device, for which the device in question could be a replacement. The use of break-even analysis in example 2, below, determines the conditions under which it is financially sensible to replace an existing furnace with an energy-efficient furnace. This example reinforces the point that break-even analysis produces a *rule for making a decision about investing in the device*.

Example 3   Break-Even Usage in a Furnace-Replacement Problem

An old home that has a 1980s-era gas-fired furnace that is only 60 percent efficient. The local natural gas utility charges $0.90 per therm (100,000 BTU). The owner can replace that furnace with an Energy Star rated furnace that has an efficiency of 95 percent. The new furnace will cost $2,500 installed, and it will have a useful life of 20 years. The current long-term mortgage interest rate of 6 percent is an appropriate reference for a required rate of return on the investment in the furnace.

(a) What level of annual heat energy loss from the home (therms/year) would make the investment in the energy-efficient furnace immediately worthwhile?

(b) What level of natural gas energy consumption with the current furnace, shown on a year's worth of gas bills, corresponds to that annual heat energy loss, and what is the current annual cost of that amount of natural gas?

Solution

(a) Write Q for the quantity of heat required to replace the heat lost from the home during a year, measured in therms/year. The current consumption of natural gas is $Q/60\%$ therms, so the annual expenditure on natural gas is $0.90 \times Q/0.60 = 1.5 \times Q$ dollars. That is the total annual operating cost of the old furnace. Now look at the energy-efficient furnace. Its efficiency is 95 percent, so it will have an annual variable (fuel) cost of $0.90 \times Q/95\% = 0.947 \times Q$. The annual fixed cost of the furnace is found using Excel's PMT function and the 6 percent discount rate for investments in real estate. The expression =PMT(6%,20,2500) in Excel returns an answer of $217.96 per year as the annualized installed cost of the new furnace. The break-even equation says that at the output rate Q, the total annual operating cost of the old furnace is equal to the total annual operating cost of the new furnace,

$$1.5 \times Q = 0.947 \times Q + 217.96$$

Solve this equation for Q to find the level of heat energy usage by the house that marks the boundary between the decision to keep the old furnace and a decision to buy a new furnace,

$$(1.5 - 0.947) \times Q = 217.96$$
$$0.553 \times Q = 217.96$$
$$Q = 217.96 / 0.553$$
$$Q = 394.1 \text{ (therms per year)}$$

(b) If the house needs 394.1 therms of heat energy per year, the old furnace will consume 394.1/60% = 656.8 therms of natural gas per year. (Recall that natural gas quantities can be measured physically in thousands of cubic feet, abbreviated as Mcf, but on utility bills they are often measured in the equivalent heat energy of the natural gas itself, hence in therms.) The corresponding annual natural gas expenditure is calculated using the utility's price of $0.90 per therm, 656.8 × $0.90 = $591 per year. So if the house had a gas bill of more than $591 per year, it would make financial sense to replace the old furnace immediately with an energy-efficient furnace. If the annual bill is below $591 per year (about $50 per month), it would be better to wait until the old furnace stops working and then replace it.

Sensitivity Analysis on the Furnace Model

We can determine the conditions under which Iowans would buy thermally efficient windows by performing *sensitivity analysis* on the solution to the previous example. In a sensitivity analysis, we change some of the assumptions (parameters) of the economic model, recalculate the solution, and then see if the break-even point would change enough that an energy-efficient furnace would make sense immediately.

1. Cost of natural gas

2. Cost of the furnace

3. Discount rate

4. Useful life of the new furnace

Example 3   Sensitivity Analysis on the Solution (Continued)

One assumption that could be changed in a sensitivity analysis of this solution is the *cost of natural gas*. We ask, "What would the price of natural gas have to be in order to make the window replacement economically sensible?" To find the answer, we resolve the break-even equation with the price of natural gas written as P (and measured as $/BTU) rather than as a given number, but we use the Iowa figure for degree days (7363 heating + 300 cooling = 7663). Here is the calculation.

$$\text{Savings per year} = \text{Total cost per year}$$
$$P \times 10 \times 24 \times 7663 \times 0.778/85\% = 11.63$$
$$P \times 1,687,662 = 11.63$$
$$P = 11.63\ /1,687,662$$
$$P = 0.000,0069\ \$/BTU$$

so
$$P = 0.69\ \$ \text{ per therm.}$$

Recall that the current price of natural gas was $0.66 per therm in the statement of the problem. The *break-even price* calculated here, of $0.69 per therm, is only a little higher than the current price. It is quite possible that the real price of natural gas could increase to that level in the future, in which case people in Iowa would start replacing their existing windows with energy-efficient windows.

Crossover Points and Arrayed Technologies

In automotive applications, electric vehicles have the advantage that their fuel cost per mile driven is quite low compared with hybrids and to cars with gasoline engines, but the plug-in hybrid electric vehicle (PHEV)

Table 7.1 Fixed and variable costs of vehicles

Device	Retail price ($)	20-Year level cost ($/yr) at 6% interest	Average variable cost ($/mile)
PHEV Leaf	47,000	4,100	0.035
Hybrid Prius	25,000	2,180	0.069
CGV 32 mpg	15,000	1,308	0.105

such as the Nissan Leaf or Chevrolet Volt is more expensive to buy than a hybrid like the Toyota Prius, and the hybrid is more expensive than the conventional gasoline vehicle (CGV). Table 7.1 shows data on variable costs taken from the *Wikipedia* article on plug-in electric vehicles[12] and purchase prices taken from the manufacturers' websites.

The table shows a clear progression of increasing average variable costs and decreasing fixed cost (levelized purchase price). This is the condition that makes the various devices an *arrayed technology*.

In such a situation, the devices do not compete with each other. They are complementary, each being optimal for a particular range of use per year. Thus, for each pair of adjacent devices, there is a *crossover point* in usage (miles per year) that marks the boundary between the region of usage in which one or the other device is optimal. The basic relationship among these technologies can be inferred without doing the calculations. The PHEV costs so much to acquire, and so little to run, that it is best for high-mileage users or for high-mileage purposes, because the high annual fixed cost gets spread over a large number of miles. The CGV costs so little to acquire but so much to run that it is best for low-mileage users or low-mileage purposes. The hybrid is in the middle.

We find the mileage crossover points by setting the annual total cost of the hybrid equal to that of its neighbor:

High crossover point
$$2180 + 0.069 \times M = 4100 + 0.035 \times M$$
$$0.034 \times M = 1920$$
$$M = 56{,}470 \text{ miles per year.}$$

Low crossover point
$$2180 + 0.069 \times M = 1308 + 0.105 \times M$$
$$872 = 0.036 \times M$$
$$M = 24{,}222 \text{ miles per year.}$$

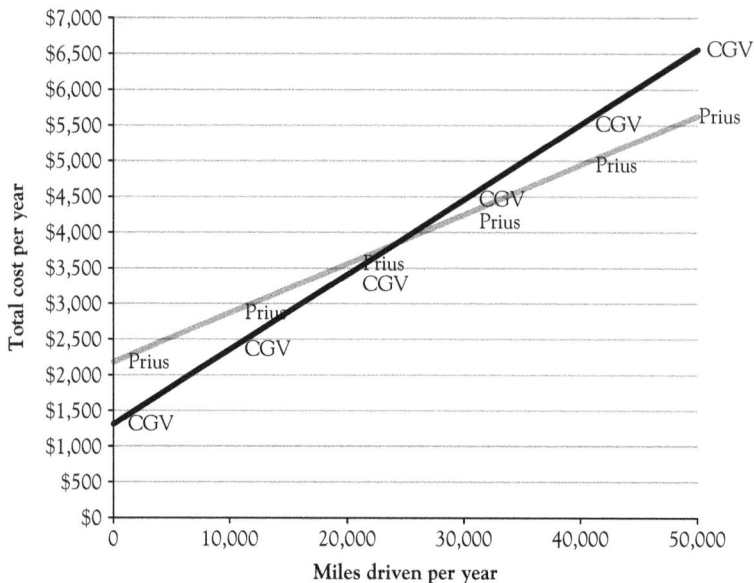

Figure 7.9 Crossover point between the CGV and the Prius

Figure 7.9 shows the graph of the two equations that define the low crossover point. Each line corresponds to a vehicle. The height of the line at $M = 0$ shows the annualized fixed cost of the vehicle. The slope of the line is the variable cost of the vehicle per mile driven. The CGV has the equation $C = 1308 + 0.105 \times M$, so its line starts at \$1,308 and rises by \$0.105 for every mile driven (\$105 per 1,000 miles). The Prius has the line that starts at \$2,180 but rises at a slope of only \$69 per 1,000 miles. The two lines intersect (the two vehicles have the same annual total cost) at 24,222 miles.

This shows that, from a purely financial point of view, without considering the greenhouse gas emissions of the various devices, the CGV is optimal for user of less than 24,166 miles per year, the Prius is optimal for users in the range between 24,166 and 56,470 miles per year, and the Leaf is optimal for users who drive more than 56,470 miles per year.

What If the Lifetimes of the Devices Depend on Usage?

The analysis of vehicles in Table 7.1 assumed that each vehicle would have a 20-year life no matter how much it was used, so each vehicle's purchase price was levelized over a 20-year life. To some extent, the useful

life of an automobile is indeed driven by calendar time. Metal components rust, and rubber components dry out with the passage of time. But
the engine and drive-train components have lifetimes that depend to a
significant extent on the number of miles driven. If an expensive car like
the Leaf is driven heavily, it might not last 20 years, or it would require
substantial reinvestment—periodically replacing the battery and even
the motor—to keep it working. With that model for the lifespan, driving
the Prius more each year just makes it more expensive to keep the car up.

Figure 7.10 shows how the crossover graph looks when the lifespan
of each vehicle is 200,000 miles, so the purchase price is levelized over
a number of years determined by the annual driving distance. We see
that the curves do not cross, and the CGV remains the less expensive
vehicle.

The lifespan model (calendar time versus usage) is therefore a very
important assumption in the economic analysis of competing technologies. An example is seen in the promotion of the Toyota fuel cell vehicle
(FCV) on the company's website. Comparing their FCV with a battery–
electric vehicle (BEV), they display a graph that looks very much like
Figure 7.9. It shows the FCV having a higher fixed cost than the BEV, due
to the higher sticker price on the FCV, but a more shallow-sloped total
cost line reflecting a lower variable (operating) cost per mile and therefore a crossover point in miles driven per year (not marked numerically
on Toyota's graph), beyond which the FCV would be the less expensive
vehicle in total.[13]

Two questions come to mind in reviewing such a graph. One is that
our analysis in Table 6.4 of the previous chapter showed that the cost of
the energy delivered to the motor is much higher for an FCV than for a
battery-powered vehicle, and we may reasonably expect that the motor
and other components of an electric vehicle are similar for the fuel cell
electric vehicle (FCEV) and BEV types, so the overall efficiency in miles
per kilowatt-hours is likely to be similar for the two vehicle types. Thus,
the higher variable cost (per kWh) of the FCEV energy-delivery system would not likely be compensated for by a lower vehicular efficiency
(miles/kWh) due to other design features and thereby result in a lower
variable cost per mile driven. These points call into question Toyota's
apparent assumption that the operating cost of the FCV is less per mile

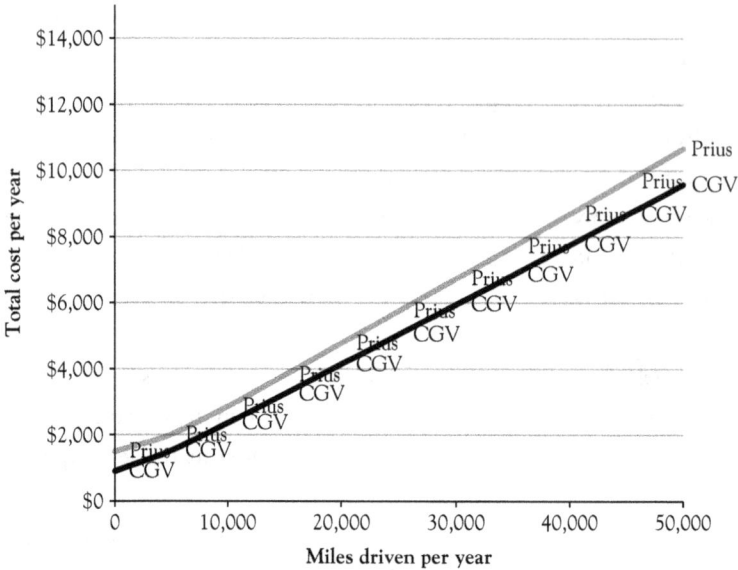

Figure 7.10 Total cost curves of the CGV and the Prius with 200,000-mile lives

than a battery-powered car. However, the main point to be seen here is that even if the FCV had a lower operating cost than the BEV, having a higher purchase price would probably cause the total-cost curve of the FCV to remain above the BEV at all levels of annual mileage, as the Prius is above the CGV in Figure 7.10.

Take-aways

The extensive examples about wind power, solar power, and home heating in this chapter brought out several important points.

- A device that produces a product for sale (such as a commercial wind turbine) or that enables the owner to avoid the expense of purchasing a similar product (such as a home solar panel) creates revenue, or its equivalent in savings, for the owner. The *break-even point* of the device is the *annual rate of output* that produces enough revenue or savings to cover the annualized fixed cost and the variable cost of the device at that output rate.

- Operating at an output rate below the break-even point, the device results in a financial loss. Above the break-even point, the device produces a profit.

- The decision to replace an existing device (usually one that is less efficient) by a newer device (that costs money but is more efficient) can be analyzed as a break-even problem. There, the *revenue* from the new device is the savings (difference) in total variable operating cost owing to its greater efficiency, and the only cost is the annualized purchase price of the new device. In many examples, the annualized purchase price of the new device is too high to be compensated for by its lesser operating cost per unit produced. This explains why firms continue with old, inefficient equipment until it fails entirely.

- In the decision context where some type of technology must be purchased and the choice is among two or more devices, the decision can be made by analyzing the total cost of ownership and operation (annualized fixed cost plus variable cost) for various levels of output per year. The total cost curves may show crossover points where two technologies have the same total cost per year; below the crossover point (at lower levels of annual use), one device is superior, and above it the other device is best.

- The simple break-even analysis and crossover analysis (Figure 7.9) hinges crucially on an assumption that the lifetime of a device does not depend on the rate at which it is used. In contexts where the useful life of a device depends on usage, the relationship between usage and lifetime must be modeled mathematically and annual costs calculated accordingly, as described for Figure 7.10.

CHAPTER 8

Basic Financial Analysis of Technology

Overview

In Chapter 7, we saw how to levelize the present purchase price of a device over its useful life in order to evaluate the costs and benefits of the device on an annual basis. In this section, we take the opposite perspective, starting with a known cash flow over time and working back to its equivalent amount as a single payment in the present. When the cash flow describes the benefits and costs of using a device, the equivalent single payment in the present represents the *value* of the device, which is the maximum amount a person should be willing to pay for it.

The examples in this chapter are set in a personal context, where a homeowner is considering an investment in an energy-saving technology. This permits a moderately realistic simplification of the financial analysis, which emphasizes the basic elements of the problem. This chapter does not present an industrial-strength financial analysis—the type that a consultant would be paid to conduct. The full analysis needed for a commercial feasibility study comes in Chapter 9. Nevertheless, this chapter treats several questions that are important for someone who is learning the basics of financial analysis:

- What is the meaning of the *present value* of a cash flow, and how can it be calculated?
- What, if anything, are the differences between an interest rate, discount rate, hurdle rate, rate of return, and yield? And, for heaven's sake, why can't economists just pick one phrase to use?

- What is an annuity, why is it important, and how do you calculate its present value?
- What different perspectives on profitability are given by the concepts of net present value (NPV) and internal rate of return (IRR)? Which one do financial decision makers tend to use?
- How do the spreadsheet functions PV, RATE, NPER, and PMT help in the analysis of financial decisions?
- Can the basic financial spreadsheet functions handle a problem, as often found in solar and wind power investments, where the benefits of the device are significantly affected by a future inflation in the price of energy from conventional sources?

This chapter continues the previous chapter's use of spreadsheets and reinforces the principles of good spreadsheet design and the use of sensitivity analysis as a way to address uncertainties in a decision context.

The Present Value of a Cash Flow

Recall that break-even analysis gives a rule for making a decision about whether or not to invest in a device. If the usage of the device would be less than the break-even point, the device would not make enough profit or savings to cover its costs. Above the break-even point, the device will make a profit. However, in many investment contexts, a deeper question is central to the analysis, which might be asked in one of two ways, "How much is the device *worth to us* if we operate it at our expected rate of use," or "What rate of return on our investment would we get if we buy that device?" To answer these questions, we must use the concept of the present value of a cash flow.

The economic perspective on technology boils the description of a device down to a statement of its cash flows. How much profit will the device make each year? Will the device have a salvage value at the end of its useful life? Those future cash flows need to be evaluated against the cost to purchase and install the device today, so the financial analysis of a technology investment requires a method to translate future amounts of money into their present-equivalent values. To that end, we now take a short excursion into the field of finance.

Discount Rates and Interest Rates

Discounted cash flow analysis recognizes that people prefer to enjoy a good or service now rather than wait and enjoy it later. People are impatient about their enjoyment of life, so $100 in the future is not worth as much as $100 that one can spend today. The link between money in the future and money in the present is provided mathematically by a *discount rate*. People who have not studied financial analysis find it easier to understand the discount rate by first understanding its close cousin, the *interest rate*, which shows how money in the present becomes money in the future.

Example 1   Future Bank Account Balance

Suppose you put $100 in a savings account that pays 4 percent interest per year
  (a) How much will you have in the account after one year?
  (b) How much after two years?

Solution

  (a) After one year, the account will have the original $100 plus 4 percent of $100 (0.04 × $100 = $4) for a total of $104.

  This answer was calculated as $100 + 4 = 104$, recognizing that the bank adds the interest to the account at the end of the year. However, a better insight into finance comes from thinking about the interest rate as growing the account multiplicatively rather than by adding interest. By the distributive law in algebra, we can rewrite the calculation of the year 1 account balance as

$$100 + 4\% \times 100 = 100 \times (1 + 4\%)$$

  In this view, the $100 becomes $104 by being *multiplied* by the *growth factor* (1 + 4%) or 1.04.

(b) The amount of money in the account after two years depends on the rule by which interest accumulates. In almost all[1] modern financial applications, interest on an account balance accrues by *compounding growth*, which means that the second year's interest is paid on the amount in the account at the start of the second year, not on the original amount in the account. Thus, at the end of year 2, the account will have

$$104 \times (1 + 4\%) = \$108.16$$

The original 104 can itself be written as $100 \times (1 + 4\%)$, so the year 2 balance can be calculated as

$$100 \times (1 + 4\%) \times (1 + 4\%) = \$108.16$$

This is the picture of compounding growth. The original $100 blows up by the growth factor 1.04 once at the end of year 1 and then a second time at the end of year 2. Using an exponential expression simplifies the presentation and the calculation,

$$100 \times (1 + 4\%)^2 = \$108.16$$

The interest rate 4 percent mathematically transforms $100 now into $108.16 after two years under the rule for compounding growth. A higher interest rate would grow the account more quickly, so today's $100 would become more than $108.16 at the end of year 2. A lower interest rate would grow the account more slowly and result in less than $108.16.

The *future value equation* shows how to calculate the future value (F) of *any* present value (P) that grows for T years at a *compounding* interest rate of r (percent per year). The general equation is expressed as the product of the present value P and the compounded growth factor,

$$F = P \times (1 + r)^T$$

---

[1] As an exception to the rule, county treasurers in Iowa charge simple interest, not compounding interest, on late payments of property taxes.

The next example shows that it is not just your savings that can grow at an interest rate. Interest rates apply to credit card balances as well.

Example 2   Future Credit Card Balance

Suppose you owe $1,500 on your credit card, and the card company charges you 24 percent interest per year. Consider three questions:

(a) How much will you owe on the card after one year if interest is charged only at the end of the year?
(b) How much will you owe on the card after one year if interest is charged monthly?
(c) How much would you owe after five years if interest is charged monthly and you did not make any payments on the account?

Solution

(a) If the credit card were to charge interest annually at 24 percent per year, on a $1,500 debt after one year the balance would be $1,500 \times (1 + 24\%) = 1,500 \times 1.24 = \$1,860$.
(b) If the credit card balance is *compounding monthly*, the credit card interest is added at the end of each month and grows from that amount in the following month. The way to solve this problem is to use months as the unit of time and use $24\%/12 = 2\%$ per month as the interest rate. In that formulation, the balance after 12 months will be

$$
\begin{aligned}
&= 1,500 \times (1 + 2\%)^{12} \\
&= 1,500 \times (1.02)^{12} \\
&= 1,500 \times 1.268 \\
&= \$1,902
\end{aligned}
$$

Compare that to the $1,860 that was calculated using one year of interest without compounding. This example shows that when the credit card company compounds its interest monthly, rather than only once a year, it gets $42 more from the credit card holder.

(c) With interest charged monthly at 24 percent per year (2 percent per month) on a $1,500 debt, after five years (60 months) the balance would be $1,500 \times (1 + 2\%)^{60} = 1,500 \times 3.281 = \$4,921.50$. The debt would have more than tripled.

Yearly Rates and Monthly Rates

One of the most important steps in solving finance problems is to reconcile the unit of time used for the future value and the interest rate. The key point in the correct solution of the example above was to see the phrase *compounding monthly* and therefore to determine the equivalent *monthly interest rate* from the yearly interest rate. The method used to do so in example 2 is called the Main Street Rule. It is appropriate to consumer-lending problems such as credit cards, bank accounts, and home mortgage loans. For example, if a bank advertises a rate of 6 percent per year, compounding monthly, you divide the annual rate 6 percent by 12 to get the monthly rate, $6\%/12 = 0.06/12 = 0.005 = 0.5$ percent per month.

In more sophisticated financial contexts, such as bond pricing, commercial leasing, and corporate investments, the conversion between interest rates of different time periods must follow the Wall Street Rule, which correctly accounts for a compounding of interest between the time periods. Consider the question of what monthly interest rate m would result in a 6 percent *annual* rate of return after monthly compounding. The monthly growth factor $(1 + m)$ would have to compound 12 times into the annual growth factor $1 + 6\%$,

$$(1 + m)^{12} = 1 + 6\%$$

Solve this for m,

$$(1 + m)^{12} = 1.06$$
$$(1 + m)^{12/12} = 1.06^{(1/12)}$$
$$1 + m = 1.00487$$
$$m = 0.00487$$
$$m = 0.487\% \text{ per month.}$$

The Wall Street Rule gives the monthly interest rate that corresponds exactly to the annual interest rate. Why doesn't 0.5 percent monthly compound up to a 6 percent annual rate? The answer is that the effect of compounding is to pay interest on the interest that accumulates during the periods of the compounding. A 0.5 percent monthly interest rate has a growth factor that, in fact, compounds over 12 months to $(1 + 0.5\%)^{12}$ or 1.0617. Thus, the 0.5 percent monthly interest rate actually yields 6.17 percent interest at the end of one year.

When banks advertize home mortgage loans at *6 percent interest, paid monthly* they are allowed to calculate the monthly interest rate as 6%/12 = 0.5% even though it means that the borrower is really paying 6.17 percent interest per year. In consumer finance, the actual yield is called the *annual percentage yield* (APY), which banks are required to disclose when they advertise their loans in this way.

The Present Value of a Single Future Value

A discount rate is just an interest rate looked at from the opposite perspective on time. For example, suppose you have a legal contract according to which you will receive $1,000 exactly five years from now. How much would you sell that contract for today? Today's selling price for the contract would be *your present value* of the future $1,000. A person's answer to the question about that selling price tells a lot about how they make the trade-off between money now and money in the future.

Example 2a $1,000 Contract

Suppose that Thomas owns a contract that will pay $1,000 exactly five years from now. Thomas also has opportunities to invest money today in ways that would earn a return of 6 percent per year. What is the contract worth to him today, if both the contract and the investment opportunity are perfectly safe?

Solution

The contract should be worth whatever amount of money Thomas *could grow to be* $1,000 in five years. The future value equation in this context would appear as

$$F = P \times (1 + r)^T$$
$$1,000 = P \times (1 + 0.06)^5$$

To answer the present value question, we would have to solve this future value equation for P. To save time, we solve for P in the general future value equation to get the *present value equation* that calculates the solution directly,

$$P = \frac{F}{(1 + r)^T}$$

$$P = \frac{1,000}{(1 + 0.06)^5}.$$

$$P = \frac{1,000}{(1.06)^5}.$$

$$P = \frac{1}{(1 + r)^5}$$

$$P = 747.27$$

The conclusion is that Thomas would value the contract at $747.27 even though it promises to pay $1,000 in five years. The $747.27 present value is the *discounted value* of the future $1,000.

Another way to write the present value equation is as a multiplication,

$$P = F \times \frac{1}{(1 + r)^T}$$

This version of the equation shows that the present value is equal to the future value F *multiplied* by a number, called the *discount factor*, which is less than one.

Example 2b $1,000 Contract

Carl owns a contract that will pay $1,000 exactly five years from now, and he is willing to sell that contract for $600 today. What does that say about Carl's personal discount rate?

Solution

When a finance problem involves a present value and a single future value, at just one point in time, the future value equation shows how the present value, future value, time, and discount rate are all related,

$$F = P \times (1 + r)^T$$

In this case, the F, P, and T are all known, and only the discount rate r remains to be calculated. Substituting the values for these variables leaves the equation

$$1{,}000 = 600 \times (1 + r)^5$$

This is a power equation. To solve it algebraically, we divide through by 600,

$$(1 + r)^5 = \frac{1{,}000}{600}$$

calculate the quantity on the right,

$$(1 + r)^5 = 1.6667$$

Raise both sides of the equation to the one-fifth power,

$$(1 + r)^{5 \times 1/5} = (1.6667)^{1/5}$$

calculate,

$$(1 + r)^1 = 1.1076$$

Knowing that any number raised to the one power is just that number, we see

$$1 + r = 1.1076$$

subtract one from both sides to see the discount rate,

$$r = 0.1076 \text{ or } 10.76 \text{ percent}$$

Examples 1 and 2 demonstrate an important point. Carl puts a *lower* value ($600) than Thomas ($747.27) on the promised future $1,000, because Carl has a greater *urgency* for money, which corresponds to a *higher* discount rate for Carl (10.76 percent) than for Thomas (6 percent).

The Present Value of an Annuity

In our analysis of investments in devices such as solar photovoltaic (SPV) units or wind turbines, we saw that the initial investment in the device produces a flow of revenue or savings over the useful life of the device. In our analysis, we assumed that the revenue would be the same each year. This means that the cash flow from the device is a series of identical payments spaced equally in time over the life of the device. Such a cash flow is called an *annuity*. Just as we could calculate the present value of a single future value, it is possible to calculate the present value of a series of future values. The mathematics to calculate the present value for an annuity is more complex than for a single future value, but spreadsheet programs have programmed the formula into a function that will do the calculation. The syntax in Excel for the *present value function* is

$$= \text{PV}(rate, nper, pmt)$$

The *rate* is the discount rate used in the evaluation; *nper* is the number of periods in the annuity, such as the number of years of useful life of a device; and *pmt* is the periodic payment as a return to the investor, such as the annual profit resulting from the operation of the device.

Example 3   The Value of a Residential SPV System

According to NREL's PVWatts calculator, the annual average insolation rate in Tampa, Florida, is 5.37 kWh/m²/day. Consider a fixed 1 kW solar panel that is pointed south and tilted at latitude. It is wired to a battery bank and an inverter that have a composite efficiency (derate factor) of 77 percent in transforming the panel's direct current (DC) electric energy into alternative current (AC) electric energy for use in a house. The retail price of electric energy in Florida is $0.1165 per kWh. Assume that the

SPV system will have a useful life of 25 years and that the insolation is constant at its annual average.[2] Use 6 percent per year as a discount rate for evaluating the investment in the SPV system.

(a) How much is the SPV system worth to a Tampa homeowner, per kilowatt of capacity?
(b) If the homeowner can get a 30 percent tax credit for this investment, what retail price should he or she be willing to pay for the SPV system?

Solution

(a) The SPV system will have an annual production of $5.37 \times 365 =$ 1,960 kWh of DC energy. After conversion losses, the resulting AC energy is $1,960 \times 77\% = 1,509$ kWh. Valued at $0.1165 per kWh, this output is worth $175.83 *per year* to the homeowner. That annuity of $175.83 per year for 25 years, evaluated using a 6 percent discount rate, is worth *an investment* of up to

$$= PV(6\%, 25, 175.83)$$
$$= (\$2,248)$$

Excel returns a negative number as the answer, meaning that it would be worth *spending* (cash outflow, negative) $2,248 per kW in order to get the flow of savings (cash inflow, positive) from the SPV unit over its useful life.

(b) A net cost of $2,248 per kW after a tax credit of 30 percent corresponds to a retail price of 2248/(1 − 30%) = $3,211 per kW.[3]

---

[2] The assumption of constant insolation across the year typically results in an overestimate of annual production by 5 to 10 percent. The PVWatts calculator produces a monthly estimate of output that sums to a more realistic estimate of the annual production. The difference is due to PVWatts accounting for the loss of efficiency (temperature derating) of an SPV system at a rate of −0.5 percent per °C of temperature above the standard testing condition of 25°C (77°F).

[3] In states that have income tax, the federal tax credit creates an additional cost in state taxes, but we ignore that here to simplify the exposition. See Chapter 9 for the full treatment of tax credits.

Sensitivity Analysis on the Solution

What would be the value of the system if it were located in Los Angeles, which has an average annual insolation of 5.63 kWh/m²/day and pays a retail price of $0.171 per kWh?

The best approach to sensitivity analysis is to set up a spreadsheet that can solve the problem in general. With the old parameters, it appears as shown in Figure 8.1.

Substituting the new insolation value as 5.63 and the new price as $0.171, we get a new solution (see Figure 8.2)

◇	A	B	C
1			
2	**SPV System Financial Valuation**		
3	Rated capacity	1	kW
4	Useful life	25	years
5	Derate factor (DC to AC)	0.77	
6	Location's Insolation	5.37	kWh/m2/day
7	Energy price or savings	0.1165	$/kWh
8	Discount rate	6%	per year
9	Tax credit for homeowner	30%	of installed cost
10			
11	Annual production of AC energy	1,509	kWh per year
12	Annual savings in energy cost	$175.83	per year
13	PV of annual savings	$ 2,248	
14	Max retail price before tax credit	$ 3,211	

Figure 8.1 SPV model parameters

◇	A	B	C
1			
2	**SPV System Financial Valuation**		
3	Rated capacity	1	kW
4	Useful life	25	years
5	Derate factor (DC to AC)	0.77	
6	Location's Insolation	5.63	kWh/m2/day
7	Energy price or savings	0.171	$/kWh
8	Discount rate	6%	per year
9	Tax credit for homeowner	30%	of installed cost
10			
11	Annual production of AC energy	1,582	kWh per year
12	Annual savings in energy cost	$270.58	per year
13	PV of annual savings	$ 3,459	
14	Max retail price before tax credit	$ 4,941	

Figure 8.2 SPV sensitivity analysis results

There in Los Angeles, the retail price of the system could be as high as $4,941 per kW, and it would still be economical for homeowners.

Measures of Profitability

The break-even analysis gives a rule for deciding when to invest in a device, whether it would be profitable or unprofitable, but it does not tell *how* profitable an investment would be. However, there are two measures of profitability that financial analysts focus on. NPV is one, and the rate of *return on investment* (ROI) or IRR is the other. Each gives a different perspective on how profitable an investment is, and in doing so they indicate whether the investment is profitable or not.

These measures of profitability are useful only to the extent that the analysis correctly considers all costs associated with the technology and all benefits that come from using the technology. The market prices of inputs and the price of the output are an economist's guide to costs and benefits. Sustainable technologies typically address a wider concern, one that accounts for the environmental consequences of using a technology. Car owners can pollute the air with carbon dioxide and oxides of nitrogen, but they don't have to pay for it directly. Everyone pays for it through the effect of pollutants on global warming and acid rain and ozone depletion. Economists and policy makers are looking for ways to incorporate these environmental effects into the financial analysis of technologies. In Chapter 10, we will look at those policies and practices in some detail. Here, we assume that the costs and benefits have been completely accounted for.

The investment decision can be made in either of two ways:

1. Setting a target rate of return and evaluating the NPV of the cash flows for the technology using that rate of return, looking to see if the NPV is positive; or
2. Setting a target rate of return and evaluating the IRR of the cash flows for the technology to see if the IRR is greater than the target rate of return.

For investment projects whose cash flow starts out negative (a payment for equipment) and then becomes positive and stays positive (due to benefits from using the equipment), these two ways of making the investment decision give the same answer. NPV and IRR give two different perspectives on the degree of profitability of an investment, so it is useful to evaluate a technology investment by both methods.

The valuation question presented in example 3 and solved using the PV function did not require any information about the cost of the device; its value was determined entirely by the future cash flow. However, the measures of profitability require specific knowledge of the installed cost of the device as well as the cash flow. The cost of the device becomes a key point of reference in measuring its profitability.

Net Present Value

The NPV of a device is the present value of its benefits minus the investment that is required. We saw above that the spreadsheet function PV can calculate the present value of a benefit flow that has the form of an annuity—identical benefits spaced equally in time over a specific lifetime. Subtracting the investment amount from that present value gives the *net* present value.

Example 4a   The Profitability of a Residential SPV System (NPV)

Consider a fixed 1 kW solar panel that is pointed south and tilted at latitude. Its wiring, battery bank, and inverter have a composite efficiency (derate factor) of 77 percent. The installed cost of the system is $4,800 (mid-2013), and it has a useful life of 25 years. The homeowner can get a 30 percent tax credit for this investment. The system is located in Los Angeles, where the average insolation is 5.63 kWh/m²/day and the retail price of electric energy is $0.171 per kWh. Use 6 percent per year as a discount rate for evaluating the investment in the SPV system.

(a) What is the NPV of the investment in this system? What should be the decision regarding investment in the device?

Solution

(a) We saw in example 3 that the flow of revenues (savings) from using this system would have a present value of $3,459. The installed cost of the system, net of the 30 percent tax credit, is $4,800 – $1,440 = $3,360. The NPV of the investment is therefore a positive number, $3,459 – $3,360 = $99. Projects that have a positive NPV add to the wealth of the owner. Because the NPV is positive, the project is financially viable, in Los Angeles.

Internal Rate of Return

The other way to look at an investment project is to ask, "If we make the required investment in this project, and we get the flow of cash that we are expecting as a return on the investment, what *rate of return* does that give us?" That rate of return is analogous to the interest rate that you would be getting if it were a bank that accepted your deposit of the investment amount and paid you back according to the schedule of the expected cash flow of the project. This rate of return is determined strictly by the investment amount and the amount and timing of the cash flows in return, not by a bank the way an interest rate would be, so in this context the rate of return may be called the *internal rate of return* of the investment and is abbreviated as IRR.

The decision rule for investment is that the IRR of a project should be at or above the decision-maker's discount rate in order to justify the investment. In this context, the decision-maker's discount rate is sometimes called a *hurdle rate*. If the IRR of a project can clear the hurdle, the project gets funded.

The IRR is easy to calculate using a spreadsheet function when the cash flow consists of a single present-value investment and then an annuity-type cash flow as the return on the investment—a flow of identical payments at equal intervals of time over a specific project lifetime. The rate of return of such a project is calculated in Excel using the RATE function with the syntax

$$= \text{RATE}(nper, pmt, pv)$$

where *nper* is the number of periods in the lifetime of the project, *pmt* is the amount of the payment in each period as the return on the investment, and *pv* is the present value that is paid as the investment amount. Recall two key points about Excel: (1) the present-value investment is interpreted as a cash outflow (negative), and the payments in return are a cash inflow (positive), so that sign convention must be used when presenting the parameters to the RATE function, and (2) the payment *pmt* must be on the same time unit as the *nper* lifetime of the project, not dollars per month on the payment with years on the lifetime.

Example 4b   The Profitability of a Residential SPV System (IRR)

Consider a fixed 1 kW solar panel that is pointed south and tilted at latitude. Its wiring, battery bank, and inverter have a composite efficiency (derate factor) of 77 percent. The installed cost of the system is $4,800, and it has a useful life of 25 years. The homeowner can get a 30 percent tax credit for this investment. The system is located in Los Angeles, where the average insolation is 5.63 kWh/m^2/day and the retail price of electric energy is $0.171 per kWh. Use 6 percent per year as a hurdle rate for evaluating the investment in the SPV system.

(a) What is the IRR on the investment in this system? What should be the decision regarding investment in this device at this location?

Solution

(a) This problem is the same as in examples 3 and 4a. The installed cost of the system, net of the 30 percent tax credit, is $3,360. The cash flow of revenues (savings) from using this system consists of $270.58 *per year* over the 25-year useful life of the device, which is an annuity type of cash flow. The IRR is calculated by the RATE function using 270.58 (positive) as the *pmt* and –3360 (negative) for the present-value investment to respect the sign conventions that Excel uses,

$$= \text{RATE}(25, 270.58, -3360)$$

In the absence of any other formatting for the cell in which that formula is typed, Excel will return an answer that is rounded to the nearest whole-number percent,

6%

In an investment context, a rate of return should be shown with at least two significant digits. Formatting the cell to show one more digit, as a decimal value in the percentage, reveals a more precise answer

6.4%.

This is the IRR of the SPV project. It is higher than the 6 percent hurdle rate established for this decision, so the conclusion is that the SPV system is profitable enough to clear the hurdle. This is the same conclusion we reached by the NPV method.

Using PV and RATE in Break-Even Analysis

The standard break-even question is about the rate of *output* from a device that would provide a flow of revenue over time sufficient to justify the expenditure on the device. We used the PMT function to find the required level of annual revenue to be generated from the device and used that, and the price per unit of output, to calculate the annual break-even output. In our analysis of break-even problems, we also saw that the break-even output rate could be related to other operating characteristics such as a break-even capacity factor for a wind turbine or a break-even insolation where a solar panel is located. Now we will see that the break-even question can also be applied to various parameters of the problem, "What purchase price would enable this project to break even?" or "What discount rate would let this project break even?" Such questions can be answered using the spreadsheet functions PV and RATE.

These questions about a change in a parameter that is necessary to achieve a specific goal are a type of sensitivity analysis, but they are not "What would happen if the parameter were ___?" They ask what specific value of a parameter is necessary to reach a particular goal, such as break-even profit. As such, we might call it goal analysis rather than sensitivity analysis.

Example 5a   Wind Power Break-Even Installed Cost (Goal Analysis)

A 50 kW wind power system will last 20 years and produce electric energy that can be sold for $0.11 per kWh. At the given location, the wind system is expected to achieve a capacity factor of 35 percent. The required rate of ROIs of this type is 9 percent per year. How low must the installed cost be to permit this system to break even?

Solution

The installed cost determines the annualized fixed cost of the wind power generator. We first find the annualized fixed cost F that enables the wind system to break even at a 35 percent capacity factor and work backward from that to the installed cost of the generator. At a 35 percent capacity factor, the output of the wind power system will be 50 kW × 365 × 24 × 35% = 153,300 kWh. We begin with the basic break-even equation,

$$\text{Revenue per year} = \text{Total cost per year}$$
$$(153,300) \times 0.11 = F$$
$$F = 16,863 \text{ (dollars)}$$

Our goal analysis question can be restated as, "For what installed cost is the annualized cost $16,863 per year over a 20-year life?"

The answer is given by the PV function in Excel. Its syntax is =PV(*rate,nper,pmt*), where *rate* is the discount rate used in the financial evaluation (here 9 percent), *nper* is the number of periods in the useful life (here 20 years), and *pmt* is the annual payment amount (our $16,863 target for the annualized installed cost.) Typing =PV(9%,20,16863) into Excel returns the answer $153,935.

Note two points about using Excel's financial functions. (1) you cannot use a comma in the number 16,863 when typing it into the *pmt* location of the Excel formula. Excel uses commas to separate the data in its functions. If you type "16,863", Excel would think that your *pmt* is 16 and an optional parameter called *fv* is 863. It would give the answer $300.04, which is not what you should expect as a price for any 50-kW wind power generator. (2) The PMT and PV numbers are always of opposite sign, so if you type 16863 as the *pmt*, Excel will give (153,934.67) in red color as its answer. The parentheses are an accountant's way of designating a negative 153,934.67. For our purposes we may ignore the parentheses and red color, noting the answer as $153,934.67. Alternatively, we could write the *pmt* as –16863, to which Excel would respond with the answer 153,934.67 in black color, meaning a positive number.

This answer, $153,935 is a little over three-quarters of the $200,000 installed cost that was first given in the presentation of this problem and which reflected a capacity cost of $4 per watt, which was not unreasonable for 2013. The installed cost of $153,935 is 77 percent of that original installed cost, so it represents a decrease of 27 percent in the price. In 2013, homeowners and businesses could take 30 percent of the cost of a wind power generator as a tax credit, so that 30 percent tax credit would be enough by itself to make the wind system financially viable in regions that could support a 35 percent capacity factor.

Example 5b   Wind Power Break-Even Discount Rate (Goal Analysis)

Returning now to the original example, suppose that the wind power project costs $200,000 but is eligible for a low-interest loan from the state government, and for simplicity (at some loss of realism) let us assume the loan would be for the entire $200,000. As before, the project can sell its output at $0.11 per kWh for the next 20 years and has an expected capacity factor of 35 percent. How low must the interest rate be for the project to be financially viable?

Solution

In Example 5a, we found the annualized fixed cost that enables the wind system to break even at a 35 percent capacity factor, which is $16,863 per year. Our task here is to determine what interest rate on a

$200,000 loan over 20 years would result in an annual payment equal to that $16,863.

The answer comes from Excel's RATE function, which has the syntax =RATE(*nper,pmt,pv*), where *nper* is the number of periods in the useful life of the device (here 20 years), *pmt* is the annualized fixed cost (here the $16,863 that results in a break-even at a 35 percent capacity factor), and *pv* is the present value, the initial investment in the wind power system (here $200,000). We take care not to type commas in any of our data, and we put a minus sign in front of either the *pmt* or the *pv* parameters to conform to Excel's sign convention in these financial functions. Typing =RATE(20,–16863,200000), and after counting the zeros in those numbers for safety's sake, we hit the Enter button, and Excel returns an answer that on most computers will appear as 6%. Increase the number of decimals shown for the contents of that cell, and the answer appears as 5.59%. Thus, the interest rate on a government-subsized loan would have to be as low as 5.59% to make the wind power system financially viable.

Low-interest loans have been a part of some state programs to promote renewable energy projects. Iowa has even offered zero-interest loans.

Example 5c   Break-Even Selling Price of Electric Energy

Returning again to the original formulation of the example, at what price would the wind power system have to be able to sell its energy to make the system financially viable at a 35 percent capacity factor, without changing any other parameters in the model?

Solution

We calculated in example 5a that, to break even at a 35 percent capacity factor, the wind power system would have to generate 153,300 kWh per year. That is the target energy production in this example. We also saw in the original analysis that a $200,000 installed cost levelized over 20 years using a commercial discount rate of 9 percent per year comes to $21,909 per year. In the basic break-even equation, Revenue per year = Cost per year, the revenue is calculated as quantity × price, and our target quantity is known to be 153,300 kWh. So the only unknown is the price that satisfies the equation,

$$153,300 \times P = 21,909$$

Dividing both sides of the equation by 153,300, we find

$$P = 21909/153300 = 0.143$$

This says that the price must be $0.143 per kWh, or 14.3 cents per kilowatt-hour, for the project to be financially viable, with no change in any of the other parameters. This is higher than the assumed $0.11 per kWh in the original statement of the example.

How should we interpret this break-even price of $0.143 per kWh? It depends on the use of the output from the wind power generator. If the generator were part of a commercial operation that sells its output into the regional transmission grid, then this selling price would be a wholesale price, which will be less than the retail price that consumers pay for electric energy. However, commercial-scale wind turbines have capacities of 1,500 kW or more. A 50 kW turbine is likely to be serving a local community or a farm or factory directly, displacing the energy that the recipient(s) would otherwise purchase from a public utility company. In that context, this *selling price* is the savings to the recipients (per kWh), which is the retail price of electric energy.

How high is $0.143/kWh as a retail price for electric energy? Electric energy prices vary a lot across the United States. Retail prices in late 2013 in the continental states ranged from a low of $0.09/kWh in Washington State to $0.171/kWh in California, $0.179/kWh in Massachusetts and Connecticut, and $0.196/kWh in New York. The retail electric rate in Hawaii was $0.363/kWh.[1] So the figure of $0.143/kWh is in the range of retail prices found in the United States. This particular sensitivity analysis, on the selling price alone, shows that wind power can be *at parity* with the power from electric utility companies *if* the states that have retail rates as high as $0.143/kWh also have sites that can yield a 35 percent capacity factor with the current technology for 50 kW wind turbines.

The analysis in examples 5a to 5c can be set up easily in a spreadsheet. Figure 8.3 shows the data and the formulas used.

◇	A	B	C
1			
2	**Wind Power Financial Viability Model**		
3	Rated capacity	50	kW
4	Installed cost	200000	dollars
5	Useful life	20	years
6	Selling price (wholesale)	0.11	$/kWh
7	Discount rate	0.09	per year
8			
9	Annualized installed cost	=-PMT(B7,B5,B4)	per year
10	Break-even output rate	=B9/B6	kWh per year
11	Maximum output rate	=B3*365*24	kWh per year
12	Break-even annualized cost	=B10*B6	$/yr
13	Break-even capacity factor	=B10/B11	
14			
15	Target break-even capacity factor	0.35	
16	Annual production for target cap factor	=B15*B11	kWh per year
17	Target annual revenue at cap factor	=B16*B6	
18	#1. Break-even installed cost	=-PV(B7,B5,B17)	
19	B/e installed cost as % of orig	=B18/B4	
20	#2. Break-even interest rate	=RATE(B5,B17,-B4)	
21	#3. Break-even wholesale price	=B9/B16	per kWh

Figure 8.3 Wind power model for example 5

◇	A	B	C
1			
2	**Wind Power Financial Viability Model**		
3	Rated capacity	50	kW
4	Installed cost	200,000	dollars
5	Useful life	20	years
6	Selling price (wholesale)	0.11	$/kWh
7	Discount rate	9%	per year
8			
9	Annualized installed cost	$21,909	per year
10	Break-even output rate	199,175	kWh per year
11	Maximum output rate	438,000	kWh per year
12	Break-even annualized cost	21,909	$/yr
13	Break-even capacity factor	45.5%	
14			
15	Target break-even capacity factor	35%	
16	Annual production for target cap factor	153,300	kWh per year
17	Target annual revenue at cap factor	$ 16,863	
18	#1. Break-even installed cost	$153,934.67	
19	B/e installed cost as % of orig	77.0%	
20	#2. Break-even interest rate	5.59%	
21	#3. Break-even wholesale price	$ 0.143	per kWh

Figure 8.4 Wind power model sensitivity analysis

Typing those formulas into the spreadsheet results in the values shown in Figure 8.4. These are the numbers that solved the original problem and each of the sensitivity analyses above.

◇	A	B	C
1			
2	**Wind Power Financial Viability Model**		
3	Rated capacity	50	kW
4	Installed cost	200,000	dollars
5	Useful life	20	years
6	Selling price (wholesale)	0.11	$/kWh
7	Discount rate	9%	per year
8			
9	Annualized installed cost	$21,909	per year
10	Break-even output rate	199,175	kWh per year
11	Maximum output rate	438,000	kWh per year
12	Break-even annualized cost	21,909	$/yr
13	Break-even capacity factor	45.5%	
14			
15	Target break-even capacity factor	20%	
16	Annual production for target cap factor	87,600	kWh per year
17	Target annual revenue at cap factor	$ 9,636	
18	#1. Break-even installed cost	$87,963	
19	B/e installed cost as % of orig	44.0%	
20	#2. Break-even interest rate	-0.35%	
21	#3. Break-even wholesale price	$ 0.250	per kWh

Figure 8.5 Wind power model sensitivity analysis

Having set up such a spreadsheet, it would be easy to reanalyze the problem for a location that has a different capacity factor, such as 20 percent. We simply type over the 35% in cell B15 with the entry "20%". The result shows immediately, with new solutions to the questions about break-even installed cost, interest rate, and price (Figure 8.5).

This spreadsheet shows in cell B18 that the installed cost of the wind power system would have to be extremely low, $87,963, to be financially viable given the other assumptions of the model. It shows in cell B20 that a negative interest rate would be required to make the project viable at such a low capacity factor. However, cell B21 shows that there is hope for wind power projects even at a capacity factor of 20 percent, if they are located in Hawaii, the only state where the retail price of electric energy is more than $0.25 per kWh.

How to Account for the Inflation of Energy Prices over Time

Consider the cash amount A in the *present* that grows compounded at an inflation rate i. The inflated future value T years from now is given by the familiar future-value equation, $F = A(1 + i)^T$. Now, discount that future value back to the present using a discount rate r, by the familiar procedure "divide by $(1 + r)$ raised to the power T." That gives a formula for the present value of that future amount $A(1 + i)^T$,

$$P = \frac{A(1+i)^T}{(1+r)^T}$$

After several steps of algebra, this formula for the present value P can be rewritten as

$$P = \frac{A^T}{\left(1 + \dfrac{r-i}{1+i}\right)^T} \quad \text{(present value of inflated } A\text{)}$$

This new formula has the appearance of a type of present-value equation. It says, "divide A by one plus $\frac{(r-i)}{1+i}$ raised to the power T. In other words, the quantity $\frac{(r-i)}{1+i}$ plays the role of a discount rate. It is the *inflation-adjusted discount rate.*

The formula for the present value of the inflated A applies to every year, so if the inflated amount $A(1+i)^T$ were paid *in every year*, the sum of the present values of those payments would be the present value of the *annuity of inflating values.* By this logic, the inflation-adjusted discount rate can be used in a standard present-value-of-annuity formula to calculate the present value of a series of cash values that is inflating at the rate i (percent per year).

This fact has an important application to the financial modeling of energy-saving devices. In the examples of wind and solar power appearing in this chapter, the devices have useful lives of 20 or 25 years. Over that time, energy prices will rise substantially due to inflation, but our financial models up through example 8 assumed the same energy savings each year. To recognize the expected inflation of energy prices, we should adjust the nominal discount rate (r) by an energy-price inflation rate (i) to get the adjusted discount rate (r^*) using the formula

$$r^* = \frac{(r-i)}{1+i} \quad \text{(Inflation-adjusted Discount Rate)}$$

Expected Inflation of Prices in General and Electric Energy Prices in Particular

Economists differ in their forecasts of energy price inflation, but they seem to agree that energy prices will rise a little faster than the general rate of inflation. An inflation-adjusted rate or price is called a *real* rate or price. The U.S. Energy Information Administration's *Annual Energy Outlook 2013* predicts a rise of real electric energy prices at a rate between 0.2 and 0.4 percent per year, depending on the level of economic growth, out to 2040.[2] The general rate of inflation is also difficult for economists to forecast. Inflation was running at about 1.7 percent per year in early 2014. Long-term forecasts of the general rate of price inflation leave a lot of room for error, but the International Monetary Fund was projecting an inflation rate of about 2 percent per year in the United States through 2017.[3]

The real energy price inflation rate compounds with the general inflation rate. If we take 0.3 percent as the real energy inflation rate and 2 percent to be the general inflation rate, we calculate the *nominal* energy price inflation rate to use in our financial analysis from the compounding growth factors,

$$(1 + r^*) = (1 + 0.3\%) \times (1 + 2\%) = 1.02306$$
$$(1 + r^*) = 1.02306$$
$$r^* = 2.306\%$$

Thus, the nominal energy price inflation rate is generally expected to be slightly more than 2.3 percent. For small rates of inflation, a good approximation to the nominal energy price inflation is the sum of the general inflation rate (here 2 percent) and the real energy price inflation rate (here 0.3 percent).

In a realistic feasibility study, the analyst should first look for a forecast of local electric energy prices and use the national expectation only if no local forecast is available. The difference can be significant. In early 2014, Alliant Energy in Iowa was forecasting a 7 percent rise in its electric rates for 2014 and 5 percent increases each year for several years after that.

Those rates of increase would mount up over time to prices much higher than if the increase were only 2.3 percent per year.

Example 6   *Residential SPV Valuation with Energy Price Inflation*

Consider a fixed 1 kW solar panel that is pointed south and tilted at latitude. Its wiring, battery bank, and inverter have a composite efficiency (derate factor) of 77 percent. The SPV system has a useful life of 25 years. The retail price is $4,800, but that is subject to a 30 percent tax credit.[4] The homeowner has a large mortgage at an interest rate of 6 percent per year and could use surplus money to pay down that mortgage unless better investment opportunities exist elsewhere. Assume that energy price inflation is expected to be 2.3 percent per year for the next 25 years.

(a) Is this system financially viable in Boston, which has an insolation of only 4.61 kWh/m²/day but a residential electric energy price of $0.1784 per kWh, including sales tax?

(b) Is it viable in Chicago, which has an insolation of 4.42 kWh/m²/day and a residential electric energy price of $0.0974 per kWh, including sales tax?

Solution

We modify the financial model from example 3 by adding a line for the expected energy price inflation rate and the calculated adjusted discount rate. The data and formulas appear in the spreadsheet image in Figure 8.6.

The calculated quantities and the solution appear in lines 11 to 18 in Figure 8.7.

---

[4] We repeat here the warning that, to focus on the basic ideas, this chapter's treatment of the tax credit is omitting details that relate to state taxes. See Chapter 9 for the fully correct treatment.

◇	A	B	C
1			
2	**SPV System Financial Valuation**		
3	Rated capacity	1	kW
4	Useful life	25	years
5	Derate factor (DC to AC)	0.77	
6	Location's Insolation	4.61	kWh/m2/day
7	Energy price or savings	0.1784	$/kWh
8	Discount rate (nominal)	0.06	per year
9	Tax credit for homeowner	0.3	of installed cost
10	Expected energy inflation rate	0.023	
11	Inflation-adjusted discount rate	=(B8-B10)/(1+B10)	
12	Retail price per kW of capacity	4800	$/kW
13	Net price per kW after tax credit	=B12*(1-B9)	
14	Annual production of AC energy	=B6*365*B5	kWh per year
15	Annual savings in energy cost	=B14*B7	per year
16	PV of annual savings	=-PV(B11,B4,B15)	
17	Net PV of investment in the device	=B16-B13	
18	Rate of return on investment	=RATE(B4,B15,-B13)	per year

Figure 8.6 Excel formulas in the residential SPV model

11	Inflation-adjusted discount rate	3.62%	
12	Retail price per kW of capacity	4,800	$/kW
13	Net price per kW after tax credit	$ 3,360	
14	Annual production of AC energy	1,296	kWh per year
15	Annual savings in energy cost	$ 231.14	per year
16	PV of annual savings	$ 3,762	
17	Net PV of investment in the device	$402	
18	Rate of return on investment	4.69%	per year

Figure 8.7 Excel results in the residential SPV model

The positive $402 NPV indicates that the residential SPV system is financially viable in Boston, given the assumptions in this model.

Age Derating of SPV Systems

However, example 6 is not the final word in the financial analysis of an SPV system. SPV systems tend to lose efficiency with age. The PVWatts calculator assumes that an SPV system will lose 1 percent of its rated capacity per year of age. This will result in a compounding decline in the annual output of the system. Mathematically, decline is negative growth, so a 1 percent rate of decline corresponds to a –1 percent *inflation* in the annual output of the SPV unit and therefore, under the residential system of pricing per kilowatt-hour, a –1 percent inflation in the annual savings from the use of the SPV unit. This –1 percent rate compounds with the general inflation rate of 2 percent and the real inflation in energy prices to yield a new inflation rate for the annual revenues in the financial analysis,

$$1 + i = (1 + 2\%) \times (1 + 0.3\%) \times (1 - 1\%)$$
$$1 + i = 1.0128$$
$$i = 1.28\%.$$

Without the aging effect, the compounding growth rate of the annual revenues from the SPV unit was 2.3 percent. With the 1 percent decline due to age, the growth rate becomes 1.28 percent. That is a little less than the 1.3 percent that one would calculate by subtracting the rate of decline from the inflation rate, 2.3 – 1 percent. This shows again that the sum of the component growth rates is only an approximation to the adjusted discount rate.

Example 7   SPV Derating with Age

Revise the solution of example 6 to incorporate a 1 percent per year derating of the SPV unit due to age.

Solution

Replace the old revenue inflation rate of 2.3 percent with the new revenue inflation rate of 1.28 percent. The solution appears as seen in Figure 8.8.

The SPV unit in Boston squeaks by with a $12 NPV and a 4.69 percent IRR, which was barely above the required 4.66 percent rate of return calculated as the inflation-adjusted discount rate. As such, it warrants a *Yes* vote in the investment committee.

	A	B	C
1			
2	**SPV System Financial Valuation**		**Example 7**
3	Rated capacity	1	kW
4	Useful life	25	years
5	Derate factor (DC to AC)	0.77	
6	Location's Insolation	4.61	kWh/m2/day
7	Energy price or savings	0.1784	$/kWh
8	Discount rate (nominal)	6%	per year
9	Tax credit for homeowner	30%	of installed cost
10	Expected revenue inflation rate	1.28%	
11	Inflation-adjusted discount rate	4.66%	
12	Retail price per kW of capacity	4,800	$/kW
13	Net price per kW after tax credit	$ 3,360	
14	Annual production of AC energy	1,296	kWh per year
15	1st yr Annual savings in energy cost	$ 231.14	per year
16	PV of annual savings	$ 3,372	
17	Net PV of investment in the device	$12	
18	Rate of return on the investment	4.69%	

Figure 8.8 SPV model solution

How to Select the Right Discount Rate for Financial Analysis

The question of what discount rate to use for the financial analysis of a project is fundamental in the theory of finance. Here, we refer to selecting the *nominal discount rate*, not adjusted for inflation. The short answer is that the appropriate discount rate depends on the level of risk inherent in the project, but *risk* has a precise meaning in that answer. It is a matter best left for study in a finance course, and there are very good textbooks on the subject.[4] We will be content to survey the main ideas here.

In a feasibility study for a corporate investment in a sustainable technology, the chief financial officer of the company making the investment will know what discount rate to use. That rate will be the weighted-average *cost of capital* to the company, which reflects both the interest rate the company pays on its loans (the cost of debt) and the rate of return that the company's shareholders expect to receive on their investment in the firm (the cost of equity). It is also influenced by the firm's income tax rate. The key point is that the cost of capital is *not* the same as the interest paid on debt. This remains true even when a project can be financed 100 percent by loans, because the business risk of such a project must be absorbed by the rest of the company, and that increases the risk borne by the company's shareholders.

For a small business, which may not have a chief financial officer trained in the theory of finance, the discount rate should still reflect the cost of capital to the firm, not just the cost of debt. The small business owner should consider what alternative investments, of comparable risk, can be made with available funds and what rate of return those alternatives might provide. The best of those alternatives is the point of reference for any investment in sustainable technologies.

For private individuals and small businesses, the investment in sustainable power technologies tends to be for the purpose of reducing the purchase of energy from conventional sources at retail prices. Such a cost-reducing project has very low business risk, because the energy will have to be purchased under all conditions. Moreover, many private individuals have one good reference point for the discount rate to use in low-risk investments—the interest on their home mortgage loan. A common feature of home mortgage contracts is that they give the borrower the right to pay down the principal amount of their mortgage at any time and by any amount. When a person pays down his or her mortgage, the payment results in a reduction in future payments, which yields a rate of ROI *equal to the interest rate* on the mortgage loan. Therefore, a homeowner's personal discount rate for very safe investment should be *at least as high* as their mortgage interest rate.

A full treatment of risk in sustainable technology investments is beyond the scope of this text. In the financial analyses presented so far, we assumed away any uncertainty about the amount of benefit (energy cost reductions) that would result from operating a renewable energy device. We picked a best estimate and used that as if it were a certainty. Sensitivity analysis on such a model shows the effect of alternative assumptions, but that is not the same as incorporating *riskiness* into a measure of financial value. A full treatment of idiosyncratic risk in nondiversifiable investments through the concept of certainty-equivalent is available in most texts on decision analysis.[5]

Take-aways

This chapter began to show the power of financial analysis in technology investment decisions. The context was mostly personal decision making, as for solar panels on one's house. This kept the technical details to a minimum so the basic financial principles would predominate.

- In financial analysis, the market value of an asset *does not depend* on how much you paid for it. The market value is determined entirely by the after-tax cash flow that will come in the future from owning and operating the asset. This is why it is necessary to forecast the quantity and selling price of the output of a technology.
- Financial decisions require the decision maker to have in mind a target rate of ROIs and to test all investment opportunities against that target. Depending on the context, the target may be called a *discount rate, hurdle rate, yield, or expected rate of return*. This discount rate expresses the decision maker's sense of urgency about money—the higher the discount rate, the more urgently the decision maker wants money. Essentially, it expresses the *price* (in percent per year) that the decision maker is willing to pay for cash flows. A higher discount rate reflects a higher price of money and a higher sense of urgency about money.
- The simplest financial model of a future cash flow is an *annuity*, which is a constant cash flow at equal intervals of time up to an end point. In our use, the end point is the lifetime of the device. We use years as the unit of time, and the (annual) cash flow numbers are the sales (or cost savings) minus any operating expenses. *In this chapter, we ignored federal and state income taxes. For a more realistic treatment, see Chapter 9.* Spreadsheets like Microsoft Excel, Open Office, and Apple Numbers have built-in functions that can calculate the present value (PV), the rate of return (RATE), the annual payment (PMT), and even the number

of years (NPER) for cash flows that have this annuity
structure.

- The *rate of return* (or *internal rate of return*) on an
  investment is a measure of how profitable the investment
  is. It is like the interest rate paid by a bank—the higher
  the rate, the more profitable the investment (if risks are the
  same). To calculate a rate of return, you need to know both
  the amount of the initial investment (purchase price of a
  device) and the cash flow that results from owning and using
  the device. The RATE function does this for annuity-type
  cash flows.

- Another measure of profitability is the NPV of an investment.
  It is the present value of the future cash flows minus the
  amount of the investment. NPV is expressed in dollar terms
  rather than as a percentage (rate of return).

- The simple, annuity cash flow may seem too simplistic for
  real technology investment models, but using the trick of
  an *inflation-adjusted discount rate*, the spreadsheet annuity
  functions can actually be made to handle cash flows that grow
  at a compounding rate—meaning a specific percentage each
  year—(the effect of inflation on energy prices) and even those
  that decline by a specific percentage each year (as in the age
  derating of SPV output).

- Investments in technology are subject to uncertainties about
  future production, future prices, and many other factors.
  A good financial analyst identifies those uncertainties, puts
  some estimates on the range of uncertainty (e.g., low and
  high values), and then performs *sensitivity analysis* on the
  basic valuation model by substituting alternative values for
  the uncertain quantities and seeing what effect that has on the
  profitability of the investment.

- What discount rate should be used for an investment
  decision? For people, not corporations, a good guide is the
  interest rate on one's home mortgage, because a person
  could choose to pay down their mortgage, and *earn* a savings

equal to the interest rate, rather than invest in a solar panel. For corporations, the determination of a hurdle rate for investment decisions is best left to financial professionals.

Chapter 9 presents what we might call an industrial-strength financial analysis of a technology investment, meaning one that is realistic enough that it could be used by a consultant for a client or for an internal corporate investment proposal. A realistic analysis will consider the effect of state and federal income taxes on a project, which leads to an analysis of the interactions between depreciation methods, state and federal tax credits, and utility rebates. Fasten your seat belt, then turn the page.

CHAPTER 9

Valuation of Commercial Projects

Overview

Commercial investments are more complex than personal investments, because the profit from the project is subject to income tax. A commercial solar photovoltaic (SPV) system must be evaluated differently from a home SPV system, for example, because the *profit* from the home SPV system does not increase the homeowner's taxable income. The homeowner was using after-tax income to pay the previous electric energy bills (and sales tax on those bills), so a reduction in the expenditure for energy just means more income being available to spend on other things, not more taxable income in total.

In contrast, a business that owns a renewable energy system must pay income tax on the profits (revenues minus operating expenses) from the operation of the device. However, the tax laws recognize that equipment used in a business has a finite useful life, so the equipment loses its value over time. Therefore, when a device is being used in a business to generate revenues, the owner is allowed under U.S. tax law to deduct a fraction of the original installed cost every year as a *depreciation expense*. The accounting for depreciation and taxes is a significant difference between the personal and the commercial evaluation of a renewable energy system. Our main task in this chapter is to account for the revenues, costs, tax credits, and taxes paid on a renewable energy system owned by a business.

Another consideration that reflects the difference between personal and commercial evaluation is that even if a business is using a renewable energy system to reduce their own energy purchases, rather than to sell the energy, the calculation of economic savings for a business may be quite different from that of a residential system. Large commercial and industrial firm pay for purchased electric energy using a system called *peak-load pricing*, which is quite different from the energy-pricing system (per kWh) used for residential customers.

In this chapter, we see how to incorporate taxes and depreciation into the analysis of a renewable energy investment and how they interact with federal and state tax credits and utility rebates. In the context of solar power feasibility study, we see the importance of estimating annual output using monthly data, and we look in particular at how commercial peak-load pricing changes the analysis of the profitability of a solar power system.

There are software packages that do feasibility analysis for renewable energy systems. These include the System Advisor Model (SAM) at the National Renewable Energy Lab (NREL) website (sam.nrel.gov) and commercial packages for solar power systems such as Clean Power Finance (www.cleanpowerfinance.com). However, it is essential for the feasibility analyst to understand what information the software is calling for to set up a feasibility study. And it is even more important to understand what the software is doing with that information to calculate the results, because one can catch mistakes in the data entry if one knows what results to expect in the base case and sensitivity analysis. This chapter uses spreadsheet software to set up the data for a feasibility analysis and to do the essential calculations. As such it is good for training and is also a good supplement to the use of commercial packages.

Depreciation

Depreciation is a concept in accounting and taxation that recognizes the tendency of devices to lose their productive value over time. This loss of value is recognized under tax law as an *expense* of the business that may be deducted from revenue in the calculation of taxable income. It is not a cash expense; it is simply permitted in the calculation of taxable income. The amount of the depreciation expense that may be taken each year for tax purposes is determined by the *tax life* or *recovery period* that is assigned to the device or asset under the tax law. Renewable energy systems are classified as *5-year property*, as if they would last only five years, even though they may have a useful life of 25 years or more.

This textbook is not meant to teach all the rules of depreciation, but a brief overview will help one understand how the economics of sustainable technologies differ for businesses and individuals. The tax laws permit businesses to calculate depreciation in one of two ways. In the simpler method, called *straight-line* (SL) *depreciation*, the permitted depreciation expense in each year is the original cost of the asset (its *cost basis*) divided by its tax life. For renewable energy properties, a five-year tax life means that 20 percent of the cost basis of the property may be deducted as a depreciation expense each year.

The more complex method, called modified accelerated cost recovery system (MACRS), allows more depreciation in the early years of the tax life, and the percentage of the cost basis allowed as a depreciation expense changes from year to year. Thus, the MACRS deduction must be calculated using a table of MACRS values. The MACRS percentages for a five-year property are shown in Table 9.1.

In this chapter, for simplicity of exposition we use SL depreciation in the solution of the examples. Chapter 10 will show an example of MACRS depreciation.

The example of the five-year tax life in Table 9.1 is significant to this chapter, because the *accelerated depreciation* policy of the U.S. federal government allows businesses to depreciate *renewable energy property* over a short period of time, substantially less than its useful life. As of 2013, the tax law permitted depreciation using a five-year tax life, which is substantially less than the commonly assumed 20-year life of wind turbines and 25-year useful life of SPV systems.

Table 9.1 MACRS and SL depreciation for five-year property

Year	SL (%)	MACRS (%)
1	20	20.0
2	20	32.0
3	20	19.2
4	20	11.5
5	20	11.5
6		5.8

MACRS, modified accelerated cost recovery system; SL, straight line.

Also, under the *Expiring Provisions Improvement Reform and Efficiency (EXPIRE) Act* that was working its way through the Senate and House in mid-2014, investments in renewable power systems that are placed in service before the end of 2015 will qualify for a *bonus depreciation* deduction that permits the owner to depreciate *in the first year of use* 50 percent of the amount of the firm's investment in the system. The other 50 percent of the cost of the system becomes the *adjusted cost basis* of the property to be used in calculating the annual amounts of ordinary depreciation over the five-year tax life of the property, including that of the first year.

Example 1   SL and MACRS Depreciation on a Solar Carport

Headley Corporation wants to install a 33 kW solar power system in its parking lot, elevated so the panels form a sun roof over parked cars. A local contractor bid $164,213 to build the system. (*This example ignores the federal tax credit, which is left for a later example in this chapter.*)

(a) What is the amount of the bonus depreciation that may be taken in the first year of use of the solar carport?

(b) What is the amount of the adjusted cost basis after the bonus depreciation is taken?

(c) What is the amount of depreciation that Headley Corporation may take on the solar carport in each of the first five years using the SL method?

(d) What is the amount of depreciation that Headley Corporation may take each year using the MACRS method?

(e) What is the total amount of depreciation that Headley may take in years 1 to 5, including the bonus depreciation and SL or MACRS?

Solution

(a) **Year 1 Bonus Depreciation:** The bonus depreciation is equal to 50 percent of the expected price of the system, $50\% \times 164,213 = \$82,106.50$. This will be added to the amount of depreciation that may be taken in year 1 under the SL or MACRS methods.

Table 9.2 SL depreciation (example 1)

Year	SL (%)	Depreciation ($)
1	20	16,421.30
2	20	16,421.30
3	20	16,421.30
4	20	16,421.30
5	20	16,421.30

(b) The adjusted cost basis after the bonus depreciation is 164,213 − $82,106.50 = 82,106.50, which is the remaining half of the original purchase price.

(c) **SL Method:** The ordinary depreciation to be taken each year under the SL method is 20 percent of the adjusted cost basis, 20% × 82,106.50 = $16,421.30. This amount may be taken in years 1 to 5 as in Table 9.2.

(d) **MACRS Method:** Under MACRS, the percentage of the adjusted cost basis that may be depreciated changes each year as shown in Table 9.1. The year 1 depreciation percentage under MACRS is the same as the first-year SL percentage, 20%, so the MACRS depreciation in year 1 is 16,421.30. It is in years 2 to 6 that the MACRS and SL methods differ. Notice that the *five-year* MACRS table has some depreciation in year 6. Multiplying each MACRS percentage in years 2 to 6 by the adjusted basis 82,106.50 gives the depreciation amounts shown in Table 9.3.

(e) The complete year 1 depreciation is the bonus depreciation plus the SL or MACRS year 1 amount. Since SL and MACRS both use 20% for year 1, they give the same total depreciation in year 1, which is 82,106.50 + 16,421.30 = 98,527.80. In years 2 to 6, SL and MACRS differ as shown in Table 9.4.

This analysis is not the final word on depreciation for the Headley Corporation case in example 1. Federal tax credits have an impact on depreciation, as we shall see in the following section.

Table 9.3 MACRS depreciation (example 1)

Year	MACRS (%)	Depreciation ($)
1	20.0	16,421.30
2	32.0	24,246.24
3	19.2	14,547.74
4	11.5	8,713.49
5	11.5	8,713.49
6	5.8	4,394.63

Table 9.4 SL and MACRS depreciation (example 1)

Year	SL ($)	MACRS ($)
1	98,527.80	98,527.80
2	16,421.30	26,274.08
3	16,421.30	15,764.45
4	16,421.30	9,442.25
5	16,421.30	9,442.25
6		4,762.18

Federal and State Tax Credits and Utility Rebates

A 30 percent federal *investment tax credit* (ITC) has been available for many types of renewable energy investments. This credit allows the taxpayer to reduce their tax payment by the amount of the credit. The benefit of this credit comes when the taxpayer would have to pay taxes, which typically would be some time in the year or so after the investment, depending on which month the investment took place and when the taxpayer will file their tax return. The federal ITC vests over five years. This means, for example, that if the owner of a renewable energy project were to sell the project after three years, the owner would have to refund 40 percent of the tax credit that had been taken.

A *production tax credit* is available, as an alternative to the 30 percent ITC, to producers who sell their energy to others rather than using the energy internally. This production tax credit pays $0.023 per kilowatt-hour to producers using wind, closed-loop biomass, and geothermal technologies. A $0.011/kWh production tax credit is available for open-loop biomass, landfill gas, municipal solid waste, and some hydro-electric and marine–hydrokinetic systems.[1] Notice that the production tax credit is not available for SPV nor solar thermal electric (STE) nor solar hot water systems. The credit is available for the first 10 years of operation of the eligible renewable energy system.

The Federal ITC and Depreciation

A person or company that elects to take the federal tax credit[1] must subtract one-half of the tax credit from the cost basis on which bonus depreciation and then SL or MACRS depreciation will be taken.

Example 2   Headley Solar Carport Depreciation After Federal ITC

Headley Corporation will take the 30 percent federal tax credit on the solar carport project.

(a) What will be the amount of the tax credit?
(b) What will be the amount of bonus depreciation it can take in year 1?
(c) What will be its complete depreciation schedule with SL depreciation of the adjusted cost basis?
(d) What will be the depreciation schedule with MACRS?

Solution

(a) The federal ITC will be 30% × 164,213 = $49,263.90.
(b) The amount of bonus depreciation is calculated against the original cost basis ($164,213) adjusted by one-half of the federal ITC. 164,213 – 24,631.95 = $139,581.05. The bonus depreciation is 50 percent of this amount, 50% × 139,581.05 = $69,790.53.

---

[1] For corporations there is an option of an investment tax credit (ITC) or a production tax credit (PTC). Each is voluntary, but any company seeking to reduce the cost of their project will take one or the other. For individuals, only the ITC is allowed.

Table 9.5 SL and MACRS depreciation (final solution)

Year	SL ($)	MACRS ($)
1	83,748.63	83,748.63
2	13,958.11	22,332.97
3	13,958.11	13,399.78
4	13,958.11	8,025.91
5	13,958.11	8,025.91
6		4,047.85

(c) The adjusted cost basis for SL depreciation is what remains after the 50 percent bonus depreciation, so that too is $69,790.53. SL depreciation is 20 percent of that amount for each year, $13,958.11. The full year 1 depreciation will be the bonus 69,790.53 plus the SL 13,958.11 = 83,748.63. Years 2 to 5 will be $13,958.11.

(d) The MACRS percentages applied to the adjusted cost basis of $69,790.53 yield the yearly depreciation amounts shown for years 2 to 6 in the final solution (Table 9.5). The year 1 figures include the bonus depreciation.

The Federal ITC and State Tax Obligation

For individuals and corporations, the amount of *federal* income tax paid is deductible from taxable income on the taxpayer's *state* income tax return. Therefore, a reduction in federal tax paid, due to the federal investment tax credit (FITC), results in a higher state-taxable income. The owner of a renewable energy project will end up paying extra *state taxes* on the amount of the federal tax credit, so this must be accounted for in the cash-flow analysis of the project.

Thus, the FITC is *as-if taxable* on the owner's state tax return. If S is the owner's marginal state income tax rate, and FITC is the amount of the federal investment tax credit, then the increase in state tax paid due to the FITC is $S \times$FITC. It is commonly thought that the FITC is like the government paying 30 percent of the cost of the renewable energy project. It is not quite that simple, because while the federal government is giving, the state government is taking some back. The net cash-flow effect of the FITC is therefore FITC $- S \times$FITC $= (1-S) \times$FITC.

This state tax effect is not too severe, because most states have rather low tax rates compared to the federal tax rate. For all but two states, the state income tax rate for the wealthiest taxpayers is just in the single digits.[2]

State ITC and Federal Tax Obligation

Some states offer credits against one's state tax obligation for investments in renewable energy projects. For example, Iowa's tax credit is 18 percent of the purchase price, but it is limited to $20,000 per project. Many states do not offer an ITC, but they offer other incentives, such as low-interest loans, or they require public utilities to give rebates for renewable energy investments. Details of all states' rules are available at the DSIRE website, www.dsireusa.org.

State taxes paid by a corporation are deductible as a business expense, and for individuals they are deductible if one itemizes deductions on Form 1040 Schedule A rather than taking the standard deduction. By the same logic seen in the analysis of the federal tax credit, a state-tax credit is *as-if taxable* on the company's federal tax return: The state investment tax credit (SITC) reduces the deductible state tax expense, so the after-tax cash-flow effect of the state tax credit is really $(1-F) \times$ SITC, where F is the taxpayer's marginal tax rate.

This effect can be significant, because the top federal income tax rate is nearly 40 percent. Thus, what might appear to be a generous state tax credit is reduced by 40 percent due to federal income taxation.

The state tax credit does not affect the adjusted basis of the project for depreciation.

Example 3   Headley Solar Carport Net Cost After FITC and SITC and Rebate

The Headley Corporation solar carport project was bid by a developer at a price of $164,213. Headley will take the 30 percent federal tax credit on the solar carport project. Located in Des Moines, Iowa, they will also take an Iowa state tax credit that by law is equal to 18 percent of the price, or $20,000, whichever is less. Headley Corporation is subject to Iowa's top income tax rate, 9 percent. Its federal income tax rate is 39.6 percent.

(a) What will be the amount of the federal tax credit, and what is its after-tax cash flow?

(b) What will be the amount of the state tax credit, and what is its after-tax cash flow?

Solution

(a) The amount of the federal ITC will be 30% × 164,213 = $49,264. The net cash flow, after accounting for 9 percent state tax paid, is 49,264 × (1–9%) = 44,830.

(b) For the state tax credit, we first calculate 18 percent of the purchase price and test that against the per-project maximum of $20,000. 18% × 164,213 = $29,553. This exceeds the Iowa maximum per project, so the amount of the tax credit to be taken is $20,000. After the federal-tax effect, what remains as cash flow from the state tax credit is 20,000 × (1–39.6%) = $12,080.

Utility Rebates

Many public utility companies offer rebates to their clients who install renewable energy systems. The details for each state appear on the DSIRE website (www.dsireusa.org). Unlike tax credits, which directly reduce the amount of one's tax and thereby represent an after-tax benefit, utility rebates must be treated as a form of taxable income to the owner of the renewable energy system. Thus, the after-tax benefit of the rebate depends on the owner's marginal federal and state tax rates.

Another feature of the public utility rebates is that they may depend on the production of energy during the first year of operation of an installation. In Iowa, for example, the rebate offered by Alliant Energy in Iowa for SPV systems through 2013 was one dollar per kilowatt-hour of production in the first 12 months of operation, subject to a maximum of $25,000.

Recall that the tax-credit basis of a project is the amount of the project's cost on which the 30 percent federal tax credit or state tax credit may be taken. The effect of a utility rebate on the tax-credit basis of a project may depend on the structure of ownership of the project. If the owner is a limited liability company (LLC), the rebate does not reduce the tax-credit basis. If the owner is an S-corporation or C-corporation, the rebate may reduce the tax-credit basis. Project owners should consult an attorney or tax professional on this point.

Example 4   After-Tax Value of the Utility Rebate

Headley Corporation wants to install a 33 kW solar power system in its parking lot, elevated so the panels form a sun roof over parked cars. The system is expected to have a derate factor of 0.815. The weather conditions in Des Moines, Iowa, provide an average insolation of 4.8 kWh/m²/ day over the year. Headley's federal tax rate is 39.6 percent, and its state tax rate is 9 percent. The company uses an 8 percent discount rate for financial decisions.

(a) What is the expected annual output of the SPV system?
(b) What will be the amount of the rebate from Alliant Energy?
(c) What will be the amount of the rebate net of federal and state taxes?

Solution

(a) The insolation expressed in kWh/m²/day is also known as the peak sun hours per day and can be multiplied by the kilowatt capacity of an SPV system to yield the output of the system per day. Here, that output will be 4.8 × 33 = 158.4 kWh/day. Multiplied by 365 days in the year, the output comes to 57,816 kWh. The usable alternating current (AC) output from the solar system is this output derated to reflect the loss of energy in the wiring, inverter, and other components of the system, so the usable output is 57,816 × 0.815 = 47,120 kWh per year.

(b) At a rebate rate of one dollar per kilowatt-hour of first-year production, the Headley solar carport would seem to qualify for a rebate of $47,120, but the rebate is limited to $25,000, so that is the amount Headley will receive.

(c) The $25,000 rebate will be treated as taxable income, so the tax on the $25,000 rebate will be $25,000 × (39.6% + 9%) = $12,150. The net rebate is therefore $25,000 − $12,150 = $12,850.

Present Value of the Investment Net of Tax Credits, Rebates, and Bonus Depreciation

The cash-flow analysis in a feasibility study breaks down fundamentally into two parts, one being the initial investment at time zero and the other being the flow of after-tax cash during subsequent years arising from the revenue or cost savings from the technology and the expenses of operating the technology. In the approach taken in this chapter, we model the future cash flows as two annuities, one that is constant—an annuity—during the depreciation period (years 1 to 5 for renewable energy projects) and another that is constant—a second annuity—during the postdepreciation period (years 6 to N) that goes to the end of the project's economic life.

In this approach, cash flows that take place at or very near the start of the project are treated as components of the initial investment. These include the net benefits from federal and state tax credits and utility rebates. They also include the after-tax cash flow from the bonus depreciation that American law allowed through 2013 and may continue to permit in the near future. The initial cost of the project is assumed to be paid on the day the project is purchased from a developer or on the day that it is completed if it is built on contract. The federal and state tax credits are typically received within 6 to 12 months of the investment. Rebates may come within three months of when the project is functional and put into service. Each of these should be discounted back to the present, year 0. The sum of their present values becomes the net initial investment in the project.

The feature that was not discussed in the previous sections is the bonus depreciation. Depreciation is a tax-deductible expense that serves to cancel out income that would otherwise be subject to income tax, so it is said to *shield* income from taxation. If D is the amount of the depreciation, and T is the owner's tax rate, then the amount of taxes saved is $T \times D$. This tax rate is the sum of the owner's federal and state tax rates, because depreciation shields income from both federal and state taxation. Taxes that are not paid, but would otherwise have had to be paid, are a genuine cash flow, so the depreciation has an after-tax cash-flow effect equal to $T \times D$ at the time the income taxes are due. Properly, if those taxes are due 6 to 12 months after the start of the project, the amount of that tax shield should be discounted back 6 to 12 months to the project's year 0.

Bonus depreciation is taken in *year 1*, as is the regular SL or MACRS depreciation on the adjusted cost basis. We will discount the bonus depreciation back to year 0 according to a reasonable estimate of when the taxes would be due. When we discuss the regular depreciation of year 1, in the section after this, we will treat it as occurring at the end of year 1, which is the timing convention for all cash flows from year 1 onward. This difference in our treatment of bonus depreciation and the year 1 regular depreciation is indeed an inconsistency, but it will accommodate the use of annuity functions in the financial calculations, reflects the fact that bonus depreciation is another form of tax incentive for renewable energy, and introduces very little error in the analysis.

In many applications of corporate finance, depreciated assets are sold after some period of time for their salvage value, and at that time the owner must pay taxes on *recaptured depreciation*. In the renewable energy projects studied here, the useful lives are very long, 20 to 25 or even 30 years, and it is reasonable to assume that the projects will have no value at the end of their economic lives and thus not create terminal cash flows related to sale and tax on recaptured depreciation. Thus, the depreciation tax shield

Example 5   Present Value of the Headley Project Net Investment

The contractor's bid to build the solar carports is $164,213. The federal tax credit net of state tax obligation is $44,830 and will be received six months after the project starts. The state tax credit net of federal tax obligation is $12,080 and will be received six months after the project starts. The utility rebate of $25,000 will be received three months after the solar photovoltaic system starts to produce energy, but the federal and state tax obligations on the rebate (totaling $12,150) will be paid six months after the project starts. The bonus depreciation is $69,791.

(a) What are the present values of each of these initial cash-flow components?

(b) What is the *net present value* (NPV) of the project cost, after accounting for all tax credits, rebates, bonus depreciation, and their effects on income taxes?

Solution

(a and b) Each amount is discounted to year 0 by multiplying it by the discount factor $(1 + 0.08)^{-T}$, where T is the time delay between the start of production and the receipt or payment of the amount. For example, the federal ITC and the state taxes associated with it are received and paid, respectively, 0.5 years after production begins. Thus, we take the net FITC amount \$44,830 and multiply it by $(1 + 0.08)^{-0.5}$ to get \$43,138. A spreadsheet handles these calculations easily. Table 9.6 shows the result of the calculations.

The cash-flow effect of the bonus depreciation tax shield is (39.6% + 9%) × 69,791 = \$33,918. In other words, through the bonus depreciation policy alone, the federal and state governments are contributing \$33,918 toward the cost of this project.

Table 9.6 *Calculation of the present value of the net initial investment*

	Nominal amounts (\$)	Delay (yr)	Discounted (year 0) value
Payment for the SPV system installed	(164,213)	0	(164,213)
Federal tax credit net of state tax obligation	44,830	0.5	43,138
State tax credit net of federal tax obligation	12,080	0.5	11,624
Utility rebate	25,000	0.25	24,524
Federal and state taxes paid on utility rebate	(12,150)	0.5	(11,691)
Bonus depreciation tax shield	33,918	0.5	32,638
PV of net investment (net cash outflow)			(63,981)

The conclusion is that the contract price for the SPV system is $164,213, whereas the net initial investment, after accounting for all the various incentives for renewable energy, is only $63,981.

Cash Flows During Operation

The next step in the analysis is to calculate the after-tax cash flows during the depreciation period years 1 to 5 and during the postdepreciation period years 6 to N. For the Headley solar carport example, we take the project lifetime to be $N = 25$ years. The cash-flow calculation follows the logic of an income statement. Begin with the *annual revenue* or cost savings from the project, subtract its *annual operating expenses*, and subtract the annual depreciation to get the taxable income, and calculate the *tax to be paid*. The annual cash flow is the sum of the revenues (+), operating expenses (–), and the taxes paid (–). Due to depreciation, the taxable income can be negative, in which case the loss from the renewable energy system during the depreciation period shields income from elsewhere in the owner's business activities, so the *tax paid* appears as a positive number, meaning a tax benefit.

In the analysis that follows, we use SL depreciation rather than MACRS, because SL depreciation is the same in all five years of the tax life of the project. We will assume a constant flow of revenues across the years and an unvarying tax rate for the owner. As a result, the after-tax cash flow will be the same for all years in the depreciation period and likewise during the postdepreciation period. This simplifies the presentation of the cash flow, into just two columns of a spreadsheet, and (later in example 7) it will allow us to calculate the present value of the cash flow using the spreadsheet annuity function *PV*.

Example 6   Cash Flow from Operations in the Headley Case

The solar carport project for Headley Corporation will have a useful life of 25 years. The electric energy generated will save Headley the expense of paying $0.131/kWh to the public utility, including state sales tax on the utility bill. The annual maintenance expenses of an SPV installation are typically estimated at $20/kW per year.

(a) Using the data presented in the previous examples calculate the after-tax cash flow of the project during the depreciation and post-depreciation periods.

Solution

The basic data of the Headley solar carport case and the previous analysis can be represented in a small section of a spreadsheet, as shown in Figure 9.1.

What remains is to construct the cash-flow calculations for years 1 to 5 when depreciation will be taken and years 6 to 25 when it will not. The annual income is $0.131 × 47,120 = $6,173. The annual maintenance expense will be 33 kW × $20/kW = $660. The depreciation in each of the years 1 to 5 is 20% × 69,791 = $13,958. The resulting taxable income is the same for federal and state purposes, so we use a combined tax rate of 39.6% + 9% = 48.6% to calculate taxes in one line. The result appears as shown in Figure 9.2, where we use signs on the numbers to indicate cash inflows (+) or outflows (−)

3	Capacity of the system		33	kW
4	DC-to-AC derate factor for the system		0.815	
5	Lifetime of the system		25	years
6	Annual maintenance expense	$	20	per kW capacity
7	Insolation at Des Moines, Iowa		4.8	kWh/m2/day
8	Annual energy production from the system		47,120	kWh
9				
10	Price of the system, installed	$	164,213	
11	Federal tax credit	$	49,264	
12	Iowa state tax credit	$	20,000	
13	Alliant energy rebate	$	25,000	
14	Federal income tax rate		39.6%	
15	State income tax rate		9.0%	
16	Adjusted cost basis after FITC		139,581	
17	Bonus depreciation (Year 1 only)		69,791	
18	Headley Corp discount rate		8.0%	
19		Nominal amts	Time delay	Year 0 value	
20	Payment for the SPV system installed	(164,213)	0	(164,213)	
21	Federal tax credit NET of state tax obligation	44,830	0.5	43,138	
22	State tax credit NET of federal tax obligation	12,080	0.5	11,624	
23	Alliant rebate	25,000	0.25	24,524	
24	Fed & state taxes paid on Alliant rebate	(12,150)	0.5	(11,691)	
25	Bonus depreciation tax shield	33,918	0.5	32,638	
26	PV of net investment			(63,981)	

Figure 9.1 Headley data and calculations

28	Avoided cost of electric energy ($/kWh)		$0.131	
29	**Calculation of After-Tax Cash Flow**		**Years 1-5**	**Years 6-25**
30	Annual cost savings		6,173	6,173
31	Annual maintenance expense		(660)	(660)
32	Annual depreciation	$	(13,958)	-
33	Taxable income		(8,445)	5,513
34	Tax benefit if positive (tax paid if negative)		4,105	(2,679)
35	Cash flow after tax [sum of shaded lines]		9,617	2,834

Figure 9.2 After-tax cash flow in the Headley case

The feasibility analysis concludes with a calculation of the present value of these cash flows, from which we subtract the net investment to get the NPV of the project. The PV spreadsheet function will calculate the present value of a constant cash flow, so we will use it for years 1 to 5 and then again for years 6 to 25. The syntax of the PV function is

$$= \text{PV}(rate, nper, pmt, fv)$$

where *rate* is the company's discount rate, here given as 8 percent, *nper* is the number of periods in the annuity cash flow. That will be five (years) for the depreciation period and $25 - 5 = 20$ years in the postdepreciation period. The *pmt* is the annual payment—the cash flow of the annuity. It will be 9617 in years 1 to 5 (recall that Excel cannot take commas in its spreadsheet functions) and 2834 in years 6 to 25. The final parameter *fv* is optional. It is a terminal payment at the end of year *nper*. When the *pmt* is 0, the PV function will calculate the present value of a single payment of *fv* at the end of *nper* years.

For the five-year annuity in the depreciation period and the $25 - 5 = 20$-year annuity in the postdepreciation period, we use the PV function without the optional *fv*. However, the answer calculated by the PV function is a *present* value corresponding to the *start* of the annuity period. The postdepreciation period's PV calculation will therefore give a start-of-year-6 dollar amount, which we can also interpret as end-of-year-5. The PV calculation from that delayed annuity must be discounted back five years (to year 0) so it can be added to the PV from the first (undelayed) annuity to get the present value of the entire cash flow.

28	Avoided cost of electric energy ($/kWh)	0.131	
29	**Calculation of After-Tax Cash Flow**	**Years 1-5**	**Years 6-25**
30	Annual cost savings	=B8*B28	=B30
31	Annual maintenance expense	=-B6*B3	=B31
32	Annual depreciation	=-20%*B17	0
33	Taxable income	=SUM(B30:B32)	=SUM(C30:C32)
34	Tax benefit if positive (tax paid if negative)	=-($B$14+$B$15)*B33	=-($B$14+$B$15)*C33
35	Cash flow after tax	=B30+B31+B34	=C30+C31+C34
36		**Years 1-5**	**Years 6-25**
37	PV of each annuity at its starting time	=-PV($B$18,5,B35)	=-PV($B$18,B5-5,C35)
38	PV of each annuity as of Year 0	=B37	=-PV($B$18,5,0,C37)
39	Sum of annuities PV at Year 0	**=B38+C38**	
40	Net Present Value of the Project	=B39+$D$26	

Figure 9.3 Formulas for Excel's PV functions in the Headley case

28	Avoided cost of electric energy ($/kWh)	$0.131	
29	**Calculation of After-Tax Cash Flow**	**Years 1-5**	**Years 6-25**
30	Annual cost savings	6,173	6,173
31	Annual maintenance expense	(660)	(660)
32	Annual depreciation	$ (13,958)	–
33	Taxable income	(8,445)	5,513
34	Tax benefit if positive (tax paid if negative)	4,105	(2,679)
35	Cash flow after tax	**9,617**	**2,834**
36		**Years 1-5**	**Years 6-25**
37	PV of each annuity at its starting time	$38,399	$27,820
38	PV of each annuity as of Year 0	$38,399	18,934
39	Sum of annuities PV at Year 0	**$57,333**	
40	Net Present Value of the Project	($6,648)	

Figure 9.4 Values of Excel's PV functions in the Headley case

The formulas for these functions are shown in Figure 9.3, and their calculated values appear in Figure 9.4. Look in particular the formulas for cells C37 and C38 to see how the present value of the delayed annuity is calculated in two steps.

The values calculated by these formulas appear in Figure 9.4.

The NPV of the project is therefore the PV of its cash flows $57,333 minus its net investment $63,981 (from Figure 9.1), which is *negative* $6,648. A negative NPV indicates a project that is not profitable enough to yield more than Headley's hurdle rate of 8 percent. The decision, based on this analysis, would be to decline the project. That, however, would ignore an important element in many renewable energy projects, which is the future inflation of energy prices.

Accounting for the Inflation of Energy Prices

In Chapter 8, we noted that energy prices are expected to rise at a rate between 0.5 and 1 percent above the general rate of inflation over the next 20 years. In Iowa, the 2014 forecast was for electric energy price increases of 5 to 7 percent by the public utility over the next several years. A reasonable approximation for Headley Corporation's energy price inflation over the next 25 years might be 3 percent per year. If energy prices are to rise at 3 percent per year for 25 years, the solar carport will have much more value in future years than it does now, so the present value of its cash flow should be higher. This needs to be accounted for in the feasibility analysis.

In Chapter 8, we saw that the spreadsheet functions for annuities can be tricked into accounting for compound growth of the cash-flow values by using an inflation-adjusted discount rate. The adjusted rate has the formula $r^* = (r-g)/(1+g)$, where r is the company's nominal discount rate (here 8 percent) and g is the compound growth rate of the cash flow (here 3 percent). The adjustment for Headley is $r^* = (0.08-.03)/(1.03) = 0.0485$, meaning $r^* = 4.85\%$. Using this discount rate in the PV formulas of the Headley case gives a very different answer, shown in Figure 9.5.

Accounting for the expected inflation of energy prices over the next 25 years made a big difference in the present value of the future cash flow and therefore in the NPV. The NPV is now a positive $6,033, showing that the project is indeed worthy of investment.

36		Years 1-5	Years 6-25
37	PV of each annuity at its starting time	$38,399	$27,820
38	PV of each annuity as of Year 0	$38,399	18,934
39	Sum of annuities PV at Year 0	**$57,333**	
40	Net Present Value of the Project	($6,648)	
41			
42	Assumed growth rate for energy prices	3%	
43	Adjusted discount rate for Headley Corp	4.85%	
44			
45	PV of each annuity at its starting time	$41,806	$35,752
46	PV of each annuity as of Year 0	$41,806	28,208
47	Sum of annuities PV at Year 0	**$70,014**	
48	Net Present Value of the Project	$6,033	

Figure 9.5 Headley solar carport NPV with energy price inflation

Wait—What About the Age Derating of SPV Cells?

It is well known that SPV cells lose capacity at a rate of about 1 percent per year. This is known as the *age derating* of the SPV cells. This would cause the output of the SPV system to decrease over time and therefore lower the present value of its future cash flows. Because the age derating is taken to be a compounding process, we can incorporate this by a second refinement to the discount rate. We take the previously adjusted discount rate 4.85 percent and adjust it by a *negative growth rate*. This will use the same formula as before, except that g will be –1 percent not +3 percent, so we have to carefully account for the minus signs in the formula,

$$r^{**} = [4.85\% - (-1\%)]/[1+(-1\%)] = (4.85\% + 1\%)/(1-1\%)$$
$$= 0.0585/0.99 = 5.91\%.$$

The result of using this discount rate in the PV formulas, and in the discounting of the postdepreciation annuity present value back to year 0, appears in Figure 9.6.

The project's NPV comes out at a positive $1,183, which means that the project will create value for Headley Corporation. It does not look quite as good as it did when age derating was ignored, but it is still a viable project.

45	PV of each annuity at its starting time	$41,806	$35,752
46	PV of each annuity as of Year 0	$41,806	28,208
47	Sum of annuities PV at Year 0	$70,014	
48	Net Present Value of the Project	$6,033	
49			
50	Age derating of SPV panels	-1%	
51	Final adjusted discount rate	5.91%	
52		Years 1-5	Years 6-25
53	PV of each annuity at its starting time	$40,607	$32,730
54	PV of each annuity as of Year 0	$40,607	24,558
55	Sum of annuities PV at Year 0	$65,164	
56	Net Present Value of the Project	$1,183	

Figure 9.6 Headley solar carport NPV with energy price inflation and age derating

However, notice how important the various financial incentives for renewable energy were: the federal and state tax credits, the rebate, and the bonus depreciation. They reduced what would have been a $164,213 price tag to $63,981 (in Figure 9.1). Without any of those, this project would not have been viable in Des Moines, Iowa. In locations with higher insolation than Des Moines, the solar cells would have higher annual output and the project would be inherently more profitable, so it might fly without as much of the incentives. The purpose of these incentives is to make solar power feasible in a wider area than otherwise and thereby stimulate the demand for, refinement of, and therefore eventually lower the installed cost of SPV technology.

Feasibility Analysis with Peak-load Pricing of Electric Energy

Example 6 assumed that the company investing in the solar panels would pay a retail rate for electric energy. However, large users such as factories, hospitals, and colleges, which may use 200,000 kWh or more per month, tend to pay on a two-part tariff that consists of an *energy charge* (priced per kWh) and a *demand charge* (priced per kW of peak demand). The demand charge is what sets industrial and large commercial pricing apart from residential pricing. Industrial pricing as a two-part tariff is generally called *peak-load pricing* though this concept may be implemented by utility companies in a few different ways with many variations within each. Here, we consider the version in which the demand charge is based on the *user's highest power demand* (kW) in any 15-minute interval during the season in which the utility company tends to have its peak regionwide power demand. In many parts of the United States, that is the summer season (June to August), when the utility's peak power demand is driven by the use of air conditioning.

Large users that are subject to such a two-part tariff tend to pay a comparatively low energy rate, such as $0.03/kWh, but they pay a demand charge, such as $180/kW, on their peak power draw each year. Commercial and industrial users tend to have a lower average cost of electric energy than residential users due to the use of two-part tariffs. The U.S. Energy Information Agency reported in September 2013 that the U.S. average residential electric energy price was $0.1252/kWh, but the average commercial rate was $0.1059/kWh (15 percent lower than residential) and the average industrial rate was $0.0712/kWh (43 percent lower than residential). Industrial users are surely on a two-part tariff, as are some but not all commercial users.

The effect of peak-load pricing is to penalize users who have a high peak relative to their average consumption. Utility companies implement this policy, because the utility has to build sufficient capacity to meet the peak power needs of its service area. Users who all peak for a short time during the year, and at the same time, cause the utility to have to build capacity that is used during that peak but lies idle for the rest of the year.

The concept of a capacity factor applies as well to a user of electric energy as to a producer, and it helps us to understand the pricing of electric power and energy to industrial users. For users, the concept is called the *load factor* and is defined to be the total energy used as a percentage of the peak power demand applied across a whole year.

Example 7   Load Factor and Average Energy Cost in Peak-Load Pricing

Suppose that a large commercial customer is subject to an energy charge of $0.03/kWh and a demand charge of $180/kW of peak power demand during the year, both figures including state sales tax.

(a) If the customer has an average electric energy charge, including state sales tax, of $0.08/kWh, what is the user's capacity factor?

(b) If the user's load factor is 35 percent, what is the average cost of electric energy per kilowatt-hour?

Solution

(a) The *load factor* of an electric power user is analogous to the capacity factor in production, but here it is expressed in relation to a customer's demand for electric energy. The key to solving this problem is to use the definition of the load factor (L, %) as the total energy used (E, kWh) divided by the total energy that might have been used if the peak power (P, kW) had been drawn during every hour of the year. In symbols,

$$L = \frac{E}{24 \times 365 \times P}$$

$$L = \frac{E}{8760 \times P} \qquad \textit{(Definition of Load Factor)}$$

Under the two-part tariff, the company's annual energy bill is calculated from the $180/kW price on the peak demand (P) and the $0.03/kWh price of energy (E),

$$\text{Total Cost} = 180 \times P + 0.03 \times E \qquad \textit{(Total Cost Equation)}$$

The total cost can also be expressed as the company's average price per kilowatt-hour multiplied by its usage, which in our example is $0.08 \times E$. The total cost equation can therefore be rewritten as,

$$180 \times P + 0.03 \times E = 0.08 \times E$$

The definition of the load factor L above shows that $8760 \times C = E/P$. We can also get an expression for E/P from the total cost equation above. We will subtract $0.03 \times E$ from both sides of the total cost equation, and then divide through:

Starting with $180 \times P + 0.03 \times E = 0.08 \times E$

Subtract $0.03 \times E$, $180 \times P = 0.05 \times E$

Divide by P, $\dfrac{180}{0.05} = \dfrac{E}{P}$

Calculate the fraction, $\dfrac{E}{P} = 3{,}600$

The equation that defines the load factor can be rewritten as

$$8760 \times L = E/P$$

Substituting this $8760 \times C$ for E/P in the equation $E/P = 3,600$, we see that, for this company, the load factor is

$$8760 \times L = 3,600$$

$$L = \frac{3,600}{8,760} = 41\%$$

(b) Here, the user's load factor is given as 35 percent, and the two-part tariff has a capacity charge of $180/kW and an energy charge of $0.03/kWh. The task is to find the average cost of energy paid by the user. We do so using the total cost equation in which we write the average cost per kilowatt-hour as a variable a,

$$180 \times P + 0.03 \times E = a \times E \quad (\textit{Total Cost Equation})$$

Now divide through by the energy usage E to reveal an equation for the average cost per kilowatt-hour,

$$\frac{180 \times P}{E} + 0.03 = a$$

Then divide both top and bottom of $\dfrac{180 \times P}{E}$ by P to put this expression in a form that uses E/P. The result is our average cost equation,

$$\frac{180}{E/P} + 0.03 = a \quad (\textit{Average Cost Equation})$$

From the definition of the capacity factor, we know that $E/P = 8760 \times L$. The problem stated that the load factor is 35 percent, so $E/P = 8760 \times 35\% = 3066$. We substitute that number for E/P in the average cost equation and calculate a,

$$\frac{180}{3066} + 0.03 = a$$

$$0.0587 + 0.03 = a$$

$$a = 0.0887$$

> This tells us that the company was paying an average price of $0.0887/kWh even though its energy charge was only 0.03/kWh. The demand charge was evidently responsible for $0.0587/kWh in its total energy cost.

Example 7 shows that a large part of an industrial consumer's energy bill can come from the demand charge. The key feature of a solar power system is that it will produce its power precisely on the clear, hot summer days when air conditioning is causing the firm's electric power demand to peak. The SPV system therefore *shaves the peak* and reduces the firm's demand charge, which could imply a significant savings.

However, there is one factor that works against the value of the SPV unit for industrial customers. The problem is that the efficiency of a solar panel decreases at higher temperatures, and on the hottest day of the year, when air conditioning loads are driving electric energy to its annual peak, the SPV system will be at its *worst efficiency*. The standard testing condition for rating a solar panel's power output is 25°C (77°F). Above that temperature, the panel's output will be less than its rated capacity, and below that temperature its output will be better. We noted in our consideration of constraints in an earlier chapter that the effect of temperature on the efficiency of an SPV unit is given by its *temperature coefficient*. Solar cells based on crystalline technology typically have a temperature coefficient of about 0.5 percent (loss) per degree Celsius above 25°C. On a hot summer day, a solar cell can reach temperatures as high as 70°C (158°F),[3] so the loss of efficiency can be significant.

NREL's PVWatts and SAM *Software for Renewable Energy Project Modeling*

The NREL, through funding from the U.S. Department of Energy, supports a basic online solar energy calculator called PVWatts (http://pvwatts.nrel.gov/) and a sophisticated energy production and financial modeling system called SAM (https://sam.nrel.gov/).[4] PVWatts accounts for the effect of temperature, using monthly average temperatures, when estimating the monthly energy production from an SPV unit at a particular location in the United States and summing the monthly production to get an estimated annual production.[5] PVWatts also assumes that the SPV unit's temperature will be the same as the ambient air temperature, although in full sun an SPV unit can heat up as high as 70°C (158°F).[6] Each of these is an important limitation to the PVWatts model, because an SPV unit's operating temperature affects its efficiency (the *temperature derating* effect), and the temperature effect has a much more dramatic consequence for the financial viability of a project when the quantity used to calculate the user's full-year electric bill from the alternative source is the user's summer peak demand *across 15-minute intervals*. In that context, the monthly average temperature is not important. What is important is the month's *maximum* temperature over 15-minute intervals, because that will determine the output of the SPV unit at the time when the firm's peak demand charge is determined. The feasibility analyst must therefore estimate the maximum air temperature in the peak month, consider the amount of wind at such a time (which would cool the SPV unit), and then estimate the resulting temperature of the SPV unit at that time.

Example 8   PVWatts Monthly and Annual Production Data

(a) Use PVWatts to calculate the monthly energy production from a 1 kW SPV unit located in Austin, Texas, facing south with a fixed tilt at latitude and having a derate factor of 0.77.

(b) Calculate the *effective* insolation by taking the annual total energy production, dividing by the derate factor, and dividing again by 365. How does that compare to the average insolation?

Solution

(a) Giving these data to the PVWatts calculator (pvwatts.nrel.gov), produces the monthly production values and summary calculations of average annual insolation and total energy seen in Table 9.7. Dividing 1,238 by the derate factor 0.77 and by 365 gives 4.40 kWh/m²/day. This is not the same as the 4.92 kWh/m²/day annual average reported in the table. In fact, it is only 4.40/4.92 = 0.90 = 90% of the stated average insolation.

Table 9.7 Output from PVWatts

Month	Solar radiation (kWh/ m²/day)	AC energy (kWh)
January	3.52	80
February	4.30	87
March	5.13	113
April	4.94	102
May	5.17	109
June	5.71	115
July	6.38	131
August	6.00	125
September	5.96	121
October	4.65	98
November	3.60	76
December	3.66	81
Average insolation	4.92	
Total energy		1,238

(b) The reason that the effective annual insolation rate calculated here is less than the average annual insolation rate reported by PVWatts for Austin, Texas, is that Austin is very hot most of the year. PVWatts includes a temperature-derating factor in its calculation of the monthly output of an SPV unit. When the monthly average temperature is above the SPV standard testing and rating condition of 77°F (25°C), the temperature derating will cause the DC output to be lower than the rated capacity of the SPV unit. In Austin, almost all months of the year have average temperatures greater than 77°F. In colder climates, the winter months will get a *positive* temperature effect, and the summer months get a negative effect. However, the angle of the sun in the winter is less advantageous for solar production than it is in the summer, so most temperate locations in the United States have a net temperature derating, many as high as 5 to 10 percent.

Example 8 yields an important lesson about using PVWatts output for spreadsheet modeling. If the average insolation that appears in the output were used directly to calculate the annual output of an SPV unit, the result would overestimate the real output. A better estimate is obtained by taking PVWatts' report of total energy output for 1 kW, dividing that by the derate factor, and dividing again by 365.

NREL SAM

NREL's SAM is a sophisticated energy production and financial modeling program available free of charge through the NREL website. It can be used for a variety of renewable energy technologies, including SPV, STE, wind, and biomass. When downloaded to the user's computer, it can draw data about tax incentives from the DSIRE website, retail electric energy prices from a public database, renewable energy technology data from NREL databases, and weather data from a list of sources. Its financial modeling is adaptable to residential and commercial energy pricing (per kWh), which may vary by time of day. It does not model peak-load pricing.

Detailed Example of SPV Feasibility with Peak-Load Pricing

The following example traces the effect of peak-load pricing in a hypothetical example that is meant to simulate a large commercial user in Southern California, where the average commercial price of electric energy is $0.1614/kWh and the average industrial price is $0.122/kWh.

Example 9   Commercial SPV Feasibility with Peak-Load Pricing

A large commercial user of electric energy is located in Southern California and would like to build a 100 kW SPV system that will last 30 years and cost $4,000/kW, installed. The annually averaged insolation at its location is 5.63 kWh/m²/day.

The company will use the 30 percent federal tax credit for solar power systems and assumes that 50 percent bonus depreciation will be available. There is no SITC for renewables, but the California Solar Initiative (CSI) is a state-mandated public utility rebate program that now pays $0.025/kWh to commercial users for the first five years of operation of an SPV system that is 30 kW or larger. (The program started in 2007 with payments of $0.39/kWh, but the rate has decreased as the state approaches its goals for renewable power capacity.)

The firm is subject to a two-part tariff that charges $220/kW of peak demand in the year and $0.05/kWh of energy used, inclusive of state sales tax. The company expects energy prices to rise at 2.5 percent per year for the next several decades.

The firm's usage pattern has a load factor of 35 percent and a total energy use that averages 200,000 kWh per month. The company's peak in August is due to its high need for air conditioning, which runs on electric energy. The peak always occurs on a sunny day, so if the company were to install 100 kWh of SPV panels, it would not only be able to supply energy over the year but reduce its peak power demand charge. However, on a hot August day, the solar panel would likely be operating at a temperature of 55°C.

The company uses a nominal discount rate of 8 percent per year on cost-saving projects. Its federal income tax rate is 39.6 percent and its state income tax rate is 8.84 percent.

(a) What is the peak power demand of this company? Would a 100 kW solar array overpower the firm?

(b) What is the present value of the net initial investment?

(c) Is this SPV project financially viable?

(d) *Sensitivity analysis on the solution.* What difference would there be in the profitability of the project if the developer could build the project at $3,750/kW rather than $4,000? Hold to the $3,750 capacity cost, but consider the result if the CSI meets its capacity goal before the project is submitted for a CSI rebate, and the rebate is no longer available? Hold to the $3,750 capacity cost, and keep the CSI rebate, but take away the bonus depreciation. What effect would that have?

(e) What is the average cost of electric energy for this firm?

(f) What conclusions would the analysis give if the peak-load pricing were ignored and the analysis conducted in the manner of example 6, using only the average cost of electric energy as the cost savings from using the SPV unit?

Solution

(a) The company's peak power demand can be calculated from the company's load factor and the total energy consumption. The definitional equation says

$$L = \frac{E}{8760 \times P} \quad \text{(\textit{Definition of Load Factor})}$$

but the E is the annual energy usage by the firm. We are given that the monthly average usage is 200,000 kWh, so we use 35 percent for the load factor and $200,000 \times 12$ for E, then solve for P,

$$0.35 = \frac{200,000 \times 12}{8760 \times P}$$

$$P = \frac{200,000 \times 12}{8760 \times 0.35}$$

$$P = 782.78 \text{ kW}$$

As the peak power demand is about 783 kW, the 100 kW solar array will satisfy only a small fraction of that demand. It will not overpower the firm.

The basic data from the problem can be set up in a spreadsheet as shown in Figure 9.7.

(b) We begin with an analysis of the net initial investment, meaning net of the federal tax credit and depreciation tax shield. Figure 9.8 shows the result as a net investment of $215,498 in year 0 dollars. A key difference between this example and the Headley Corporation case of example 8 is that the California rebate is earned each year for five years, so there is no one-time rebate. Correspondingly, in Figure 9.8, cell B26 is zeroed out, and the rebate percentage in B17 is used in a special line of the income statement (cell B44) shown in Figure 9.9.

(c) The annual benefits and costs depend on both the production of energy and the power output of the SPV system at the time of the company's peak load in August. The demand charge is $220/kW/yr and the energy charge is $0.05/kWh. Annually, the SPV system

	A	B	C
1	**Chapter 9 Example 9**	SPV with PLP	
2	Rated capacity	100	kW
3	Installed cost per kW of capacity	4,000	$/kW
4	Useful life of SPV unit	30	years
5	Tax life of the SPV unit	5	years
6	Annual maintenace cost per kW	$20	per kW capacity
7	Derate factor (DC to AC)	0.77	
8	Age derating of the solar cells	-1%	per year
9	Temperature coefficient of the solar cells	0.5%	per oC above 25oC
10	Expected solar cell temp during peak	55	oC
11	Location's Insolation	5.63	kWh/m2/day
12	Energy price per kWh	0.122	$/kWh
13	Demand price per kW/yr	0	$/kW per yr
14	Discount rate used by the firm	8.0%	per year
15	Federal tax credit rate	30%	% of installed cost
16	State tax credit rate	0%	% of installed cost
17	Rebate or other taxable incentive	0.025	$/kWh for 5 years
18	Bonus depreciation percentage	50%	change to 0 if no B.D.
19	Firm's federal income tax rate	39.60%	
20	Firm's state income tax rate	8.84%	
21	Nominal inflation of energy prices	2.5%	
22	Total installed price of the system	$ 400,000	

Figure 9.7 Data for example 9

22	Total installed price of the system	$	400,000	
23	Cost basis after federal tax credit	$	340,000	
24	Federal tax credit amount	$	120,000	
25	State tax credit amount	$	-	
26	Taxable rebate/other amount (one-time)	$	-	
27	Bonus depreciation amount	$	170,000	
28	**Calculation of PV of Net Investment**	Nominal amts	Time delay	Year 0 value
29	Payment for the SPV system installed	(400,000)	0	(400,000)
30	Federal tax credit NET of state tax obliga	109,392	0.5	105,263
31	State tax credit NET of federal tax obliga	-	0.5	-
32	Rebate/other amount (one-time only)	-	0.25	-
33	Fed & state taxes paid on rebate/other	-	0.5	-
34	Bonus depreciation tax shield	82,348	0.5	79,239
35	PV of net investment			**(215,498)**

Figure 9.8 Calculation of the PV of net investment

will produce 100 kW × 0.77 (derate) × 5.63 (kWh/kW/day) × 365 days = 158,231 kWh (cell B39 in Figure 9.9). The amount of power that can be shaved from the firm's peak is the AC output of the SPV system, which is significantly affected by the operating temperature at the time of the August peak demand. That AC output will be the rated capacity of 100 kW multiplied by the derate factor

0.77, multiplied again by the temperature derating factor, which is calculated from an efficiency loss of $(55 - 25) \times 0.5\% = 15\%$. The AC output on the peak summer day will therefore be $100 \times 0.77 \times (1-15\%) = 65.45$ kW. That saves $65.45 \times 220 = \$14,399$ per year on the demand charge. The savings on the energy charge is 158,231 kWh $\times 0.05$ \$/kWh $= \$7,912$. The total annual savings is therefore $\$22,311$.

This analysis calculates the annual energy production using the *effective annual* insolation for the location given in the statement of the problem. This number was taken from PVWatts as in example 8 and thereby reflects a temperature derating based on the *average monthly* temperature at the location. Although PVWatts does account for the fact that the normal operating cell temperature (NOCT) is hotter than the air temperature, even that allowance is based on an average over time. When a company pays for electric service under peak-load pricing, most of its annual cost is accounted for by the power drawn during the hottest 15-minute interval of the year, and PVWatts does not track such data. That is a time when there is likely to be full sun and little or no wind to cool the SPV unit. In our analysis of production during the peak 15-minute period, we had to make a specific assumption about the panel temperature, here 55°C (131°F), although the air temperature in a peak Iowa summer day will not be more than 104°F (40°C).

The CSI rebate provides 0.025 (\$/kWh) $\times 158,231$ kWh $= \$3,956$ per year for the first five years, which, conveniently for this analysis, coincide with the depreciation period.

Maintenance expenses are estimated at $20/kW per year, meaning $2,000. The calculation of annual cash flows and of their present values appears in Figure 9.9.

The project shows an NPV of *positive* $11,873, which indicates a *Go* decision on the project. Another perspective on the profitability of this project is seen in the calculation of the project's internal rate of return (IRR). For a cash flow that consists of an initial investment and a (constant) annuity of benefits in the future, the spreadsheet RATE function will calculate a rate of return. However, this cash flow consists of two annuity segments, so RATE will not work. Instead, we use the spreadsheet's Goal Seek routine. The project's rate of return is defined as the discount rate that would cause the NPV to be zero. The firm's discount rate is located in cell B14. The NPV of the project is in cell B53. We pass these cell addresses to the Goal Seek routine in its dialog box as shown in Figure 9.10.

Hitting *OK* starts the Goal Seek routine, which changes the content of cell B14. When Goal Seek reports a solution, as shown in Figure 9.11, one must hit *OK* to hold the solution. Then look for that solution in cell B14 of the financial model. In this case, the

35	PV of net investment			(215,498)
36	Net growth rate for revenues	1.47%	per year	
37	Growth-adjusted discount rate	6.43%	per year	
38	AC power during summer peak	65.45	kW	
39	Annual production of AC energy	158,231	kWh per year	
40	**Annual Cash Flows**	**Years 1-5**	**Years 6-N**	
41	Annual savings in energy charges	$ 7,912	$ 7,912	
42	Annual savings in demand charges	$ 14,399	$ 14,399	
43	Total annual savings	**$ 22,311**	**$ 22,311**	cash
44	California Solar Initiative rebate	$ 3,956		cash
45	Annual maintenance expense	$ (2,000)	$ (2,000)	cash
46	Depreciation expense (straight-line)	$ (34,000)		
47	Profit before tax	**$ (9,734)**	**$ 20,311**	
48	Tax saved (paid)	$ 3,855	$ (8,043)	cash
49	Cash flow after tax	**$ 28,121**	**$ 12,268**	
50	PV of cash flow at start of segment	$ 117,082	$ 150,610	
51	PV of cash flow at time of investment	$ 117,082	$ 110,289	
52	PV of cash flow, both segments	$ 227,371		
53	Net Present Value of the project	$ 11,873		

Figure 9.9 Calculation of cash flows and net present value

Goal Seek

Set cell: B53

To value: 0

By changing cell: $B$14

Cancel   OK

Figure 9.10 Goal seek

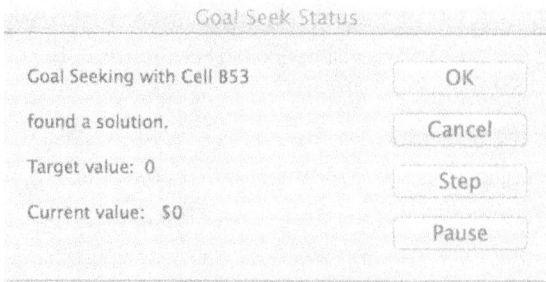

Goal Seek Status	
Goal Seeking with Cell B53	OK
found a solution.	Cancel
Target value: 0	Step
Current value: $0	Pause

Figure 9.11 Goal seek finds a solution

number 8.6 percent would be found in cell B14, so the project has a profitability of 8.6 percent per year. This is above the firm's 8 percent hurdle rate, which we would expect, because the NPV was positive. (Note: After each use of Goal Seek, the new value, here 8.6 percent, will remain until the old value, here the firm's 8 percent discount rate, is restored by hand.)

(d) *Sensitivity analysis on the solution.* Sensitivity analysis is easy to perform when the solution is set up in a spreadsheet such as this. After setting the firm's discount rate in B14 back to 8 percent, we conduct the following analyses.

Loss of Bonus Depreciation. Setting the bonus depreciation percentage in cell B18 to 0, we look at cell B53 and find that the NPV has gone from the base case result of +11,873 to –11,309. The project is not viable without the bonus depreciation! The corresponding IRR is only 7.5 percent per year, not high enough to clear the firm's hurdle rate of 8 percent.

Lower Installed Cost. Holding to the loss of the bonus depreciation, would the project become profitable again if the installed cost could be negotiated from $4,000/kW down to $3,750/kW? We set the discount rate in B14 back to 8 percent and change the capacity cost in B3 to 3,750. The result is an NPV of *positive* $105, which is barely above zero, but it does indicate a *Go* decision. The corresponding IRR is 8.01 percent, which is barely above the firm's hurdle rate 8 percent, as the NPV was just barely above zero.

Loss of the CSI. What would happen to this project if the CSI meets its capacity goal before the project can be submitted for a CSI rebate, and the rebate is no longer available? Let us continue with the assumption that the bonus depreciation is not available. At the installed cost of $3,750, the project was essentially at break-even. A loss of the CSI rebate would send the NPV negative and the rate of return below 8 percent. The question now will be, "What (lower) capacity cost would just compensate for the loss of the CSI?" In other words, without the CSI, what is the break-even capacity cost? To find the answer, we reset the discount rate cell B14 back to 8 percent, keep the capacity cost in B3 at 3,750, but set the CSI rate in cell B17 to 0. The result in cell B53 is an NPV of negative $9,843, as expected. We find the break-even capacity cost using Goal seek's dialog box, "Set cell B53 (NPV) to 0 by changing cell B3 (capacity cost)." The result in B3 is $3,534, meaning that the capacity cost would have to be at or below $3,534 to make the project viable if the CSI rebate is not available.

(e) The average cost of energy to this user is given by a generalized form of the text's *average cost equation.* In example 7, where the demand charge was $180/kW and the energy charge was $0.03/kWh, the average cost equation appeared as $a = \dfrac{180}{E/P} + 0.03$, where E is the annual energy production (kWh) and P is the peak demand (kW). If we write d for the demand price and e for the energy price, the general form of the average cost equation is $a = \dfrac{d}{E/P} + e$. In this problem, $d = \$220/kW$, $e = \$0.05/kWh$, $E = 200{,}000$ kWh/month $\times$ 12 months $= 2{,}400{,}000$ kWh/year, and P was calculated in part (a) to be 783 kW. The average cost is therefore $a = \dfrac{220}{2400000/783} + 0.05 = 0.072 + 0.050 = 0.122$, meaning $0.122/kWh.

(f) If the firm had been subjected to ordinary pricing at $0.122/kWh, it would have paid 158,231 (kWh) $\times$ 0.122 ($/kWh) = $19,265 per year for the energy produced by the solar panels. Using the peak-load pricing formula and explicit temperature derating at the time of the summer peak, we found in the spreadsheet line 43 a total avoided cost, hence savings, of $22,311. This shows that the average energy price underestimated the savings that would result under peak-load pricing. By using $0.122 for the energy price in cell B12 and 0 for the demand charge in B13, the spreadsheet would show that the average energy price model predicts an NPV of *negative* $12,013 in the base case. This would have indicated an incorrect *No Go* decision rather than the favorable decision derived using peak-load pricing correctly in part (c).

Example 9 shows the power of spreadsheet modeling and the importance of sensitivity analysis on a financial model.

Take-aways

This chapter presented realistic examples of feasibility analysis for sustainable technologies. The following are the key points to remember.

- A realistic analysis, adequate for making business decisions about investments in sustainable technologies, must take into consideration federal and state tax credits, utility rebates, rules for depreciation, and other incentives that impact the after-tax cash flow of a project. The DSIRE website (www.dsireusa.org) is a good starting point for state and federal rules that relate to renewable energy, but the incentives for renewable energy have expiration dates written into the law, so financial analysts should consult accountants and attorneys for the most up-to-date information.
- The bonus depreciation that existed through 2013 and was proposed for renewal in 2014 has been the subject of criticism by conservative politicians and may be vulnerable to expiration, yet as we saw in example 9, it has an effect on the profitability of renewable energy projects that may be significant.
- The profitability of a project is best understood from two complementary perspectives, NPV expressed in dollars and IRR expressed as a percentage per year. NPV greater than zero indicates a viable project, as does IRR greater than the firm's hurdle rate. In most practical situations, these two

methods give the same answer about whether to invest in a project or not.[2]

- The PVWatts solar energy calculator and the more complete SAM production–finance model and other commercial software packages like Clean Power Finance are important resources for projects in which the owner pays for electric energy by the kilowatt-hour, as is typical for residential and many commercial customers. However, it is vital that the technology analyst understand the assumptions that go into those models. A good practice for cross-checking the output of a commercial software package is to set up a spreadsheet to do one's own calculations and to perform a sensitivity analysis on the spreadsheet solution.

- PVWatts and SAM do not calculate the financial results of an SPV installation if the owner pays for electric energy under peak-load pricing, also called a two-part tariff, as it is typical for industrial and large commercial customers. The financial analyst conducting a feasibility study in this context should use PVWatt's monthly output data to calculate a savings on the annual energy charge. However, to account for the temperature derating of an SPV unit at the time of the owner's peak electric demand, the analyst needs to build a special spreadsheet, and make specific assumptions about the panel's operating temperature at the peak time, like those

---

[2] There is an exception to the rule that NPV and IRR give the same decision. The IRR method must be used with care in cases where a project has more than one IRR. This can happen in practice if the cash flow changes sign several times. The author has seen one such example, caused by a 15-year bank loan financing a 25-year project. The investment in year 0 was a negative number, of course; the years 1–5 cash flows were positive due to the five-year depreciation; years 6–15 had negative cash flow due to the bank loan; and years 16–25 had positive cash flow. The result was one IRR near 3% and another near 60%. A sensible IRR of around 11% was found by explicitly using the cash flow during the depreciation period to pay down the principal on the bank loan as much as possible.

shown in example 9, to calculate the savings on the annual demand charge and its financial consequences.

To this point in the book, we have looked at technology decisions in strictly economic terms, although *sustainability* introduces considerations that go beyond market economics, such as a clean environment for future generations. In the next chapter, we look at how public policy supporting sustainable technologies has tried to give an economic value to the sustainable attributes of technology.

CHAPTER 10

Accounting for Environmental Benefits

Overview

Renewable energy systems are not just another way for investors to make a profit, although up to this point in the book we have treated them as such. Relative to power systems based on fossil fuels, renewable power systems decrease greenhouse gas (GHG) emissions and decrease toxic emissions to the environment. Sustainable technologies of types other than power systems also aim to reduce the toxic effects of human activity. Such benefits to the environment, which impact present and future human life, should count for something in the financial evaluation of sustainable technologies.

Our approach in this chapter is to put a financial value on the environmental benefits of sustainable technologies using the emerging markets in *environmental attributes*—represented by renewable energy certificates (RECs) and carbon permits—to price those benefits. However, these markets in environmental attributes are not ordinary commodity markets that are driven by the forces of supply and demand, so the price signals sent from these markets must be interpreted cautiously.

The markets for RECs and carbon permits have been established by governmental authorities with the goal of reducing the production of GHGs. In the case of RECs, the buyers are retail electric power companies. In the carbon markets, the buyers are industrial producers of GHGs, including traditional electric power companies but extending to all large industrial users of fossil fuels. RECs and carbon permits represent two very different instruments of public policy for controlling GHG emissions. We will consider each one in turn.

Renewables Portfolio Standards and the Market for RECs

In their desire to reduce GHG production within their geographic domains of authority, some states have enacted laws that establish minimum standards for the percentage of electric energy sold in the state that must come from renewable sources. These laws are called *renewables portfolio standards* (RPS). As of late 2013, 29 states had enacted a mandatory RPS, and eight states had stated voluntary goals. However, the laws vary from state to state. In fact, no two states have identical standards. The key provisions in the RPS are (1) what percentage of the electric energy sold to users in the state must come from renewable sources and in which years going into the future, (2) which technologies qualify as a renewable source, (3) the geographic location of renewable electric power generation facility whose energy output may qualify as meeting the standard, (4) the penalty price to be paid by a load-serving entity (LSE) for not meeting the standard, (5) whether any technologies have their own specific minimum requirements, called a *carve-out* or *tier* structure in the standard, and (6) rules for *banking* unused RECs.

The states' standards typically state a long-term goal for the year 2020 and include a yearly progression of yearly targets that reach the long-term goal. A few states put their long-term goal in 2025, and one in 2035. Among the 17 states that have a goal for 2020, the average standard for 2014 is 10.1 percent renewable energy, and for 2020 it is 19.0 percent, showing that the typical standard calls for nearly a doubling of the percentage of energy to be supplied from renewable sources over that six-year period.

The states typically allow a wide range of renewable resources to qualify for their standard. Almost all will accept solar thermal electric, photovoltaics, landfill gas, wind, biomass, hydroelectric, geothermal electric, municipal solid waste, anaerobic digestion, tidal energy, wave energy, and fuel cells using renewable fuels. Somewhat less common are solar water heat, solar space heat, solar thermal process heat, and cogeneration (combined heat and power). Only Ohio admits advanced nuclear technology in its RPS.

A state's RPS seems to be intended to promote the use of renewable power systems within the state, although generation outside the state by

LSEs that sell into the state tends also to be permitted. The smaller states, as in New England and the Mid-Atlantic region, have formed trading groups that permit their RPS to be satisfied by generation outside their state but within the group, although the amount of renewable energy generated out of state is typically limited to a percentage of the total requirement.

The RPS is typically enforced by an alternative compliance payment (ACP), which is a penalty fee to be paid by an load-serving entity that fails to meet the RPS through its owned generation or RECs that it purchases. The typical fee is $50 per MWh of deficiency ($0.05 per kWh).

Tiered structures that specify standards for different technologies are not uncommon in states' RPSs, especially when the RPS allows for energy-efficiency improvements such as cogeneration. Tiers are also used to distinguish pre-existing versus new generation. Several states have carve-outs for distributed generation, which includes solar photovoltaic units on a customer's property and net-metered to the customer. Sixteen states had a carve-out for solar energy in 2012.[1] For 10 states whose solar carve-outs were reported by DSIRE in 2014, the average requirement was 0.5 percent of energy sold, ranging from 0.07 to 2.00 percent.[2] The ACP for solar tends to be very high at present, $300 to $500 per MWh ($0.30 to $.50 per kWh), which is more than twice the price of the underlying energy, but it is usually slated to decline to the regular ACP over a 10- to 15-year period. Some states achieve a similar effect, promoting solar power, by giving solar RECs (SRECs) a *credit multiplier* in their use to meet the requirements of an RPS.

The common provision for banking RECs is two years after the year of issuance, meaning that an REC can be used in three years, the year of issuance and the following two compliance years. Some states have no banking provision. Only one has five-year banking, and in another the RECs have indefinite life.

The Creation and Retirement of RECs

The typical state RPS law applies to all LSEs, which are companies that sell electric energy to end-users in the state, although the law may have different rules for investor-owned, municipal, and cooperative utilities. Thus, every company that sells electric energy to end-users in the state must report its total sales of electric energy in the state (in megawatt-hours, MWh), and it must account for the origin of the sold energy, both geographically and technologically.

The accounting for the origination of the energy is accomplished in the United States and Canada through nine regional tracking systems or registries. Four are regional (New England, Mid-Atlantic, Upper Midwest, and West). Four are state-specific (Texas, North Carolina, Michigan, and Nevada), and one is the North American Renewables Registry (NARR), covering states and provinces not covered by the regional markets.[3] According to the Green Power Network, "REC tracking systems provide a basis for creating, managing, and retiring RECs, ensuring that each REC is counted only once." Each REC that is issued accounts for 1 MWh of energy produced from a qualifying renewable power system. The certificate is dated by the year of production and is qualified by the state in which the production took place and the type of technology used.

These broad regional systems for the registry of RECs should not be confused with trading groups. RECs are usually restricted to use in their state of origin, although the New England and Mid-Atlantic states allow for some interstate reciprocity.

The REC as a concept owes its existence to the remarkable idea that green energy can be separated into *green* and *energy*. The certificate of origin (validating renewability) can be sold separately from the energy itself. Thus, a renewable power system simultaneously creates two products, the energy and the REC. When the energy from a renewable power system is sold with its REC, it is called *bundled*. The idea that the REC can be unbundled from the energy and sold separately is what creates the need for a registry. It also implies that any energy sold from a renewable power system without its REC must be classified as *nonrenewable* energy.

REC Markets and Prices

As of 2014, the market for RECs is highly fragmented, because it is not one market. There is a different *market* for each state's RECs, and each state may have several tiers to its RECs or RECs designated to a specific

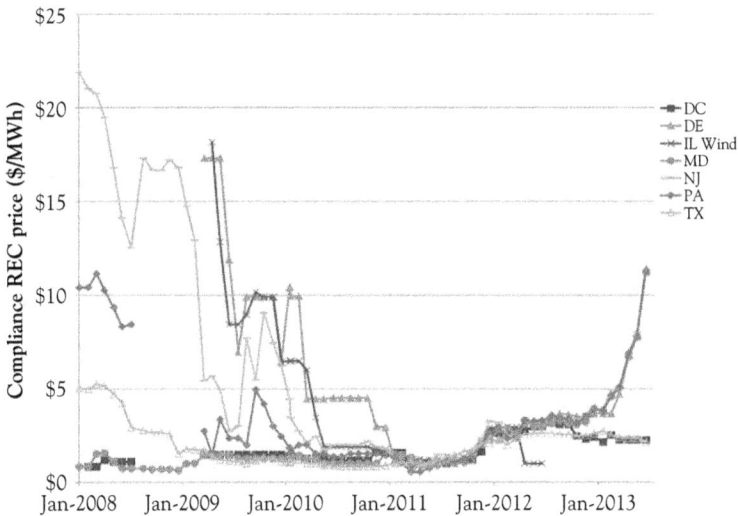

Figure 10.1 REC prices in the compliance market

Source: U.S. Department of Energy EERE green power network.

technology, such as the SRECs. There is no single exchange on which RECs trade. The exchange mechanisms that bring buyers and sellers together are the companies that broker or trade in RECs, so RECs sell *over the counter* in private deals. Some of the brokers have been willing to publish information about REC prices, which we will discuss for the example of Figure 10.1. To better understand those price patterns, we must first look at the structure of the REC markets.

The Simplest Model of an REC Market—Price Discontinuity

The simplest model of an REC market reveals a lot about its underlying dynamics. Imagine an REC that sells in a single state. The state has imposed annual requirements for the percentage of renewable energy in the mix sold by entities that serve loads in the state; those requirements increase year by year up to the target amount and year specified in the state RPS law, such as 20 percent by 2020. The state imposes an ACP of $50 per MWh that a load-serving entity (LSE) must pay if it is short in meeting its commitment. In any compliance year, the LSEs are given until March 31 of the following year to produce RECs for that compliance year that are sufficient to cover their requirement.

The problem with this market model is that the price of an REC is either zero or $50. The reason is that during the compliance year, both supply and demand are fixed. The supply of RECs is determined by the total capacity of the renewable power systems in the state, and as it usually takes more than a year to take a power project from idea to production, that capacity will not change during the year even if suppliers see high prices. Likewise, the demand for RECs is determined strictly by the amount of energy consumed within the state, and that will hardly be affected during the year by users' anticipation of higher or lower REC prices. The consequence is that supply stands at the total capacity of the renewable power systems, and demand stands at the year's RPS multiplied by the annual energy demand of the state. If the supply of RECs is more than the demand, the price of the RECs becomes zero, and unused RECs expire worthless. If the supply of RECs is less than the demand, then all available RECs are bought up and retired, and for the remainder, LSEs are forced to pay the alternative compliance rate. Anticipating that, buyers in the market see the alternative compliance price as a ceiling price for any RECs that remain for sale in the market.

In this simple model, investors who are considering the construction of new renewable power projects are left to guess, for each of the 20 to 25 years in which their project will produce RECs, whether there will be a surplus or shortage of RECs in relation to the standard. That task may be so daunting to many investors that they would likely ignore the value of RECs altogether when making their investment decisions.

Policies for a REC Market that Promotes Price Stability

If the market prices for RECs were more stable from year to year, investors would be able to use REC prices in their financial feasibility analyses, thereby incorporating into their decisions the value of a renewable power project's benefits to the environment. One policy that promotes somewhat more stable REC prices is the *banking* of unused RECs for future use. Most states allow a REC to be retired either in the year in which it was generated or in the following two compliance years.[1] One state permits

---

[1] A compliance year may be a calendar year or a fiscal year, such as April 1–March 31, depending on the RPS.

five-year banking, and another does not set a limit. The consequence of this practice is that, even if there is a surplus of RECs in the current compliance year, if there is *any possibility* of a deficit of RECs in the next compliance year or the year after that, this year's RECs will trade at a positive value. In one-year banking, they would trade at a value equal to the ACP multiplied by the probability of a deficit and discounted one year. With two-year banking, the price would be the maximum of a similar formula for each year. In general, for a REC with a life of N years, if p_i is the probability of a deficit in the ith subsequent year, and ACP_i is the alternative compliance payment in that year, and r is the discount rate for investments of similar risk, then the price of the REC in the year of its issuance will be $P = \max_{i=0,\ldots N} \left\{ \dfrac{p_i ACP_i}{(1+r)^i} \right\}$. The price is determined by the largest of these quantities, so when investors respond by preparing more renewable capacity for that critical year, the probability of a deficit in that year will fall, and other years will become critical in addition to the original one. Thus, the longer the banking period, the more stable the REC prices will be.

The other policy that impacts the stability of REC prices is the fungibility of RECs across states. The broader the geographic market, the larger the market will be in terms of energy sold (MWh) per year. The price of the common REC will be driven by the aggregate expected supply in relation to the aggregate compliance requirements across the region of the common market. The addition of any new capacity will be relatively small in relation to the large market, as compared to the statewide markets, so expectations about the aggregate surplus or deficit in the supply of RECs will change more slowly for a large market than for a small one.

The Compliance Markets

The type of market described in the previous section is called a *compliance market*, because the buyers (LSEs) purchase RECs in order to comply with the requirements of their RPS. As we have seen, the compliance market has unusual supply-and-demand properties, because the RECs have no inherent value on which buyers' preferences might differ. The demand for RECs by LSEs is fixed by the RPS and is independent of their price. The price history for RECs in several states in the Mid-Atlantic group and in Texas over the period 2008 to 2013 is shown in the graph in Figure 10.1.[4]

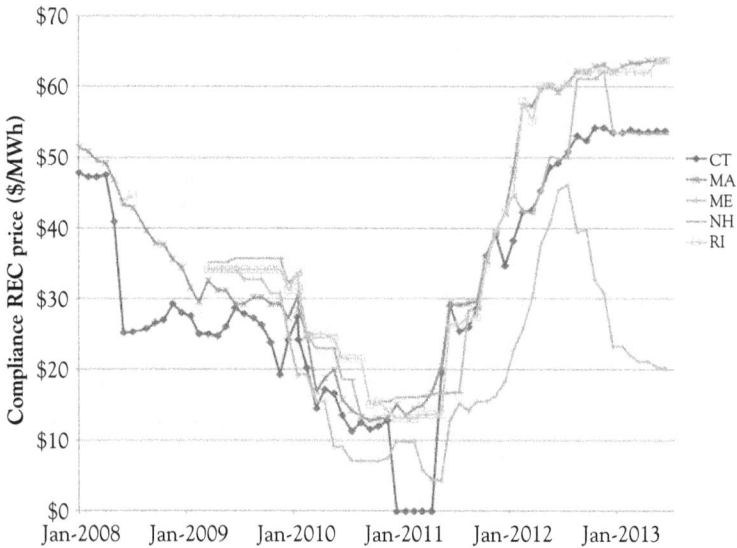

Figure 10.2 **REC prices in the New England compliance market**

Source: U.S. Department of energy EERE green power network.

The graph in Figure 10.1 shows that the spot-market price for RECs could vary quite a lot state by state at any given time, but when all states were seeing a surplus of RECs, they all had prices near zero. This was not the case in New England, whose prices in 2013 tended to stay high, as seen in Figure 10.2.

North Carolina differs from all other states in that it permits an REC from *any state* to be used in satisfaction of up to 25 percent of the North Carolina RPS. North Carolina also allows RECs to be purchased within three years of their generation, and according to DSIRE, "they must be retired within seven years from when their cost was recovered." That creates a very wide market from which North Carolina's LSEs can buy their RECs for that 25 percent of their requirement, so North Carolina's LSEs can get their RECs at very low prices.

The Voluntary Markets

In contrast, RECs behave like an ordinary commodity in the *voluntary market*, where the buyers are individuals, companies, organizations, and governments that value renewable energy for its ability to lighten their carbon footprint. Any person or organization that wants to claim carbon-neutrality in their energy consumption can achieve that by buying RECs. These buyers are collectively called the voluntary market. They pick up surplus RECs in states that have achieved their RPS, and they buy RECs from renewable power generators in states that do not have an enforced RPS. For example, a wind power producer in any of the 21 states that do not have an enforced RPS can register its RECs with the NARR and sell them to the *national wind* market. The buyers in this market are not required to hold RECs, so the price of RECs in the voluntary market is upheld only by the desire of buyers to be carbon-neutral or at least to impose a lighter carbon footprint on their environment. The Green Power Network has published a graph showing prices in the voluntary market (Figure 10.3).

Notice that, while prices in the compliance market were above $10/MWh for significant parts of the last five years, the voluntary market prices never got above $10. In fact, each of the national markets shown

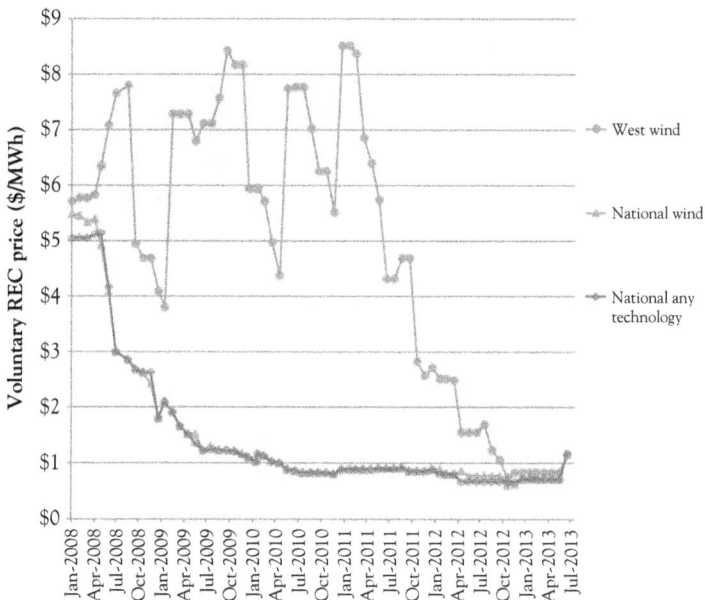

Figure 10.3 **REC prices in the voluntary market, 2008–2013**

Source: U.S. Department of energy EERE green power network.

above had prices around one dollar per megawatt-hour during 2013, which is essentially zero to the producer, because the brokerage commission in the sale of RECs is approximately one dollar per megawatt-hour.

These prices for RECs in the voluntary market stand in sharp contrast to the prices that environmentally conscious energy consumers pay to participate in *green energy* programs through their local utility companies. Many load-serving entities offer their customers the opportunity to pay an extra fee per kilowatt-hour to *source* their energy from renewable power projects. In the upper Midwest, Alliant Energy sells its customers a Second Nature program in which for an extra $0.02 per kWh, the customer can enjoy 100 percent renewable energy. The U.S. Department of Energy calls that a *green pricing* option.[5] Of course, Alliant Energy cannot physically direct electrons to flow from a renewable power plant to a customer's home, and the location of its renewable energy facilities may be hundreds of miles away from a customer who subscribes to their Second Nature program. However, Alliant was selling the *Second Nature* program to its customers in 2013 for $0.02 per kWh, which is $20 per MWh. That year, a customer who wanted to feel the joy of renewable energy could have bought RECs in the compliance and voluntary markets at prices near one dollar per megawatt-hour.

If customers in the retail electric energy markets were to become more sensitive to the environmental effects of their consumption in the future, and if marketers can sell the concept of carbon neutrality through RECs to the same types of people who would otherwise buy with a green pricing option, then the national voluntary markets for RECs would see greater demand and higher prices.

Solar RECs

Approximately 10 states created a market for SRECs by carving out a specific percentage in the overall requirement that must be met by solar energy. Solar energy was such a priority in these states that the solar alternative compliance payments (SACPs) were as high as $700 per MWh and were commonly above $300 per MWh in recent years. Such prices are more than double the cost of producing the underlying solar energy, so they have induced substantial investor interest in solar power systems.

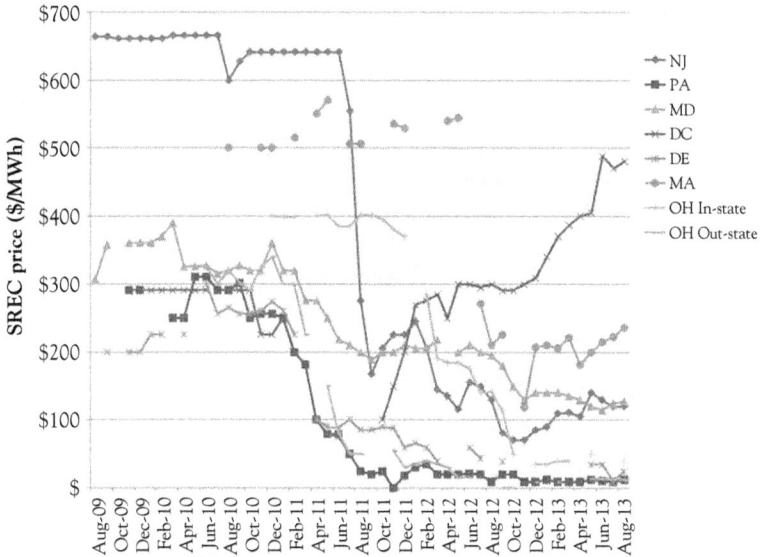

Figure 10.4 SREC prices in the compliance market, 2009–2013

Source: U.S. Department of energy EERE green power network.

The graphs in Figure 10.4 show that the price of SRECs depends critically on the conditions of surplus or deficit in the state. Pennsylvania's SRECs were trading near zero when Washington DC's SRECs were priced between $300 and $500 per MWh.

The example of SRECs shows that a financial analysis of a renewable power investment should not ignore the environmental attributes of the project. Although the solar alternative compliance payments, which the state RPSs mandate, will decline over the next 10 to 15 years toward the ACP of other renewable sources, we should also expect that these REC markets will rationalize somewhat and that prices will permit a more reliable forecast of the effects of environmental attributes on investments.

We end this chapter with a reflection on where the American system of statewide energy policies might be headed during the 20- to 25-year lifetime of a wind or solar project that is being planned today. To frame that discussion, we examine one other policy tool that runs parallel with the RPSs, the cap-and-trade system for regulating the emission of GHGs in a region. However, the importance of SRECs as a revenue source for current solar photovoltaic projects requires us to consider how to model general cash flows for discounted cash flow analysis, so we will take a short methodological side trip before completing our analysis of the policy frameworks under which environmental attributes may be valued and incorporated into investment decisions.

Cap-and-Trade Regimes and the Market for Carbon Credits

The global warming potentials (GWPs) of the six gases identified in the Kyoto Protocol are measured relative to the GWP of carbon dioxide. Thus, the standard measure for the GWP of any combination of emissions is metric tons of CO_2-equivalent (CO_2e).

One approach taken in many regions of the world to control global warming is an emissions trading system (ETS). Under the authority of the government, ETS is set up with a governing body that has the power to define the criteria by which organizations become subject to the rules of the ETS, set limits on the total tonnage of CO_2e that may be emitted by participating organizations in each year over a planning period, issue permits for that amount of tonnage, and verify the quantities of emissions and permits of each participating organization. The ETS allows the organizations sell their permits if they have more than they need or purchase permits if they have less. In the early years of an ETS usually issues the permits, or allowances, based on past emissions, but over time the ETS may sell some of the required permits and use the proceeds to fund initiatives or research that reduce the production of GHGs.

The European Union Emissions Trading System

The European Parliament and Council established its ETS in 2005. It governs emissions in the 28 EU countries and the three EEA-EFTA states of Iceland, Norway, and Liechtenstein. The criteria for participation depend somewhat on the industry, but in general the ETS applies to any company in manufacturing and power generation that has a rated combustive power capacity totaling 20 MW or higher across its installations.

In 2013, this brought more than 11,000 power plants and factories into the European Union Emissions Trading System (EU ETS), and it covered 45 percent of the total GHG emissions in the EU.

The European Commission, through its European Climate Change Program set a limit of 2.084 billion tonnes of CO_2e emissions for 2013, and that limit will decrease by 1.74 percent per year.[6] Thus, by 2020, GHG emissions from the participating sectors will be 21 percent lower than in 2005. Airlines are subject to a cap 5 percent below their average emissions in 2004 to 2006. The emissions of all participating organizations must be audited annually. Any firm that fails to procure allowances covering its emissions must pay a compliance penalty of 100 euros per tonne.

By 2013, more than 40 percent of the allowances, elsewhere termed permits or credits, had to be acquired at auction. All power generators had to buy their allowances. Manufacturing firms were given free allowances for 80 percent of their requirement in 2013, but that percentage will decline to 30 percent by 2020. Almost all of the auctioned allowances are first issued to the member states on the basis of their share of verified emissions from EU ETS installations in 2005, but a small percentage is allocated to the poorest EU member states as a source of revenue for projects that will reduce their carbon intensity and help them adapt to climate change.[7]

A remarkable feature of the EU ETS is that manufacturers can fulfill their obligation for carbon permits by purchasing *carbon credits* in any of several varieties. *Certified Emission Reduction* (CER) units account for one metric tonne of CO_2e that is sequestered or avoided *in a developing country* and is certified under the EU's Clean Development Mechanism (CDM). Projects that reduce emissions in developing countries may produce credits called *Emissions Reduction Units* (ERUs), which are certified under a mechanism known as the Joint Implementation. Participants in the EU ETS may fulfill up to 50 percent of their obligation by purchasing CERs, although that limit does not apply to CERs from the least developed countries nor those from the EU-27 countries.

As already noted, CERs and ERUs are derived from projects that offset carbon emissions by mitigating the emission of carbon, such as reforestation or the chemical destruction of the most severe of the Kyoto gases. However, the development of certain renewable energy resources also qualifies as an offset of CO_2e emissions, so CERs constitute another source of revenue for such projects. In order for renewable energy projects to be eligible for CER or ERU certification, they must be able to quantify the amount of CO_2e emissions that the project will offset, and the project must be *additional* to what is otherwise required by law or regulation. The amount of CO_2e emissions offset by a wind or solar project depends on the source of the electric energy that the project replaces and the emissions factor ($MtCO_2e/MWh$) of that source. Biomass projects whose feedstock would otherwise decompose into methane, which has a GWP 25 times that of CO_2, have the additional value of destroying a powerful GHG. A biogas digester that fuels an electric generator using food waste as feedstock would be an example.

The market price of a carbon allowance or carbon credit in the EU ETS is determined jointly by supply and demand in the market. This is a compliance market, so if the EU's cap on CO_2e in a particular year is lower than the expected emissions of participating installations in that year, then the participants will have to bid for allowances at auction and for CERs on the market. The supply of CERs depends on the number and size of the projects that have been approved for CER credits. In 2008, the EU carbon market had excess demand, resulting in prices around 20 euros per tonne. The recession in subsequent years reduced industrial production, and thus industrial emissions, below the target, and many firms registered their CO_2e mitigation projects under the rules of the CDM, so prices fell dramatically. In 2013, CER prices were around 0.40 euro.

United States: California's ETS

The state of California's Air Resources Board (ARB) has the authority to set GHG emissions standards, verify emissions, and implement a system of allowances and credits. Its goal is to reduce emissions to the 1990 level by 2020. All firms with annual emissions of at least 50,000 metric tons per year must participate. All firms with annual emissions of 25,000 $MtCO_2e$ or more must report their emissions. Presently, the ARB issues allowances to polluters in the amount of 90 percent of their requirement and auctions the remainder. Up to 8 percent of a participant's requirement may be met through offsets.

In late 2013, the ARB ran an auction of current-year 2013 allowances and a forward sale of 2016 allowances, which cleared at prices of $11.48 and $11.10 per $MtCO_2e$.

United States: Regional Greenhouse Gas Initiative

The Regional Greenhouse Gas Initiative (RGGI) started operations in 2009. Its participants, called *compliance entities* because they are forced by state law to participate, are the owners of fossil-fuel power plants having a capacity of 25 MW or higher in the six New England states plus New York, Maryland, and Delaware. New Jersey was an initial participant but withdrew in 2011.

The purpose of the RGGI is "to provide administrative and technical services to support the development and implementation of each RGGI state's CO_2 Budget Trading Program."[8] The RGGI develops and maintains a system under which compliance entities measure and report their GHG emissions, allowances are issued and auctioned, and ownership of allowances is tracked. The RGGI has no authority to set emissions goals. That authority rests with the participating states.

The states in the RGGI established a goal to reduce GHG emissions to their 2002 to 2004 levels by 2015 and to reduce them another 10 percent by 2020. Each state creates permits according to the cap on carbon emissions in its jurisdiction, and each power plant subject to the RGGI is required to obtain enough permits to meet its obligation to the state in which the plant is located. However, the compliance entities may use a CO_2 allowance issued by any participating state to meet their obligation, so the state programs function as an integrated regional market for carbon permits.

Most states sell their permits at auction, and the proceeds are used by the state to support greenhouse-gas mitigation programs including renewable energy initiatives.

The RGGI allows compliance entities to purchase carbon offsets to meet up to 3.3 percent of their compliance obligations. The RGGI has rules that govern the eligibility of emissions-reduction and carbon sequestration programs to produce certifiable carbon offsets.[9]

In early 2013, *the New York Times* reported that the RGGI's 2012 cap of 165 million tons, established in 2008, was much higher than the actual 2012 emissions of 91 million tons due to the recession having reduced the demand for electricity, electric utilities using lower-priced and lower-emitting natural gas as a fuel, and to a small extent due to customers' efforts at conservation.[10] As a result, RGGI permits had been selling for as little as two dollars per ton. The RGGI therefore reduced its 2013 cap on emissions to 91 million tons and agreed to 2.5 percent annual reductions after that, expecting that this would raise the price of a carbon permit by 2020 to approximately $10 per ton, which is near the price that California's carbon permits were selling at in 2013. Even so, the new rule a provision that additional allowances would be issued to bring down the price of carbon permits if auction prices exceeded $4 in 2014, $6 in 2015, $8 in 2016 and $10 in 2017.

Other Emission Trading Systems

Kazakhstan and New Zealand already have ETSs, as do California, the provinces of Alberta and Quebec, Canada, and the city of Tokyo, Japan. India's emission and energy efficiency trading system began operation in 2014 and covered eight industrial sectors with a goal to reduce its 2005 emission levels by 20 to 25 percent by 2020. Australia and South Korea will begin their own ETSs in 2015. Australia and Switzerland will link their own systems with the EU ETS by 2018. China's ETS will begin in 2016. India has been piloting an ETS since 2011. Thailand and Vietnam have plans for their own systems. Brazil has issued standards for voluntary emissions mitigation and is working to establish an ETS.[11]

The Voluntary Markets

As with the REC markets in the United States, there is a voluntary market for carbon credits, which was created by the voluntary commitments of developed nations to reduce their emissions under the Kyoto Protocol. There are private companies such as the Gold Standard (GS), the Climate Action Reserve (CAR), and the Verified Carbon Standard (VCS) that verify carbon credits that do not qualify for trading on the EU ETS, such as those sourced in developed countries outside the EU. The voluntary market saw carbon credits for renewable offsets trading between $2.00 and $4.60 per tonne in 2013.[12]

A 20- to 25-Year Forecast of the Regulatory Context for RECs and Carbon Credits

Renewables Portfolio Standards

Among the 29 states that have an enforced RPS, the earliest adoptions of the practice were in 1997, and half of the current RPS states have adopted their standards since 2005, barely eight years ago. All of the states that now have voluntary standards adopted them since 2005. One should expect that over the next 20 to 25 years, mandatory standards will appear across the country.

However, while 21 states are moving toward mandatory standards, other forces will push to reduce the fragmented policies of the states. Over the next 10 years, as many of the states with mandatory standards approach the 2020 and 2025 dates for their long-term RPS targets, there will be increasing pressure to install more capacity of renewable power systems. The *increasing* pressure will be driven in no small measure by the fact that many states' standards prescribed percentages for renewable energy that increased slowly at first, then faster and faster as the long-term target date is approached. For example, Ohio's RPS begins at 0.5 percent in 2010 and increases at 0.5 percentage points per year until 2014 when it starts increasing at 1.0 percentage point per year until 2025. Similarly, New Jersey will increase its Class 1 RPS by 0.8 percentage points each year through 2017, then the increase pops to 1.8 points per year until the target year of 2021.

Other states have significant upward discontinuities in their standards, which might result in ACPs if the supply of renewables does not anticipate the discontinuity. For example, North Carolina expects that renewables should be 3 percent of sales in 2014, then 6 percent in 2015, and 10 percent only three years after that. Washington State's RPS calls for 3 percent through 2015, after which the standard jumps to 9 percent. West Virginia expects 10 percent through 2019, then 15 percent in 2020 through 2024, and pops it 10 percentage points to 25 percent in 2025. Oregon expects renewable energy to be 5 percent of sales through 2014 but increases it by a whopping 10 percentage points for 2015. Montana's RPS is 10 percent through 2014, then it jumps to 15 percent in 2015.

As these upward discontinuities and accelerating standards put pressure on LSEs to find more and more renewable energy, we should expect significant frustration among citizens, consumers, producers, and policymakers with the extreme diversity of standards across states and the severe limitations on the eligibility of RECs to be used outside their state of origin. These aspects of state regulation fragment the REC markets and, as we saw earlier in this chapter, result in substantial volatility in REC prices. All of that makes financial planning for renewable energy projects more difficult. The result will be pressure on policy makers to permit a wider interstate eligibility of RECs. That pressure found an expression in the 2009 Waxman–Markey bill that would have created a federal RPS with the goal of 20 percent renewable energy nationwide by 2020. That bill was approved by the U.S. House of Representatives, but in the Senate it failed to get enough bipartisan support even to be put to a vote.

If the REC markets do not rationalize through a federal RPS, then they might approach that effect through the formation of regional groups. It is difficult to predict what form those regional groups might take. They might run along the lines of nine REC registries that now coordinate the production and retirement of RECs, or that function might fold into either the regional electric reliability councils or the regional power pools that administer the transmission grids. As the REC pools increase in their geographic scope, they will likely extend their banking rules beyond two years, probably to three and perhaps to five, lending added stability to REC prices.

The formulation of a national energy policy, with a national RPS, would be a big step toward rational, functioning markets for RECs. Such a step may require some external motivation, perhaps precipitated by an international event that spikes the price of oil and suddenly puts everyone's attention on the importance of renewables for energy self-sufficiency.

The broadest goal of an RPS is to slow down the process of global warming, which means reducing the production of GHGs. As the Environmental Defense Fund reminds us, "we can fight global warming by reducing emissions anywhere in the world."[13] In that spirit, the EU ETS permits polluters in the EU to fulfill their requirement for carbon permits by buying carbon credits called CERs units that originate in carbon-reduction projects in developing countries. Such a global fungibility of carbon credits reflects the global responsibility to reduce the negative impact of climate change.

An RPS can also serve the goal of decreasing a nation's dependence on foreign fossil fuels. To that end, it should not matter whether a renewable power system is installed in one state or another. A national RPS would achieve that goal.

What, then, is the purpose of a statewide RPS, which is the current practice in the United States? If it restricts the trading of RECs globally, the goal would not be to affect climate change. If it restricts the trading of RECs nationally, it would not be national security. With the restriction of REC trading to markets within a state or with its close neighbors, the goal seems to be focused primarily on creating jobs for the construction or operation of facilities in the emerging renewable energy sector within the state or region.

Policy makers whose goals are focused more on national security or on global climatic threats should frame the discussion of renewable energy in terms of its ability to offset the emission of GHGs. The way to regulate directly the industrial emission of GHGs is through a system that puts a legal limit on the total emission permitted in a region, issues or sells permits for that amount of emission, and lets those permits trade in a market.

Renewable energy projects offset the emission of GHGs and are therefore eligible for carbon credits that trade like carbon permits in these cap-and-trade systems. We turn now to look at ETSs as a way to promote renewable energy, giving particular attention to the question of whether carbon credits could supplant REC markets even in the United States.

Will REC and Carbon Markets Merge in the United States?

In a 2009 article in *GreenBiz.com*, Aimee Barnes described the REC and carbon offset markets as "two parallel and related, but distinct, environmental markets—the market for renewable energy certificates (RECs) and the market for voluntary emission reductions (VERs), also known as carbon offsets."[14] She noted that people who are looking to mitigate their carbon footprint use both without fully understanding the difference. Barnes' main point was that use of RECs is the natural method to offset the so-called Scope 2 emissions of CO_2-equivalent, which result from purchased electricity. Any customer can read from their electric bill the amount of energy they have consumed in a year, convert that number of kilowatt-hour to megawatt-hour, and buy one REC for each megawatt-hour used. The Scope 1, or direct, emissions arise from the consumer's use of fossil fuels such as gasoline in a car and natural gas in a home furnace. These emissions are best measured in tonnes of CO_2e, which is the unit in which VERs are denominated.

Electric Energy Emission Factors

One REC represents the production of 1 MWh of electric energy from a renewable source. The corresponding amount of GHG emissions avoided by the use of renewables can be calculated if one additional piece of information is available—the amount of CO_2e emitted by the electric utility for each megawatt-hour of energy produced. This conversion ratio of CO_2e per megawatt-hour is called the *emission factor* of the utility. Electric utilities have different emissions factors owing to their differences in the fuels used in and the ages of their generating plants, so a consumer who wants to calculate the carbon offset of an REC must know which utility's energy production was lessened by the presence of the renewable energy generator that originated the REC. Information about the emission factors of utilities is available from the U.S. Energy Information Agency (EIA), although the reader has to compute the composite emission factor for CO_2e from the given emissions factors for CO_2, CH_4, and N_2O.[15] This is not difficult, using the facts that CH_4 has a GWP equal to 25 times that of CO_2, and N_2O is 298.

Example 1 Calculation of a Utility Emission Factor

The U.S. EIA website reports the data in Table 10.1 for emissions factors of three GHGs by electric utilities in a sample of states. Use the facts that

Table 10.1 *Electric utility emission factors*

State	CO_2 (Mt/MWh)	CH_4 (lb./MWh)	N_2O (lb./MWh)
Massachusetts	0.579	0.0174	0.0120
Ohio	0.817	0.0130	0.0288
Iowa	0.854	0.0138	0.0298
California	0.275	0.0067	0.0037

Table 10.2 *Solution to example 1*

Massachusetts	CO_2 (Mt/MWh)	CH_4 (lb./MWh)	N_2O (lb./MWh)
Data as reported	0.579	0.0174	0.0120
Data in Mt/MWh	0.579	7.89×10^{-6}	5.44×10^{-6}
GWP of the gas	1	25	298
CO_2-equivalent	0.5790	0.0002	0.00162
CO_2e, total	**0.5808**		

the GWP of CH_4 is 25 and that of N_2O is 298 to calculate the emission factor for electric energy generated in Massachusetts.

Solution

The EIA data are complicated by the fact that the CO_2 emission factor is reported in metric tons (1,000 kg) and the CH_4 and N_2O factors are reported in pounds. So the first step is to convert the Massachusetts data from lb. to kg/MWh (multiply by 0.4536) then, dividing that by 1000, find the Mt/MWh, which turn out to be very small numbers. The next line in the solution table presents the GWP of each GHG, and the final line multiplies the data in Mt/MWh by the GWP to get the emission factors in CO_2-equivalents per megawatt-hour (Table 10.2). The sum of the CO_2e values for CO_2, CH_4, and N_2O is the emission factor for electric energy, here found to be 0.5790 + 0.0002 + 0.0016 = 0.5808 Mt/MWh.

Notice that the contributions of CO_2e from CH_4 and N_2O were extremely small compared with that of CO_2 itself. We can have almost three significant digits of accuracy even when ignoring the contributions of methane (CH_4) and nitrous oxide (N_2O).

The data about the four states in Table 10.1 show that states may vary substantially in their emissions factors. California's CO_2 emission factor (in 2002) was lower than others, because it was getting some of its power from the hydroelectric facilities in Washington State.

The Value of an REC as a Carbon Offset

If the United States were to have a national cap-and-trade system, prices of carbon permits and carbon offsets (per $MtCO_2e$) would depend on how low the cap on emissions is in relation to manufacturers' needs for emissions. We have seen that in Europe's ETS, prices in 2013 were around 0.40 euro ($0.55) per tonne, because the agreed cap was not very restrictive. However, California's ETS had 2013 prices around $11 per tonne. One REC in California, representing 1 MWh of electric energy, would convert to about 0.275 $MtCO_2e$ of emissions avoided (California's CO_2 emission factor in Table 10.1) and thus be worth about 0.275 × $11 = $3 as a carbon credit. California's tradable RECs were selling in 2011 at around $10 to $20 per MWh and were implicitly priced in the range of $25 to $50 in utility rebate programs,[16] but in 2012 trades were being executed at just under $2.[17] The latter corresponds more closely to the 2013 price of California's carbon credits, but that may be coincidental, as there seems to be no recognition in the press of any relationship between these markets.

The discussion above was motivated by a question that would become very real if California were to have both an ETS and a functioning market for RECs. Each market would have its own cap—the tonnage of CO_2e for the ETS and the percentage of renewable energy represented in the purchases of the state's electric consumers—and each market would have its own demand conditions, so the markets would seem to operate in parallel. However, if a renewable energy generator were to have the choice of selling its environmental attributes either as RECs or as VERs, the markets would be linked economically, and the owner of a renewable energy facility would face a very real question: "Should we sell our environmental attributes this year as a carbon credit for the ETS or as an REC for the RPS?" This would be a very real choice, because the environmental attributes would have to be declared for one purpose or the other. We saw in the example above that the answer depends on the price of an REC and the price of a VER (carbon credit) and on the state's emission factor that relates MWh to MtCO$_2$e.

An ETS and an RPS are two policy frameworks through which renewable energy can be promoted. We now see that these policy frameworks are related through the markets they create. Which way will the United States go, or will it evolve with two parallel but linked markets? A simultaneous evolution of the two markets is likely over the next 20 years. The price of a carbon credit reflects the beneficial impact of renewable energy systems directly on climate change. Some have argued that it does not reflect the effect of renewable energy capacity on the nation's energy security nor on the creation of jobs,[18] but the cap on emissions set by the administrator of an ETS, by stimulating a demand for nonemitting sources, does move the nation toward a lower reliance on imported fuels. Furthermore, a state's goal to create jobs in the renewables sector can be promoted by the restrictions imposed on VERs or RECs for use in satisfying an ETS or an RPS. Local job creation would be promoted if the eligibility of VERs or RECs to satisfy the ETS or the RPS, respectively, is restricted to in-state renewables projects.

The NPV and IRR Spreadsheet Functions for General Cash Flows

The previous section reported that SRECs in several markets were selling in 2013 for prices in the range of $100 to $500 per MWh, which is equivalent to $0.10 to $0.50 per kWh. Those prices are greater than the market price of the underlying electric energy and in some cases are several times the price of the energy. They should not be ignored in the financial analysis of solar PV projects. However, the penalties that states charge LSEs for not meeting the requirement, which define an upper bound to the price of SRECs, are legislated to decline over time toward the typical $50 penalty for ordinary RECs. For example, Ohio's SACP in 2014 is $300 per MWh, but it is slated to decline by $50 every two years to 2024. New Jersey's SACP is $339 in 2014 and will decline at $7 per year to $239 in 2028. Maryland's SACP is $400 in 2014 but declines to $350 in 2016, drops to $200 in 2018, and then declines steadily by $50 every two years to $50 in 2023. Such year-by-year changes in cash flow over a significant period of time should not be ignored in a feasibility analysis, but neither can they be evaluated financially using the PV, RATE, and PMT functions, which assume that the cash flow is an annuity, constant across all periods.

We have already seen that the modified accelerated cost recovery system (MACRS) creates a year-by-year difference in depreciation, which therefore requires a year-by-year modeling of the cash flow from a project. In addition, when a project is financed with debt, the interest payments are tax-deductible as a business expense, but the interest payments vary from year to year under the standard form of an installment loan. These features of business taxation together with the unique pattern of hypothesized changes in SREC prices over time reinforces the need for year-by-year modeling of the cash flow of a project. When the after-tax cash flow of an investment project varies from year to year, the project should be modeled on a spreadsheet with each year in a separate column, beginning with the time of the initial investment, which we call year 0.

In the example that follows, a corporation is considering the installation of a large SPV system in an East Coast state. There is considerable uncertainty about SREC prices over the next 10 years, but by the end of that time SREC prices are assumed to stabilize. In this example, the solution will model the cash flow in the present moment (year 0) and in years 1 to 10 individually as separate columns of the spreadsheet. However, years 11 to 25 are modeled as constant in real terms and thus their components are presented in a single column. As a result, the net present value (NPV) function is needed to evaluate the cash flow over years 1 to 10 and the PV function will evaluate the 15-year annuity in years 11 to 25. Thus, this solution is a hybrid of direct yearly modeling and modeling using a constant-dollar annuity.

Case Analysis: Utility-scale SPV with PTC, SRECs, Advantageous Debt, and MACRS Depreciation

An independent renewable energy company plans to set up a 1,000 kW fixed solar array that is pointed south and tilted at latitude. The system's availability, wiring, mismatch and inverter result in a composite efficiency (derate factor) of 77 percent. The SPV panels will have a useful life of 25 years but will be subject to age derating at 1 percent per year. The installed cost will be $2,100 per kW.

The company's chief financial officer uses a discount rate of 8 percent per year on capital investment proposals, and the company has a federal income tax rate of 35 percent and a state income tax rate of 9 percent. Energy price inflation is expected to be 2.3 percent per year for the next 25 years.

The company may elect either a 30 percent tax credit immediately or a production tax credit (PTC) of $0.023 per kWh per year over the first 10 years of the life of the system.

The insolation at the location for the project averages 4.46 kWh/m^2/day over the year. The solar penalty fee (SACP) in the state is currently $339/MWh, but the state's SRECs were selling for $125 in late 2013. Its SRECs have a four-year life. The state's solar carve-out jumped from 0.4 percent in 2012 to 2.05 percent in 2014, which may explain the uncertainty about the sufficiency of SRECs in the near future. The carve-out will rise quickly over the next five years to 3.29 percent then rise more slowly, at about 0.09 percentage points per year to 4.1 percent in 2028. The spreadsheet solution will present three scenarios (low, intermediate, and high) for the path of SREC prices over the first 10 years. After that, SREC prices are assumed to be stable in constant dollars.

Independent power producers in the region have been able to sell power to LSEs at a wholesale price of about $0.05/kWh under a 25-year contract that includes price escalation in accord with the inflation of electric energy prices but allows the producer to retain ownership of the SRECs.

A *Green Growth* state loan program will finance up to 50 percent of the cost of a renewable energy system on a four-year loan at an interest rate of 2 percent per year.

Questions

(a) What is a reasonable assumption about the prices of the state's SRECs over the next 25 years? Describe a high-price scenario (with one-third probability) and a low-price scenario (one-third probability) in addition to the expected scenario.

(b) Is this project financially viable under the expected SREC scenario? What is the NPV of the project under that scenario? What is the internal rate of return (IRR)? Does this seem like a high-risk or low-risk project?

(c) How does the financial viability of the project change under the high-price or the low-price scenario?

(d) Suppose that the utility purchasing the electric energy also wants to buy the SRECs of the project, *bundling* the SRECs with the energy at a single energy price. What initial energy price should the developers of this project negotiate for? (Recall that the initial price will escalate with inflation under the terms of the contract.)

Solution

Refer to the spreadsheet images shown on the following pages.

(a) **Scenarios for SREC prices.** The discussion of SREC markets and carbon credit markets in this chapter should leave the reader with substantial uncertainty about how the U.S. regulatory environment and SREC market will look over the next 25 years. We know that, over the next 10 years, the solar penalty fees (SACP) will decline to the ordinary REC penalty fee of about $50/MWh, so SREC prices will generally decline. However, the state popped its standard for solar energy in 2014 from 0.4 to 2.05 percent of the energy sold in the state, and its standard will rise for the next several years first by adding 0.4 percent then 0.3 percent then 0.25 percent, then 0.2 percent then 0.19 percent eventually reaching 3.5 percent of energy sold in 2020 and 4.1 percent in 2028. Its SREC price in late 2013 was $125, which is 125/339 = 37 percent of the current SACP, but the state's SRECs have a life of four years, so the 2013 price reflects traders' allowance for the possibility that the state will encounter a deficit of SRECs in 2014 to 2016.

It seems reasonable to expect that the SREC price will rise somewhat over the next five years. After that, it is even more difficult to predict, because the rules governing the state's SRECs could change if the state widens its participation in an SREC pool or if a national RPS is created and a national market emerges. After 10 years, a moderate expectation for the price of an SREC might be today's price for an ordinary REC, about $50 per MWh. A high-price scenario would anticipate a higher likelihood of an SREC shortage in the period 2015 to 2020 and a slightly higher long-term REC rate. A low-price scenario would occur if the state market were flooded with other SRECs, due to the widening of the SREC pool in which the state participates, and its long-term SREC price for years 11 to 25 would be in the low single digits. The relevant point of reference for SREC prices in each year is the penalty fee, the SACP, which is shown in row 35 of the spreadsheet. Rows 36–38 show high-, moderate-, and low-price scenarios that seem consistent with the discussion above.

(b) **Spreadsheet solution**. The spreadsheet solution will need to have one column for each of the first 10 years, because the SREC price forecast will likely vary across those 10 years, the PTC only lasts for the first 10 years of a project, the MACRS depreciation gives different values for each of the first six years, and the Green Growth loan is paid over five years. However, years 11 to 25 are so far out that it would be reasonable to model the cash flow as an annuity growing at the rate of inflation in energy prices less than the rate of age derating of the SPV cells. This simplifying assumption reduces the size of the spreadsheet by 14 columns and has the additional advantage, for teaching purposes, of permitting the entire spreadsheet to appear on the following page.

The top rows of the spreadsheet solution record the data of the problem and calculate quantities relevant to the time of the investment, such as the cash-flow consequences of the federal investment tax credit (FITC), the depreciable cost basis of the project, and its allocation as bonus depreciation and MACRS depreciation. We discuss those first, then consider the year-by-year cash flow.

Line 18. Net nominal growth rate for revenues. The values in column M, representing the annuity from years 11 to 25, will really change in time due to the compounding effects of energy price inflation (+2.3 percent per year) and the age derating of the solar cells (–1 percent per year) over the 15 years of that period. The net or

	A	B	C	D	E	F
1	Chapter 10 Example 2 - Utility-scale SPV with SRECs, Debt financing, and MACRS					
2						
3	Rated capacity	1,000	kW			
4	Installed cost per kW of capacity	2,100	$/kW			
5	Useful life	25	years		Be sure to set this cell	
6	Annual maintenace cost per kW	$20	per kW capacity		back to 8% after each	
7	Derate factor	0.77			use of Goal Seek	
8	Location's average annual insolation r	4.46	kWh/m2/day			
9	Wholesale price of energy	0.050	$/kWh			
10	Production tax credit	0.000	$/kWh			
11	Nominal discount rate	8.0%	per year		Change this cell to 0 to	
12	Investment tax credit for owner	30%	of installed cost		invoke the Production Tax	
13	State income tax rate	9%			Credit. Use 30% to invoke	
14	Federal income tax rate	35%			the Investment Tax Credit	
15	Nominal inflation of maintenance exp	2.0%	per year			
16	Nominal inflation of energy prices	2.3%	per year			
17	Age derating	1%	per year			
18	Net nominal growth rate for revenues	1.28%	per year			
19	Inflation-adjusted discount rate	6.64%	per year	Used in Years 11-25		
20	Total installed price of the system	$ 2,100,000				
21	Federal income tax credit	$ (630,000)				
22	Increased state income tax due to fed ta	$ 56,700				
23	Net system cost after federal tax credit	$ 1,470,000				
24	Green Growth loan amount	$ 735,000				
25	Green Growth loan term	$ 5	years			
26	Green Growth loan interest rate	2%				
27	Net Year 0 cash outlay for SPV system	$ 1,526,700	Year 0			
28	Depreciable cost basis after tax credit	$ 1,785,000	(Cost minus one-half the credit)			
29	Bonus depreciation in 1st year	$ 892,500	(50% of depreciable cost basis)			
30	MACRS depreciation amount	$ 892,500				
31	1st year production of AC energy	1,253,483	kWh per year			

Figure 10.5 Data and preliminary calculations for an SPV model with SRECs

composite growth rate is revealed from the product of the growth factors of each effect. The formula $(1 + 0.023) \times (1 - 0.01)$ gives the compound growth factor, 1.0128. Subtracting 1 from the growth factor reveals the growth rate, 1.28 percent per year.

Line 19. Inflation-adjusted discount rate. The discount rate to use for the period of the annuity will be the nominal rate (8 percent) adjusted for the net growth rate 1.28 percent. Using the formula r^* $= (r - i)/(1 + i)$, we get the adjusted rate, 6.64 percent (Figure 10.5).

Lines 21 and 22. Federal income tax credit. This line shows the calculation of the FITC as 30 percent of the installed price.

Line 22. State-tax consequence of federal tax credit. This line recognizes that the resulting decrease in federal income taxes has the effect of increasing income that is subject to state income tax. The $56,700 is the state tax rate of 9 percent multiplied by the amount of the federal income tax credit.

Line 23. Net system cost. The Green Growth loan is limited to 50 percent of the net system cost, which we take here to be the system cost minus the federal tax credit.

Lines 24 to 26. The Green Growth loan amount is 50 percent of the net system cost from Line 23, and other terms of the loan are presented in Lines 25 and 26.

Line 27. Net year 0 cash outlay. This is the installed cost, minus the federal tax credit, plus the state-income tax effect, minus the amount borrowed as a Green Growth loan. This is a slight simplification for teaching purposes, because we treat the tax credit and its state-tax effect as if they occur at the time of the investment, although in reality they may occur 3 to 12 months later. Those amounts could have been discounted by an appropriate fraction of a year to be more realistic, but the reader would not have been able to see the calculation as easily.

Line 28. Depreciable cost basis. This is the installed cost minus one-half of the FITC. It is interesting that the U.S. government does not require the owner to subtract the entire tax credit, but this is how the law is written.

Lines 29 and 30. Depreciation quantities. The bonus depreciation to be taken in the first year is 50 percent of the depreciable cost basis, and the remaining 50 percent is subject to MACRS depreciation on a five-year schedule, which actually runs into the 6th year.

Line 31. First-year production. This is calculated in kilowatt-hours as the capacity of the system (kW) multiplied by the insolation (kWh/day per kW capacity) × 365 days/year, multiplied by the DC–AC derate factor. The insolation data are given in monthly quantities at the PVWatts calculator at NREL's website and have been converted to a yearly average. The derate factor would be determined using production data from similar SPV installations.

The remaining part of the spreadsheet solution has the year-by-year data, which include the annual energy production and prices, the SREC prices, and the components of a cash-flow calculation. See Figure 10.6 on page 264.

Line 39. Annual energy production. This is the first-year annual energy production (cell B31) in the year 1 column, and for each subsequent year is calculated as the previous year's output multiplied by (1–$B$17). The absolute cell reference ($B$17) allows the formula to be copied and pasted across years 3 to 10.

Line 42. Annual revenue from energy sales. This is the energy production (C39) multiplied by the contract energy price (B9) as escalated by the 2.3 percent (B16) annual rise in energy prices, using absolute cell references for the model parameters and a relative cell reference to the year's energy production. It would be written in Excel as =C39*$B$9*(1+$B$15)^C34.

Line 43. Annual revenue from SREC sales. This formula uses the annual energy production from Line 39, divided by 1000 to measure energy in megawatt-hours, multiplied by the year's estimated SREC price (Line 38). Our reference to the estimated price in line 38, rather than in one of lines 35 to 37 reflects a practice of good spreadsheet design—Line 38 can easily be altered to refer to any of lines 35, 36, or 37, and showing that result in line 38 tells the reader of the spreadsheet what information has gone into line 43. The alternative would be to embed the reference to the price scenario (line 35, 36, or 37) in the formula for line 43 and change that formula to switch scenarios, but that would be more prone to error and less revealing of what the spreadsheet is using in its calculation.

Line 45. Annual maintenance expense. Maintenance expenses are likely to rise at the rate of general inflation, due to their origin in the price of labor and materials, not at the rate of energy price inflation. So this spreadsheet accounts for the rise of maintenance expenses using the general inflation rate 2.0 percent (B15).

Line 46. Operating profit. This is an intermediate calculation of profit, equal to revenues minus direct operating costs. It serves as a reference point on the way to taxable income, below.

Line 47. Interest paid. The Green Growth loan is paid in five equal installments, but the amount of interest and principal in each installment varies over the life of the loan. The amount of interest in each installment is calculated by the spreadsheet function *interest payment* (IPMT) with the syntax =IPMT(*rate,per,nper,pv*). The *rate* is the 2 percent interest rate on the loan. *per* is the period within the loan for which the interest is calculated, here taken to be the year number from Line 33. *nper* and *pv* are respectively the number of years of the loan and the amount of the loan taken at year 0 (the present).

Lines 48 and 49. Depreciation. Line 48 has the bonus depreciation in year 1. Line 49 shows the series of MACRS depreciation deductions, which are calculated using the standard table of five-year MACRS percentages. The percentages are embedded in the formulas for each year.

Line 50. Profit before tax. This is the sum from Operating Profit through interest and depreciation.

Line 51. Tax saved (paid). The sign of this number reflects whether the amount is paid out (negative, in parentheses) or received as a benefit and thus shown without parentheses. The same formula works for both cases: a negative sign on the tax rate multiplied by the profit before tax. Here, the tax rate is the sum of the state and federal rates, so the quantity gives the sum of state and federal taxes saved or paid. Implicitly, the model assumes that the corporate owner has other profits in years 1 and 2 against which the losses from this SPV system will provide tax savings in the year.

Line 52. Production tax credit. The spreadsheet model is set up so that if cell B12, the investment tax credit (ITC), is nonzero, the PTC in B10 will be zero. If B12 is equal to zero, the PTC in B10 will be $0.023 per kWh as stated in the problem. This line tracks the amount of the PTC that would be received each year.

Line 53. Profit after tax. This is the accounting profit after taxes paid or credited.

Line 54. Add back depreciation. To get the after-tax cash flow, depreciation has to be *added back* to the profit after tax, because when it was used in Lines 48 and 49 it was not a real cash flow but a mathematical construct for the calculation of income tax.

Line 55. Principal paid on loan. Unlike the interest portion of the loan payment, which is tax-deductible, the principal portion is paid out of after-tax funds, so it appears here.

Line 56. Cash flow after tax. This is the real *bottom line* of a cash-flow analysis.

Year		1	2	3	4	5	6	7	8	9	10	Years 11-25
SACP penalty fee ($/MWh)		339	331	324	317	310	303	296	289	282	275	-
High SREC price scenario	High	125	150	200	250	275	250	225	200	175	150	70
Expected SREC price scenario	Moderate	125	150	175	200	200	175	150	125	110	100	50
Low SREC price scenario	Low	125	125	140	130	120	100	80	60	50	40	30
SREC price scenario used in calcs	Moderate	125	150	175	200	200	175	150	125	110	100	50
Annual production of AC energy (kWh)		1,253,483	1,240,948	1,228,539	1,216,253	1,204,091	1,192,050	1,180,129	1,168,328	1,156,645	1,145,078	1,145,078

Year	0	1	2	3	4	5	6	7	8	9	10	Years 11-25
Annual revenue from sale of energy		64,116	64,934	65,764	66,603	67,454	68,315	69,188	70,071	70,966	71,872	71,872
Annual revenue from sale of SRECs		160,289	194,803	230,173	266,414	269,816	239,104	207,563	175,178	156,125	143,745	71,872
Total revenues		224,405	259,738	295,936	333,017	337,270	307,419	276,751	245,249	227,091	215,617	143,745
Annual maintenance expense		(20,000)	(20,400)	(20,808)	(21,224)	(21,649)	(22,082)	(22,523)	(22,974)	(23,433)	(23,902)	(23,902)
Operating profit of the SPV system		204,405	239,338	275,128	311,793	315,621	285,337	254,228	222,276	203,658	191,715	119,843
Interest paid on Green Growth loan		(14,700)	(11,875)	(8,994)	(6,055)	(3,058)						
Depreciation - "Bonus depreciation"		(892,500)										
Depreciation - MACRS 5yr		(178,500)	(285,600)	(171,360)	(102,816)	(102,816)	(51,408)					
Profit before tax (Taxable income)		(881,295)	(58,138)	94,774	202,922	209,748	233,929	254,228	222,276	203,658	191,715	119,843
Tax saved (paid)		387,770	25,581	(41,701)	(89,286)	(92,289)	(102,929)	(111,860)	(97,801)	(89,610)	(84,355)	(52,731)
Production tax credit		-	-	-	-	-	-	-	-	-	-	-
Profit after tax		(493,525)	(32,557)	53,074	113,636	117,459	131,000	142,367	124,474	114,049	107,360	67,112
Add back depreciation		1,071,000	285,600	171,360	102,816	102,816	51,408					
Principal paid on Green Growth loan		(141,236)	(144,061)	(146,942)	(149,881)	(152,879)						
Cash flow after tax	$ (791,700)	436,238	108,982	77,491	66,571	67,396	182,408	142,367	124,474	114,049	107,360	67,112

NPV of cash flow years 1-10	$1,025,723	in Year 0 dollars
NPV of cash flow years 11-25	$289,712	in Year 0 dollars
Initial cost net of ITC	$ (791,700)	in Year 0 dollars
Net Present Value of the project	$ 523,735	

Figure 10.6 Years 1–10 cash flow and years 11–25 annuity model

Lines 58 and 59. Net present value. These lines show the calculation of the NPV of the project. Line 58 uses the NPV function to calculate the present value of the series of payments in years 1 to 10. The NPV function discounts the first payment in the series by one year, so the cash flow passed to the NPV function must begin with year 1 (column C). The discounting of years 1 to 10 must be taken using the nominal discount rate 8 percent, because each of the cash flow numbers for years 1 to 10 is a nominal, meaning current-year, value.

The initial investment in the project, which is made in the present, has to be accounted for separately (in B56) where it is not discounted (Figure 10.6).

Line 59 shows how to calculate the present value of the annuity in years 11 to 25. As we saw in the wind power example of Chapter 9, this is done in two steps, although it appears here as one calculation. The first step is to take the present value of the annuity using the PV function with the adjusted discount rate (B19), which calculated from Line 18, accounts also for the inflation of energy prices and the deflation of energy production. The syntax is =PV(*rate,nper, pmt,*[*fv*]), so this is accomplished by the formula =PV(B19,15,M56). Notice that the column M revenues were the same as column L (year 10). This is because when an adjusted discount rate is used, the *pmt* number should be a *start-of-period* annuity payment to get the correct calculation out of the PV function. The number that results from the PV function will be a value set at the start of the first period in the annuity, and start-of-year-11 has the same meaning as end-of-year-10. This value therefore has to be discounted back 10 years to the present. The cash flow used in the PV function was for years 11 to 25, so the value given by the function is a year 10 dollar value. We discount it back 10 years to the present using the nominal discount rate in this problem, which is 8 percent. This is accomplished by multiplying the quantity =PV(B18,15,M48) by a 10-year discount factor $1/(1+0.08)^{10}$.

Line 60 repeats the initial investment for the sake of clarity.

Line 61 sums the initial investment (outflow, negative) with the present values of the two portions of the cash flow stream (inflow, positive) to get the NPV of the project.

If the cash flow were presented in the spreadsheet with one value for each year, then the spreadsheet function IRR could be used, starting with the year 0 value in B56 and continuing as long as the cash flow lasted. However, column M represents an annuity of 15 years, not a single value, so IRR cannot be used here. The only way to calculate the IRR in this structure of financial model is to try different values of the discount rate by hand or use the Goal Seek routine to set the NPV (B61) to 0 by changing the nominal discount rate (B11).

(c) **The NPV and IRR for the SREC price scenarios, with ITC or PTC.** Setting the SREC prices in line 38 equal to their corresponding values in line 35 (high) or line 36 (moderate) or line 37 (low) reveals the NPV for each scenario. Likewise, setting the tax credit toggle B12 equal to 0 for PTC or 30 percent for ITC shows the result of each policy option for the given SREC prices. This sensitivity analysis therefore has six cases to consider. The results for these conditions of the model are shown in the two parts of Table 10.3. Note that the results are reported rounded to the nearest dollar. It is not good practice to report decimals (cents) on numbers that are on the order of $100,000 or more.

Several conclusions follow from these tables. First, on the choice between the ITC and the PTC; the ITC is better than the PTC under each of the three scenarios. Thus, the choice of the ITC domi-

Table 10.3 Results of sensitivity analysis on the model

Production tax credit	Low SREC	Moderate	High SREC
NPV	($7,155)	$319,511	$615,965
IRR (%)	7.9	12.9	16.7
Investment tax credit	**Low SREC**	**Moderate**	**High SREC**
NPV	$197,069	$523,735	$820,189
IRR (%)	12.5	19.0	23.7

nates the PTC, so the project developer should take the ITC. Second, using the ITC, each scenario has a positive NPV, so the decision to invest in this project dominates the decision not to do so. However, the NPV varies greatly across the scenarios, corresponding to rates of return on investment that vary from 12.5 percent to almost 24 percent. The valuation of the project is subject to a lot of uncertainty.

(d) **Bundling SRECs with the energy in the power purchase agreement.** Lastly, we consider whether the project developer should bundle SRECs with the energy in its power purchase agreement with the utility company and, if so, at what price. Looking at the revenue lines in the spreadsheet solution, we see that the sale of SRECs results in two to four times as much revenue, each year, as the sale of the underlying electric energy. The regulatory and market environment of SRECs is so uncertain that even our Low and High scenarios may not represent well the range of possibilities for SREC prices. The project developer who sells only the energy on a long-term contract is not shifting much of the business risk to the utility company. Project developers need to assess their own core competence—if it is in the development of the project alone, they should sell the project as soon as it is built; if their competence is in operations, but they don't want too much business risk, they should sell the energy and SRECs on a long-term contract, perhaps not even for the full 25 years; if their competence is in operations, and they have the financial depth to take on the business risk, they may want to sell only year by year, on the spot market, not by a long-term contract. Most of the business risk here seems to be in the SREC values, so a developer should consider bundling the SRECs with the energy and selling them as a package to the utility. The expected scenario (moderate price) with the ITC yields an after-tax rate of return of 19 percent per year, but it is subject to substantial risk. The project's investors might be willing to take a lower rate of return in exchange for a fixed schedule of payments. The bundled price (per kWh) will depend on what they would view as a *low-risk or certain* return comparable to the 19 percent risky return. Put another way, given that they can obtain an NPV of $523,735 by taking on the risk of the uncertain SREC prices, how much of that value would they be willing to give up for the security of a long-term contract?[2] To answer that question, we need a reference point for the expected return on a secure investment. In this example, that reference point could be the outcome of the low estimate of SREC prices, which offers an NPV of $197,069 corresponding to a yield of 12.5 percent on the investment.

The question then is what price per kilowatt-hour, *with no SREC income*, would yield an NPV of $197,069. To find the answer, we set the nominal discount rate back to 8 percent (if it had been changed by a recent use of Goal Seek), and we must disrupt the spreadsheet solution by typing 0 over all the formulas in line 38 (SRECs prices). Then we use Goal Seek to set the NPV value in cell B61 to 197,069 by changing the energy price B9.

Doing so, we see that the energy price would have to be $0.147 per kWh, so that value should be the reference point in negotiating a long-term bundled contract with the utility company.

Take-aways

Public policy supporting sustainable technologies in the United States is still in its infancy. The United States does not have a national energy policy under which a national market might emerge for RECs or carbon credits. But global warming is a global problem, and something more coordinated than the balkanized state regulations of the present time will surely emerge. It remains to be seen whether the United States will move toward a European model, extending the California and RGGI carbon markets, or whether it will continue to focus on sustainable energy production through RECs. The key points that help us to understand those issues are the following:

---

[2] We do not assume that investors would give up all of their NPV, because the analysis has revealed that the project's investors have a business opportunity that is expected to produce a supernormal value (greater than zero) when evaluated at the market discount rate of 8 percent. They should be willing to give up some of that value, but not all of it, in exchange for a long-term contract.

- The market for RECs is created by states' laws establishing standards for the percentage of electric energy, sold in the state, which must come from renewable sources. REC prices are more unstable when utilities can purchase RECs only from within the state and when RECs expire if unused soon after they are created. Public policy about RPSs *might* be trending toward greater regionalization and a longer life for RECs, which would lead to more stable prices.

- Carbon ETSs perform a similar role to RECs but in relation to the emission of all types of GHG and from any source, not just from electric energy production. Europe uses carbon credits, also known as carbon offsets, rather than RECs as its policy instruments for controlling the emission of GHGs. California has its own ETS, which may soon link with Quebec, and the RGGI of New England and several Mid-Atlantic states is another.

- The concept that links RECs with carbon credits is the *emission factor* of an electric utility company, expressed as the number of kilograms of CO_2-equivalent GHGs emitted by the utility per megawatt-hour of electric energy.

- The path that REC prices may take over the next 10 to 20 years is highly uncertain. REC prices could add a lot of value to renewable energy projects, or they might not. A proper analysis of the feasibility of a renewable energy project over a 20- to 30-year project life must consider the possible income from the sale of RECs or carbon credits. This may require year-by-year modeling of the cash flow from a project for 10 years or so. The profitability of such year-by-year cash flows can be evaluated using the NPV and IRR spreadsheet functions.

Appendices

Appendix A   Unit Conversion Factors

Common Units of Weight

Table A-1

Entries are column unit per row unit	Pound	Kilogram	U.S. ton	Imp. ton (long ton)	Metric ton (t)
1 pound (lb.)	1	0.45360	0.0005	0.00044643	0.00045360
1 kilogram (kg)	2.2046	1	0.0002268	0.00098420	0.001
1 U.S. ton	2,000	4,409.20	1	1.12	0.90703
1 imperial ton (long ton, shipping ton)	2,240	1,016.06	0.89286	1	1.01587
1 metric tonne	2,204.6	1,000	1.1025	0.98438	1

Common Units of Area

1.0 hectare = 10,000 m^2 (an area 100 m × 100 m or 328 × 328 ft.) = 2.47 acres

1.0 km^2 = 100 hectares = 247 acres

1.0 acre = 0.405 hectares (ha.)

Common Units of Volume

Table A-2

Entries are column unit per row unit	U.S. gallon	Imp. gallon	Liter	Cubic meter (m³)	Cubic foot	U.S. bushel	UK bushel	Petrol barrel
1 U.S. gal	1	0.83267	3.78541	0.0037854	0.13368	0.10742	0.10408	0.02381
1 Imp. gal	1.20095	1	4.54609	0.00454609	0.16054	0.12901	0.12500	0.02859
1 liter	0.26417	0.21997	1	0.001	0.03531	0.02838	0.02750	0.00629
1 m³	264.172	219.969	1,000	1	35.3147	28.3776	27.4962	6.2893
1 ft³	7.48052	6.22884	28.3168	0.028317	1	0.80356	0.77860	0.17811
1 U.S. bushel	9.30918	7.75151	35.239	0.035239	1.24446	1	0.96894	0.22165
1 UK bushel	9.60760	8.00000	36.3686	0.036369	1.28435	1.03206	1	0.22875
1 Petroleum barrel	42	34.972	158.987	0.158987	5.6146	4.51168	4.37154	1

1 U.S. bushel holds 56 lb. (25 kg) of corn or sorghum = 60 lb. (27 kg) of wheat or soybeans = 40 lb. (18 kg) of barley.

Energy Conversion Factors

Table A-3

	Kilowatt-hour (kWh)	BTU	Kilocalorie (kCal)	Megajoule (MJ)
1 kWh	1	3,412.14	860.421	3.6
1 BTU	0.00029307	1	0.25216	0.001055
1 kCal	0.0011622	3.96567	1	0.0041868
1 MJ	0.27778	947.817	238.846	1
1 BOE	1,699.81	5,800,000	1,461,575	6,119.32

1,000 BTU/lb. = 2.33 gigajoules per tonne (GJ/t).

1,000 BTU/U.S. gal = 0.279 megajoules per liter (MJ/l).

Power Conversion Factors

Table A-4

Entries are column unit per row unit	kW	Joule/sec (J/s)	Horsepower	BTU/ hr
1 kW =	1	1,000	1.341	3,412.14
1 Joule/sec =	0.001	1	0.001341	3.41214
1 Hp =	0.74571	745.71	1	2,545
1 BTU/hr =	0.00029307	0.29307	0.00039	1

1 watt = 1 joule/sec.

Units of Crop Yield

1.0 U.S. ton/acre = 2.24 tonne/ha.

1 metric tonne/hectare = 0.446 U.S. ton/acre.

$100 \text{ g/m}^2 = 1.0$ tonne/hectare = 892 lb./acre.

For example, a *target* bioenergy crop yield might be: 5.0 U.S. tons/acre (10,000 lb./acre) = 11.2 tonnes/hectare ($1,120 \text{ g/m}^2$).

Appendix B   Energy Content of Fuels

Sources for this appendix include The Engineering Toolbox (www.engineeringtoolbox.com/), the Bioenergy Feedstock Development Program at Oak Ridge National Laboratory (http://bioenergy.ornl.gov/papers/misc/energy_conv.html), and The Climate Registry (www.theclimateregistry.org/downloads/2013/01/2013-Climate-Registry-Default-Emissions-Factors.pdf)

> LHV means *lower heating value*, the energy that would be captured through combustion that lets vaporized water escape.
>
> HHV means *higher heating value*, the energy that would be captured if the latent heat of vaporized water were also captured by cooling all byproducts to their original temperature.

Renewable Fuels

Table B-1

Fuel	MJ/kg (GJ/t)	BTU/lb.	Other
Charcoal	29.6	12,700	
Wood fuel (HHV, bone dry)	18–22	7,600–9,600	
Wood fuel (air dry, 20% moisture)	~15	~ 6,450	6,400 BTU/lb.
Agricultural residues (moisture content varies)	10–17	4,300–7,300	
Ethanol LHV	26.7	11,500	75,700 BTU/gal = 21.1 MJ/l
Biodiesel	37.8	16,250	(33.3–35.7 MJ/l)
Hydrogen LHV	121	51,600	33.6 kWh/kg

Fossil Fuels

Table B-2

Fuel	MJ/kg (GJ/t)	BTU/lb.	Other
Gasoline—LHV	44.4	19,085	
Gasoline—HHV	47.3	20,332	
Petro-diesel—LHV	42.8	18,398	130,500 BTU/gal = 36.4 MJ/l
Kerosene—LHV	43.0	18,484	
Natural gas—LHV	50	21,493	HHV 1,027 BTU/ft.^{3} LHV 930 BTU/ft.^{3} = 34.6 MJ/m^3
Coal* anthracite LHV	29.2	12,550	
Coal* bituminous LHV	29.0	12,460	
Coal sub-bituminous LHV	20.1	8,625	
Coal lignite LHV	16.5	7,105	

* *Typical* coal (rank not specified) usually means bituminous, common for power plants.

Appendix C   Useful Data on Materials

Densities and Specific Heats of Materials

Table C-1

Material	Density (lb./ft.³)	Density (kg/m³)	Specific heat capacity
Water (liquid)	16.02	1,000	1.00
Paraffin wax (solid)	13.30	830	0.58
Paraffin wax (liquid)	12.50	780	0.57
Vegetable oil			0.48
Wood	8.81	550	0.40
Brick	30.79	1,922	0.22
Concrete	36.85	2,300	0.21
Stone	27.23	1,700	0.20
Iron	126.08	7,870	0.11

Source: The Engineering Toolbox (www.engineeringtoolbox.com/).

Emission Factors (After Combustion)

Table C-2

Fuel	kgCO$_2$e / GJ	Other	Other Unit
Fuel oil no. 2	0.078	10.21	kgCO$_2$/gal
Gasoline	0.074	8.78	kgCO$_2$/gal
Kerosene	0.079	10.15	kgCO$_2$/gal
Natural gas (methane)	0.056	0.05	kg/scf
Coal, anthracite	0.109	2,597.82	kgCO$_2$/ton
Coal*, bituminous	0.099	2,328.46	kgCO$_2$/ton
Coal, sub-bituminous	0.102	1,673.6	kgCO$_2$/ton
Coal lignite	0.102	1,369.28	kgCO$_2$/ton
Propane (liquid)	0.065	5.59	kgCO$_2$/gal
Wood (12% moisture)	0.099	1,442.64	kgCO$_2$/ton
Biodiesel	0.078	9.45	kgCO$_2$/gal
Vegetable oil	0.086	9.79	kgCO$_2$/gal
Ethanol	0.072	5.75	kgCO$_2$/gal

* *Typical* coal (rank not specified) usually means bituminous, common for power plants.

Source: The Climate Registry's 2013 Default Emission Factors http://www.theclimateregistry.org/downloads/2013/01/2013-Climate-Registry-Default-Emissions-Factors.pdf

Fuels—Physical Density

Wood (cord) 4×4×8 ft. = 128 cubic feet (3.62 m³); contains approximately 1.2 U.S. tons (oven-dry) = 2,400 pounds = 1,089 kg.

Wood 1.0 metric tonne wood = 1.4 cubic meters (solid wood, not stacked).

Ethanol (7.94 petroleum barrels per metric tonne = 1,262 liters/tonne).

Ethanol density (average) = 0.79 g/ml (= metric tonnes/m³).

Biodiesel density (average) = 0.88 g/ml (= metric tonnes/m³).

Wood (cord) 4×4×8 ft = 128 cubic feet (3.62 m³); approximately 1.2 U.S. tons (oven-dry) = 2,400 lb. = 1,089 kg.

Wood 1.0 metric tonne wood = 1.4 cubic meters (solid wood, not stacked).

Ethanol 7.94 petroleum barrels per metric tonne = 1,262 liters/tonne; density 0.79 g/ml (= Mg/m³)

Biodiesel density (average) = 0.88 g/ml (= metric tonnes/m³, Mg/m³)

Petro-diesel density (average) = 0.84 g/ml (= metric tonnes/m³, Mg/m³)

Oil, metric tonne = 7.2 barrels oil = 42–45 GJ.

Gasoline, metric tonne = 8.53 barrels = 1,356 liter

Gasoline density (average) = 0.73 g/ml (= metric tonnes/m³)

Petro-diesel density (average) = 0.84 g/ml (= metric tonnes/m³)

Hydrogen 0.0899 kg/Sm³ = 0.0838 kg/Nm³. Sm³ is a cubic meter of gas at standard temperature and pressure (0°C, 1 atm.), Nm³ is a cubic meter of gas at normal temperature and pressure (20°C, 1 atm.).

About the Author

Scott R. Herriott is Professor of Business Administration at Maharishi University of Management (MUM). He received his BA degree in mathematics from Dartmouth College and his PhD in management science and engineering at Stanford University. He taught at the University of Texas at Austin and the University of Iowa for six years before joining MUM in 1990.

His expertise is the application of quantitative methods to business strategy with a special focus on sustainable business. He teaches economics, finance, operations management, strategic management, and sustainable business. He is the author of a dozen scientific papers on economics, organization, and business strategy. His textbooks include *College Algebra Through Functions and Models* (Cengage, 2005) this *Feasibility Analysis for Sustainable Technologies: An Engineering-Economic Approach* (Business Expert Press, 2015), and the forthcoming *Metrics for Sustainability* (Routledge, 2016).

Notes

Chapter 1

1. Laszlo et al. (2014).
2. Fritsch and Gallimore (2007).
3. U.S. Energy Information Administration (2013b).
4. National Institute of Building Sciences (2013).
5. Steven Winter Associates, Inc. (2013).
6. Torcellini et al. (2006)
7. International Energy Agency (2013).
8. U.S. Environmental Protection Agency (2010).
9. Taisei Corp (2012).

Chapter 2

1. *Wikipedia* (2013).
2. Wind Energy Center (1970).
3. Boccard (2008).
4. Shahan (2012).

Chapter 3

1. "Solar Thermal Energy" (2011).
2. "Turbine" (2011).
3. Biello (2010).
4. Allan (2007).
5. "Hydroelectric Power" (2005).
6. BuildItSolar (2006).
7. "Water Heater Energy Factor" (2014).
8. National Renewable Energy Laboratroy (2014d). See the explanation of each item at <http://www.nrel.gov/rredc/pvwatts/changing_parameters.html>
9. *Wikipedia* (2014d).
10. Gipe (2013).

Chapter 4

1. Gordon-Bloomfield (2012).
2. NASA (2014).
3. Greenstream Publishing (2014).
4. Mehalic (2012).
5. Walker(2012).
6. Solar Facts and Advice (2014).
7. Pacific Green Group (2009).
8. De Vries (2013).
9. Nowicki and Bronski (2013b).
10. WindPower Program (2014).
11. Hydropower Basics (2014).
12. United States Environmental Protection Agency (2013).
13. Turbine Output (2014).
14. TECA Corp. (2010).
15. *Wikipedia* (2014b).

Chapter 5

1. Institute of Electrical and Electronics Engineers (1990).
2. Taub (2009).
3. 1000Bulbs.com (2014).
4. Electric Vehicle Wiki (2014).
5. Apple Corporation (2013).
6. Battery University (2013).
7. Waco (2011).
8. U.S. Department of Energy (2014b).
9. Lighting Research Center (2006).
10. 1000Bulbs.com (2014).
11. Anonymous (1999).
12. Wikimedia Commons (2014).
13. "Degradation and Failure Modes" (2013).
14. Woody (2013).
15. Guevara-Stone (2013).
16. Collins (2010).
17. Anonymous (2013).
18. Natural Resource Defense Council (2008).
19. Power Engineering (2011).
20. Patel (2009).
21. Nowicki and Bronski (2013a).

22. Power Engineering (2011).
23. Power Engineering (2011).
24. *Wikipedia* (2014d).
25. The Engineering Toolbox (2014).
26. U.S. Energy Information Agency (2013).
27. Paraffin Waxes (n.d).
28. Thirugnanam and Marimuthu (2013).
29. Electricity Storage Association (2014).
30. Tsiplakides (2012).
31. U.S. Department of Energy (2014d).
32. *Wikipedia* (2014c).

Chapter 6

1. Windustry.org (2013).
2. Feldman et al. (2012).
3. Solar Energy Industries Association (2013).
4. Tomorrow is Greener (2011).
5. Lynley (2011).
6. IEA (2009).
7. U.S. Department of Energy (2014e).
8. Florida Solar Energy Center (2014).
9. U.S. Department of Energy (2014a).

Chapter 7

1. Sunrun (2014).
2. Wholesale Solar (2014).
3. SolarPowerRocks.com (2013).
4. National Renewable Energy Laboratory (2013b).
5. National Renewable Energy Laboratory (2014c).
6. GAISMA (2014).
7. National Renewable Energy Laboratory (2014e).
8. National Renewable Energy Laboratory (2013a).
9. National Renewable Energy Laboratory (2014b).
10. Watson (2010).
11. Landau (2014).
12. *Wikipedia* (2014a).
13. Toyota (2014).

Chapter 8

1. U.S. Energy Information Administration (2013a).
2. U.S. Energy Information Administration (2014).
3. Statistia (n.d).
4. Brealey, Myers, and Marcus (2012).
5. Goodwin and Wright (2009); Skinner (2009).

Chapter 9

1. DSIRE (2013).
2. Federation of Tax Administrators (2014).
3. Pacific Green Group (2014).
4. National Renewable Energy Laboratory (2014a).
5. Marion et al. (2001).
6. Pacific Green Group (2014).

Chapter 10

1. Platts (2012a).
2. U.S. Department of Energy and the North Carolina Solar Center (2013).
3. Green Power Network (2013a).
4. Green Power Network (2013b).
5. U.S. Department of Energy (2014c).
6. European Commission (2013a).
7. European Commission (2013b).
8. Regional Greenhouse Gas Initiative (2013b).
9. Regional Greenhouse Gas Initiative (2013a).
10. Barringer (2013).
11. Reuters (2013).
12. Amarjargal (2013).
13. Environmental Defense Fund (2013).
14. Barnes (2009).
15. U.S. Energy Information Agency (2002).
16. Gerza (2011).
17. Platts (2012b).
18. Blanco and Rodrigues (2008).

References

1000Bulbs.com. 2014. *Understanding Life Hours, Part 1: How Are Life Hours Determined?* http://blog.1000bulbs.com/understanding-life-hours-part-1/, (accessed July 19, 2014).

Allan, S.D. 2007. "Tesla Turbine: Engine of the 21st Century?" *PES Network, Inc.*, http://pesn.com/Radio/Free_Energy_Now/shows/2007/04/14/9700225_KenReili_TeslaTurbine/

Amarjargal, B. September 4, 2013. "CER Sales Opportunities and Challenges in Non-EU Markets: A Project Developer's Perspective." *Fourth Workshop on Enhancing the Regional Distribution of CDM Projects in Asia and the Pacific (Manila)*, www.iges.or.jp/files/research/climate-energy/mm/PDF/20130904/S2_2_Bayarmaa.pdf, (accessed December 20, 2013).

Anonymous. 1999. "Compact Fluorescent Lamp Products." *Specifier Reports* 7:1, www.lrc.rpi.edu/programs/NLPIP/PDF/VIEW/SR_SB_CFL.pdf

Anonymous. 2013. *Lamp Life*, www.venturelighting.com/techcenter/lamps/lamp_life.htm, (accessed December 26, 2013).

Apple Corporation. 2013. *Apple Notebooks*, http://www.apple.com/batteries/notebooks.html

Barnes, A. March 12, 2009. *REC vs. Carbon Offset: Do You Know the Difference? GreenBiz.com*, www.greenbiz.com/blog/2009/03/12/rec-vs-carbon-offset-do-you-know-difference, (accessed December 27, 2013).

Barringer, F. 2013. "States' Group Calls for 45% Cut in Amount of Carbon Emissions Allowed." *New York Times* (Business Day, Energy & Environment, February 7, 2013). www.nytimes.com/2013/02/08/business/energy-environment/states-group-calls-for-45-cut-in-amount-of-carbon-emissions-allowed.html?ref=energy-environment&_r=2&, (accessed December 20, 2013).

Battery University. 2013. *How to Prolong Lithium-based Batteries*, batteryuniversity.com/learn/article/how_to_prolong_lithium_based_batteries, (accessed December 26, 2013).

Biello, D. 2010. "A Spin on Efficiency: Generating Tomorrow's Electricity with Better Turbines." *Scientific American*, http://www.scientificamerican.com/article.cfm?id=a-spin-on-efficiency-with-better-turbines, (accessed July 22, 2014).

Blanco, M. I., and G. Rodrigues. 2008. "Can the Future EU ETS Support Wind Energy Investments?" *Energy Policy* 36, no. 4, pp. 1509–20.

Boccard, N. 2008. "Capacity Factor of Wind Power: Realized Values vs. Estimates." *Social Science Research Network Working Paper Series*. http://ssrn.com/abstract=1285435, (accessed December 5, 2013).

Brealey, R.A., S.C. Myers, and A.J. Marcus. 2012. *Fundamentals of Corporate Finance*. 7th ed. Homewood, IL: Irwin.

BuildItSolar. 2006. *Measuring Collector Performance and Efficiency*, www.builditsolar.com/References/Measurements/CollectorPerformance.htm, (accessed September 30, 2014).

Collins, E. 2010. "Reliability and Availability Analysis of a Fielded Photovoltaic System." *Sandia National Laboratories*, energy.sandia.gov/wp/wp-content/gallery/uploads/093004c.pdf, (accessed July 19, 2014).

De Vries, E. 2013. "Finding the Optimum Low-Wind Design Combination." *Wind Power Monthly*, http://www.windpowermonthly.com/article/1187461/finding-optimum-low-wind-design-combination, (accessed January 9, 2014).

Degradation and Failure Modes. 2013. *PV Education*, pveducation.org/pvcdrom/modules/degradation-and-failure-modes (accessed December 27, 2013).

DSIRE. 2013. *Renewable Electricity Production Tax Credit*, http://dsireusa.org/incentives/incentive.cfm?Incentive_Code=US13F, (accessed December 11, 2013)

Electric Vehicle Wiki. 2014. *Factors Affecting Battery Capacity Loss*, http://www.electricvehiclewiki.com/?title=Battery_Capacity_Loss, (accessed July 8, 2014).

Electricity Storage Association. 2014. *Pumped Hydroelectric Storage*, http://www.electricitystorage.org/technology/tech_archive/pumped_hydro_storage, (accessed January 11, 2014).

Environmental Defense Fund. 2013. *What are Carbon Offsets?* http://business.edf.org/energy-emissions/carbon-offsets/what-are-carbon-offsets, (accessed December 20, 2013).

European Commission. 2013a. *Climate Action: Allowances and Caps*. http://ec.europa.eu/clima/policies/ets/cap/index_en.htm, (accessed December 21, 2013).

European Commission. 2013b. *The EU Emissions Trading System*, http://ec.europa.eu/clima/publications/docs/factsheet_ets_en.pdf, (accessed December 20, 2013).

Federation of Tax Administrators. 2014. *State Individual Income Taxes*, http://www.taxadmin.org/fta/rate/ind_inc.pdf, (accessed July 20, 2014).

Feldman, D., G. Barbose, R. Margolis, R. Wiser, N. Darghouth, and A. Goodrich. 2012. "Photovoltaic (PV) Pricing Trends: Historical, Recent, and Near-Term Projections." *US Department of Energy. Technical Report DOE/GO-102012-3839*, *http://www.nrel.gov/docs/fy13osti/56776.pdf*, (accessed December 9, 2013).

Florida Solar Energy Center. 2014. *Hydrogen Basics-Storage.* http://www.fsec.ucf. edu/en/consumer/hydrogen/basics/storage.htm

Fritsch, A.J., and P. Gallimore. 2007. *Healing Appalachia: Sustainable Living Through Appropriate Technology.* Lexington, KY: University Press of Kentucky.

GAISMA. 2014. *Sunrise, Sunset, Dawn and Dusk Times Around the World,* www. gaisma.com/en/dir/us-ca-country.html, (accessed July19, 2014).

Gerza, A. February 9, 2011. "How Much Are California TRECS Worth?" *The Leaf Exchange,* http://www.theleafexchange.com/2011/02/how-much-are-trecs-worth/, (accessed December 27, 2013).

Gipe, P. 2013. *All about Wind Energy,* http://www.wind-works.org/ cms/index.php?id=43&tx_ttnews[tt_news]=2572&cHash= b74148dbab1938159937a994adf1f05b, (accessed July 19, 2014).

Goodwin, P., and G. Wright. 2009. *Decision Analysis for Management Judgment,* 4th ed. New York, NY: Wiley.

Gordon-Bloomfield, N. 2012. "How Long Will Your Electric Car Battery Last? It Depends Where You Live." *Green Car Reports.* http://www.greencarreports. com/news/1077329_how-long-will-your-electric-car-battery-last-it-depends-where-you-live, (accessed July 8, 2014).

Green Power Network. 2013a. *Renewable Energy Certificates: National REC Tracking Systems,* http://apps3.eere.energy.gov/greenpower/markets/certificates.shtml? page=3#fn2

Green Power Network. 2013b. *Renewable Energy Certificates: REC Prices,* http:// apps3.eere.energy.gov/greenpower/markets/certificates.shtml?page=5

Greenstream Publishing. 2014. "Solar Irradiance." *Solar Electricity Handbook 2014,* http://solarelectricityhandbook.com/solar-irradiance.html, (accessed July 22, 2014).

Guevara-Stone, L. June 26, 2013. *For As Long As The Sun Shines: The Non-Crisis of PV Module Reliability. RMI Outlet,* blog.rmi.org/blog_2013_06_26_For_ As_Long_As_The_Sun_Shines, (accessed December 29, 2013).

Hydroelectric Power. 2005. *Electropedia,* www.mpoweruk.com/hydro_power. htm

Hydropower Basics. 2014. *Microhydropower,* http://www.microhydropower.net/ basics/turbines.php

IEA. 2009. *Renewable Energy Essentials: Concentrating Solar Thermal Power,* http://www.iea.org/publications/freepublications/publication/name-3864-en.html (accessed July 14, 2014).

Institute of Electrical and Electronics Engineers. 1990. *IEEE Standard Computer Dictionary: A Compilation of IEEE Standard Computer Glossaries.* New York, NY: Computer Society.

International Energy Agency. 2013. *Pushing the Envelope: Improvements To Buildings' Outer Layer Can Slash Energy Use,* http://www.iea.org/newsroomand

events/news/2013/december/pushingtheenvelopeimprovementstobuilding souterlayerslashenergyuse.html

Landau, C.R. 2014. *Optimal Tilt of Solar Panels*, http://www.solarpaneltilt. com/#fixed, (accessed July 20, 2014).

Laszlo, C., J. Brown, J. Ehrenfeld, and Gorham, M. 2014. *Flourishing Enterprise: The New Spirit of Business*. Stanford, CA: Stanford University Press.

Lighting Research Center. 2006. *What is the life of T8 fluorescent lamps?* www. lrc.rpi.edu/programs/nlpip/lightinganswers/t8/05-t8-lamp-life.asp, (accessed December 26, 2013.

Lynley, M. April 19, 2011. *Solar Trust of America Nabs $2.1B Loan for Solar Thermal Plant*. *VentureBeat*, http://venturebeat.com/2011/04/19/solar-trust-doe-loan-thermal/

Marion, B., M. Anderberg, R. George, P. Gray-Hann, and D. Heimiller. 2001. "PVWATTS Version 2—Enhanced Spatial Resolution for Calculating Grid-Connected PV Performance." *National Renewable Energy Laboratory*. http:// www.nrel.gov/docs/fy02osti/30941.pdf, (accessed July13, 2014).

Mehalic, B. 2012. "Flat Plate and Evacuated Tube Solar Thermal Collectors." *Home Power*, http://www.homepower.com/articles/solar-water-heating/equipment-products/flat-plate-evacuated-tube-solar-thermal-collectors, (accessed June 5, 2014).

NASA. 2014. *Incoming Sunlight*, http://earthobservatory.nasa.gov/Features/ EnergyBalance/page2.php, (accessed July 22, 2014).

National Institute of Building Sciences. 2013. *Whole Building Design Guide: Existing Buildings*, http://www.wbdg.org/references/fhpsb_existing.php

National Renewable Energy Laboratory. 2013a. "Solar Resource Information." *NREL Renewable Resource Data Center*, http://www.nrel.gov/rredc/solar_ resource.html (accessed December 6, 2013).

National Renewable Energy Laboratory. 2013b. "What Influences the Amount of Solar Irradiation? Chapter 3 in Renewable Energy Resource Center." *Shining On*, rredc.nrel.gov/solar/pubs/shining/chap3.html⊠, (accessed December 6, 2013).

National Renewable Energy Laboratory. 2014a. "System Advisor Model Version 2014.1.14 (SAM 2014.1.14)." *National Renewable Energy Laboratory. Golden, CO.*, https://sam.nrel.gov/content/downloads, (accessed July 13, 2014).

National Renewable Energy Laboratory. 2014b. *Cautions for Interpreting the Results*, http://rredc.nrel.gov/solar/calculators/pvwatts/interp.html, (accessed July 20, 2014).

National Renewable Energy Laboratory. 2014c. *PVWatts*, http://www.nrel.gov/ rredc/pvwatts/, (accessed July 19, 2014).

National Renewable Energy Laboratory. 2014d. "Calculator for Overall DC to AC Derate Factor." *PVWatts,* http://rredc.nrel.gov/solar/calculators/PVWATTS/version1/derate.cgi

National Renewable Energy Laboratory. 2014e. *US Solar Radiation Resource Maps. National Renewable Energy Laboratory,* http://rredc.nrel.gov/solar/old_data/nsrdb/1961-1990/redbook/atlas/, (accessed July 19, 2014).

Natural Resource Defense Council. 2008. *The 3 R's Still Rule,* www.nrdc.org/thisgreenlife/0802.asp, (accessed July 19, 2014).

Nowicki, A., and P. Bronski. February 19, 2013a. "Are Direct-Drive Turbines the Future of Wind Energy?" *Earth Techling,* http://www.earthtechling.com/2013/02/are-direct-drive-turbines-the-future-of-wind-energy/, (accessed December 26, 2013).

Nowicki, A., and P. Bronski. February 19, 2013b. "Are Direct-Drive Turbines The Future Of Wind Energy?" *Rocky Mountain Institute, Renewable Energy, Wind Power,* http://www.earthtechling.com/2013/02/are-direct-drive-turbines-the-future-of-wind-energy/, (accessed January 9, 2014).

Pacific Green Group. 2009. *Solar Panel Efficiency versus Temperature,* http://www.pacific-greentech.com/solar-panel-efficiency.html

Pacific Green Group. 2014. *Solar Panel Efficiency versus Temperature,* http://www.pacific-greentech.com/solar-panel-efficiency.html, (accessed July 19, 2014).

Paraffin Waxes. n.d. *Southwest Wax,* http://www.southwestwax.com/paraffin.html, (accessed July 19, 2014)

Patel, P. September 23, 2009. "GE Grabs Gearless Wind Turbines." *MIT Technology Review,* www.technologyreview.com/news/415425/ge-grabs-gearless-wind-turbines/

Platts. 2012a. *Renewable Energy Certificates: A Platts Special Report,* http://www.platts.com/commodity/electric-power, (accessed July 19, 2014).

Platts. April 24, 2012b. *REC Markets Reveal Diverse Trends, Volatility,* http://www.platts.com/news-feature/2012/rec/index, (accessed December 27, 2013).

Power Engineering. March 1, 2011. *Direct Drive vs. Gearbox: Progress on Both Fronts,* http://www.power-eng.com/articles/print/volume-115/issue-3/features/direct-drive-vs-gearbox-progress-on-both-fronts.html

Regional Greenhouse Gas Initiative. 2013a. *CO_2 Auctions, Tracking and Offsets,* www.rggi.org/market, (accessed December 20, 2013).

Regional Greenhouse Gas Initiative. 2013b. *RGGI, Inc,* www.rggi.org/rggi, (accessed December 20, 2013).

Reuters. September 26, 2013. Factbox: Carbon Trading Schemes around the World. http://www.reuters.com/article/2012/09/26/us-carbon-trading-idUSBRE88P0ZN20120926, (accessed December 20, 2013).

Shahan, Z. 2012. *Wind Turbine Net Capacity Factor—50% the New Normal?* http://cleantechnica.com/2012/07/27/wind-turbine-net-capacity-factor-50-the-new-normal/#azM3wIBshMzm6v0f.99 (accessed December 4, 2013).

Skinner, D.C. 2009. *Introduction to Decision Analysis.* 3rd ed. Gainesville, FL: Probabilistic Publishing.

Solar Energy Industries Association. 2013. *Solar Market Insight Report 2013 Q2,* http://www.seia.org/research-resources/solar-market-insight-report-2013-q2, (accessed December 10, 2013).

Solar Facts and Advice. 2014. *Solar Panel Temperature Affects Output—Here's What You Need to Know,* http://www.solar-facts-and-advice.com/solar-panel-temperature.html

Solar Thermal Energy. April 29, 2011. *Wikipedia,* en.wikipedia.org/wiki/Solar_thermal_energy

SolarPowerRocks.com. 2013. *How do Solar Panels Work in Cloudy Weather?* http://www.solarpowerrocks.com/solar-basics/how-do-solar-panels-work-in-cloudy-weather/, (accessed December 6, 2013).

Statista. n.d. *Projected Annual Inflation Rate in the United States from 2014 to 2019,* http://www.statista.com/statistics/244983/projected-inflation-rate-in-the-united-states/, (accessed December 11, 2013).

Steven Winter Associates, Inc. 2013. "Net Zero Energy Buildings." *Whole Building Design Guide,* http://www.wbdg.org/resources/netzeroenergy buildings.php

Sunrun. 2014. *Cost of Solar Power,* http://www.sunrun.com/solar-lease/cost-of-solar/, (accessed July 19, 2014).

Taisei Corp. 2012. *Challenges for the Development of Zero Energy Buildings,* http://www.taisei.co.jp/english/ir/image/ar2012/taisei_annual_2012_05.pdf

Taub, E. February 11, 2009. "How Long Did You Say that Bulb Would Last?" *New York Time,* http://bits.blogs.nytimes.com/2009/02/11/how-long-did-you-say-that-bulb-will-last/?_r=0, (accessed December 26, 2013).

TECA Corp. 2010. *AHP-6200/Curves,* http://www.thermoelectric.com/2010/pr/ac/tm/indoors.htm, (accessed July 19, 2014)

The Engineering Toolbox. 2014. *Solids—Specific Heats,* http://www.engineeringtoolbox.com/specific-heat-solids-d_154.html#.UpI7uL9gid4, (accessed July 19, 2014)

Thirugnanam. C., and P. Marimuthu. 2013. "Experimental Analysis of Latent Heat Thermal Energy Storage Using Paraffin Wax as Phase Change Material." *International Journal of Engineering and Innovative Technology* 3, no. 2, pp. 372–6.

Tomorrow is Greener. 2011. *Google Invests $168 Million in Huge Mojave Desert Solar Project*, http://www.tomorrowisgreener.com/google-invests-168-million-in-huge-mojave-desert-solar-project/, (accessed July 19, 2014).

Torcellini, P., S. Pless, M. Deru, and D. Crawley. 2006. "Zero Energy Buildings: A Critical Look at the Definition." *National Renewable Energy Laboratory*, http://www.nrel.gov/docs/fy06osti/39833.pdf

Toyota. 2014. *5. Comparing an Electric Vehicle with a Fuel Cell Vehicle*, http://www.toyota-global.com/innovation/environmental_technology/fuelcell_vehicle/ (accessed July 10, 2014)

Tsiplakides, D. 2012. "PEM Water Electrolysis Fundamentals." *Newcastle University*, http://research.ncl.ac.uk/sushgen/docs/summerschool_2012/PEM_water_electrolysis-Fundamentals_Prof._Tsiplakides.pdf, (accessed July 14, 2014).

Turbine Output. 2014, http://ganz.info.hu/keptar/Termékek/Turbinák/Általános%20képek/ltalnos11.png, (accessed July 19, 2014)

Turbine. April 29, 2011. *Wikipedia*, http://en.wikipedia.org/wiki/Turbine

U.S. Department of Energy and the North Carolina Solar Center. 2013. *Database of State Incentives for Renewables and Efficiency (DSIRE)*, http://www.dsireusa.org/

U.S. Department of Energy. 2014a. "Accomplishments and Progress." *U.S. Department of Energy*, http://energy.gov/eere/fuelcells/accomplishments-and-progress

U.S. Department of Energy. 2014b. *Benefits and Challenges*, http://www.fueleconomy.gov/feg/fcv_benefits.shtml

U.S. Department of Energy. 2014c. *Green Power Pricing*, http://apps3.eere.energy.gov/greenpower/markets/pricing.shtml?page=0, (accessed July 19, 2014).

U.S. Department of Energy. 2014d. *Natural gas reforming*, http://energy.gov/eere/fuelcells/natural-gas-reforming, (accessed July 14, 2014).

U.S. Department of Energy. 2014e. *Status of Hydrogen Storage Technologies*, http://energy.gov/eere/fuelcells/status-hydrogen-storage-technologies, (accessed July 9, 2014).

U.S. Energy Information Administration. 2013a. *Electric Power Monthly*, http://www.eia.gov/electricity/monthly/epm_table_grapher.cfm?t=epmt_5_6_a, (accessed December 5, 2013).

U.S. Energy Information Administration. 2013b. *Frequently Asked Questions*, http://www.eia.gov/tools/faqs/faq.cfm?id=86&t=1

U.S. Energy Information Administration. May 7, 2014. *Annual Energy Outlook 2014*, http://www.eia.gov/forecasts/aeo/MT_electric.cfm, (accessed July 19, 2014).

U.S. Energy Information Agency. 2002. *Voluntary Reporting of Greenhouse Gases Program: Average Electricity Factors by State and Region*, www.eia.gov/oiaf/1605/ee-factors.html, (accessed December 27, 2013).

U.S. Energy Information Agency. November 14, 2013. *2013 Completions of Large Solar Thermal Power Plants Mark Technology Gains*, http://www.eia.gov/todayinenergy/detail.cfm?id=13791#tabs_SpotPriceSlider-3, (accessed January 11, 2014).

U.S. Environmental Protection Agency. 2010. *Greening Your Purchase of Copiers: A Guide for Federal Purchasers*, http://www.epa.gov/epp/pubs/copiers.htm

United States Environmental Protection Agency. August 2013. *Low-Head Hydropower from Wastewater*, http://water.epa.gov/scitech/wastetech/upload/Low-Head-Hydropower-from-Wastewater.pdf, (accessed January 9, 2014).

Waco, D. 2011. "How Long Do Solar Panels Last?" *Civic Solar*, http://www.civicsolar.com/resource/how-long-do-solar-panels-last, (accessed July 8, 2014).

Walker, A. 2012. "Solar Water Heating." *National Institute of Building Sciences*, http://www.wbdg.org/resources/swheating.php, (accessed June 5, 2014).

Water Heater Energy Factor. 2014. http://www.aricoplumbing.com/waterheater/waterheater-energy-factor.aspx (accessed March 14, 2014).

Watson, D.E. 2010. "Optimal Tilt Angle." *FT Exploring*, http://www.ftexploring.com/solar-energy/tilt-angle2.htm, (accessed July 20, 2014).

Wholesale Solar. 2014. *Solar Insolation Map*, http://www.wholesalesolar.com/Information-SolarFolder/SunHoursUSMap.html, (accessed July 19, 2014).

Wikimedia Commons. 2014. http://commons.wikimedia.org/wiki/File:Bathtub_curve.jpg, (accessed July 19, 2014).

Wikipedia. 2013. *Horsepower*, http://en.wikipedia.org/wiki/Horsepower, (accessed 5Dec2013.

Wikipedia. 2014a. *Plug-in Electric Vehicle: Lower Operating and Maintenance Costs*, https://en.wikipedia.org/wiki/Plug-in_electric_vehicle#Lower_operating_and_maintenance_costs, (accessed July 20, 2014).

Wikipedia. 2014b. *Relationship of SEER to EER and COP*, http://en.wikipedia.org/wiki/Seasonal_energy_efficiency_ratio, (accessed July 19, 2014)

Wikipedia. 2014c. *Steam Reforming*, http://en.wikipedia.org/wiki/Steam_reforming, (accessed July 18, 2014).

Wikipedia. 2014d. *Wind Turbine*, http://en.wikipedia.org/wiki/Wind_turbine (accessed December 27, 2013).

Wind Energy Center. 1970. *Wind Power: Capacity Factor, Intermittency, and What Happens When the Wind Doesn't Blow?* http://www.windaction.org/posts/3589-wind-power-capacity-factor-intermittency-and-what-happens-when-the-wind-doesn-t-blow#.VCtgjFY4Qds

WindPower Program. 2014. http://www.wind-power-program.com/large_turbines.htm, (accessed July 19, 2014)

Windustry.org. 2013. *How Much Do Wind Turbines Cost?* http://www.windustry.org/resources/how-much-do-wind-turbines-cost, (accessed 24 November 2013).

Woody, T. May 28, 2013. "Solar Industry Anxious Over Defective Panels." *New York Times Business Day,* http://www.nytimes.com/2013/05/29/business/energy-environment/solar-powers-dark-side.html?_r=0, (accessed December 29, 2013).

Index

OTHER TITLES IN OUR ENVIRONMENTAL AND SOCIAL SUSTAINABILITY FOR BUSINESS ADVANTAGE COLLECTION

Chris Laszlo, Weatherhead School of Management, Case Western Reserve University and Robert Sroufe, Duquesne University

- *Strategy Making in Nonprofit Organizations: A Model and Case Studies* by Jyoti Bachani and Mary Vradelis
- *Developing Sustainable Supply Chains to Drive Value: Management Issues, Insights, Concepts, and Tools* by Robert Sroufe and Steven Melnyk
- *IT Sustainability for Business Advantage* by Brian Moore
- *A Primer on Sustainability: In the Business Environment* by Ronald M. Whitfield and Jeanne McNett
- *The Thinking Executive's Guide to Sustainability* by Kerul Kassel
- *Change Management for Sustainability* by Huong Ha
- *The Role of Legal Compliance in Sustainable Supply Chains, Operations, and Marketing* by John Wood

Announcing the Business Expert Press Digital Library

Concise e-books business students need for classroom and research

This book can also be purchased in an e-book collection by your library as

- a one-time purchase,
- that is owned forever,
- allows for simultaneous readers,
- has no restrictions on printing, and
- can be downloaded as PDFs from within the library community.

Our digital library collections are a great solution to beat the rising cost of textbooks. E-books can be loaded into their course management systems or onto students' e-book readers.
The **Business Expert Press** digital libraries are very affordable, with no obligation to buy in future years. For more information, please visit **www.businessexpertpress.com/librarians**. To set up a trial in the United States, please email **sales@businessexpertpress.com**.

www.ingramcontent.com/pod-product-compliance
Lightning Source LLC
Chambersburg PA
CBHW060326200326
41519CB00011BA/1850